Yellow Dogs and Republicans

YELLOW DOGS AND REPUBLICANS

Allan Shivers and Texas Two-Party Politics

RICKY F. DOBBS

TEXAS A&M UNIVERSITY PRESS
College Station

First edition
The paper used in this book meets the minimum requirements
of the American National Standard for Permanence
of Paper for Printed Library Materials, Z39.48-1984.
Binding materials have been chosen for durability.
∞
Unless noted otherwise, photographs are courtesy of the Texas
State Archives.

Library of Congress Cataloging-in-Publication Data

Dobbs, Ricky F.
Yellow Dogs and Republicans : Allan Shivers and
Texas two-party politics / Ricky F. Dobbs.—1st ed.
p. cm.
Includes bibliographical references and index.
ISBN 1-58544-407-3 (cloth : alk. paper)
1. Shivers, Allan, 1907– 2. Governors — Texas — Biography.
3. Texas — Politics and government — 1865–1950.
4. Texas — Politics and government — 1951–
5. Political parties — Texas — History — 20th century. I. Title
F391.S562D63 2005
976.4′063′092—dc22
2004016550

For My Parents

CONTENTS

ILLUSTRATIONS

ACKNOWLEDGMENTS

WHEN I FIRST BEGAN STUDYING ALLAN SHIVERS'S POLITICAL CAREER, I had no clear ideas or impression of the man. I knew vaguely that he had been governor and led an insurgency that put Texas in Eisenhower's column in 1952 and 1956. As research increased my awareness, he loomed as a controversial and powerful figure in an era when giants walked the landscape of Texas politics. Over the years, Shivers has not broken through into my personal pantheon of heroes. Instead, I have come to an appreciation of his significance to the political history of Texas and the South. He helped make Texas what it is today—and that is not altogether a good thing. He also helped move the South one step farther down the road to two-party politics.

THIS BOOK COULD NOT HAVE HAPPENED WITHOUT THE HELP AND SUPPORT of many people. My wife Miriam and my daughter Claire have lived with Allan Shivers (and me) for thirteen years between them. Claire at times seemed overawed at the idea of her daddy writing a book and offered to help illustrate it. Miriam just wanted it finished so our home office could be thoroughly cleaned. Together they make life a joy and give meaning to all that I do. I am thankful for them and their loving support. My parents, Barbara and Jack Dobbs, supported, loved, and encouraged me through endless years of higher education. It is to them this book is dedicated.

Colleagues at Southwest Baptist University and Texas A&M University–Commerce also advised, supported, and encouraged me. Graduate school friends provided intangible but essential moral support when this work was germinating. Texas A&M University–Commerce has also contributed generously in release time and research funds for this project. While in graduate school at Texas

A&M University, I received travel assistance for my research. The Harry S. Truman Library funded my research at that facility. Truman Library personnel, along with archivists at the Eisenhower and Johnson presidential libraries, greatly facilitated my exploration of the past. The Texas State Archives staff in Austin provided excellent service and assistance, which underlay most of my research. Archivists and librarians at several other facilities also proved helpful, including: Baylor University, the Sam Houston Regional Library and Research Center, Southwest Baptist University, Texas A&M University, Texas A&M University–Commerce, the University of Houston, and the Center for American History at the University of Texas. I am also particularly grateful to participants who gave generously of their time and memories. The late Maury Maverick Jr. took a special interest in this project, connecting me with many people who were more than willing to tell me about my subject. Others—including the late George Christian, John Osorio, and Jake Pickle—helped temper this account of a controversial figure.

All historians owe debts to those who taught and encouraged them. Stanley Campbell and Thomas Charlton of Baylor University inspired me as gentlemen, researchers, and teachers. They showed me an alternative path to the law, my original career choice, and gently said, "we told you so," when I decided to drop law school and take up further graduate study. Both have influenced my teaching, my understanding of history, and, even more important, my understanding of life. I wish I could again thank Robert A. Calvert for all he meant to me personally and to this project. His wonderful humanity, warmth, and deep commitment to his students and friends remain pleasant memories for all who knew him.

There are others who also helped along the way. Walter Buenger, Harold Livesay, David McWhirter, and Henry Schmidt served on my dissertation committee. Gregg Cantrell, Patrick Cox, Charles Elliott, Nick Sarantakes, and Rebecca Sharpless all offered practical advice and support during the crafting of this work. Finally, the editorial staff at Texas A&M University Press contributed mightily to this book's best qualities. Any imperfections that remain are my own.

Yellow Dogs and Republicans

INTRODUCTION

FROM THE END OF RECONSTRUCTION UNTIL AT LEAST THE 1950S, THE American South was governed by a single party, the Democrats, with almost no effective competition from Republicans.[1] Politics in the Solid South were oriented toward the preservation of white supremacy, county-seat oligarchies, and rural control over political power. The one-party system relied upon a restricted franchise, an emphasis upon personalities, distracting side issues, and pervasive racial fears for its survival. These obscured apparent class divisions among whites, producing an artificially conservative southern politics and state governments characterized by low taxes and poor public services. The political class that dominated this regime was self-perpetuating and sought to insulate state-local matters from national ones to maintain the status quo. From the 1930s through the 1960s, the southern Democratic one-party system experienced the strains that would lead to its eventual collapse.

The New Deal and World War II posed critical challenges to southern political and social life. Roosevelt administration efforts to end the Great Depression not only brought federal dollars, they also showed federal concern over the organic bases of southern poverty. New Deal relief and work programs disrupted labor relations by encouraging the unionization of industrial workers and placing upward pressures on wages. For the first time since Reconstruction, the federal government took a serious interest in the situation of southern blacks. The Democratic Party became nationally dominant and less dependent upon white southerners for its survival. Although the New Deal did not end the depression, it began an era in which average Americans looked to Washington for economic security. This was true of average southerners as well. Developments such as these threatened the traditional patterns of rural life, paternalism, deference, and race relations. Wartime industrialization brought increased urbanization. The new industrialization was also fed by federal money, driven by federal planning, and absorbed excess labor from across the region and beyond. Military service and postwar veterans' benefits empowered a generation to dream far beyond anything imaginable in 1941. Some hoped to participate in politics the old-fashioned way within the old system. Still others—liberals, unionized workers, minorities—sought to shake up the one-party order and demand a place at the table of southern Democratic politics. By the time the U.S. Supreme Court handed down its landmark *Brown v. Board of Education* decision in 1954, the one-party system was in a state of simmering crisis varying in intensity across the South.

Because of its size, wealth, and relatively advanced economy and politics, Texas' experience during this era of change deserves special attention when attempting to understand the wider regional story. In 1940, the majority of Texas' population was rural, tied to the farm, and impoverished. Ten years later, the majority of the population was urban—already more so than any other state in the region. Its white citizens were among the most heavily middle class in the South. At the close of the 1950s, 66 percent of Texans owned their own homes—80 percent of which had indoor plumbing and television. Median urban white family income stood at $5,693. Suburbs with young, mainly white, populations spread outward from the centers of major cities. Working Texans saw significant increases in income and benefits, in no small part due to postwar increases in unionization. Despite restrictive labor laws, hundreds of thousands joined unions. The pressure they brought to bear on employers improved the lives even of nonunion workers.

So much change within a twenty-year period caused Texas' one-party system to shudder under the strain. Most white Texans identified with the Democratic Party. As the emerging urban middle and working classes became more prosperous and politically aware, they participated more than their parents and grandparents would have bothered. This forced changes upon a style of politics designed to prevent change. Intraparty competition became more intense and the battles more genuinely ideological as Texas' elites struggled to keep control over the vehicle of their political power. This struggle began the birth of two-party politics. At times appropriate to the situation, each southern state underwent a similar pattern of transition.

Within this vast sectional story, Allan Shivers, Texas' governor from 1949–57, stands as a significant transitional figure. He never left the Democratic Party and thereby personally completed the political transformation he helped start in Texas. Shivers did not cause the Solid South to crack and the modern two-party South to emerge, but he was an important agent in hastening its arrival. In a sense, he had one foot firmly planted in the aging one-party system and another

Allan Shivers. Shivers's youth and looks proved a strong political asset.

in the emerging two-party order. He sought primarily to dominate Texas' politics through the vehicle of the state Democratic Party, push a decidedly probusiness conservative agenda, and attract votes by using distracting nonissues and the force of his personality. He combined these elements of the old political style with the savvy use of new media and exploiting the voting strength of Texas' rising white middle class. An elitist, he managed to mediate the divide between Texas' corporate elites and this growing block of anxious arrivistes. In pursuit of these ends, Shivers made presidential Republicanism acceptable in Texas and helped do so in the South generally. This led to even greater disruption within the state party he sought to control, speeding the defection of moneyed interests to the more amenable Republicans and the coming of two-party politics.

The increasing influence of white southerners and their political values upon the national Republican Party carries echoes of the old one-party system and the style of politics practiced by Shivers and his political cohort. The federal government has become the enemy. Regulation of business and rudimentary social justice measures such as the minimum wage and collective bargaining stand in the way of boom times for all. Progressive taxation discourages economic expansion. A steady diet of taxes creates a federal government that is bigger and more intrusive. Clean-water laws endanger property rights. Direct and even indirect efforts by government to address racial injustice actually cause *more* racial tension. The federal courts have arrogated too much power to themselves. All of these have been woven together with varying levels of subtlety, but when carefully analyzed and thought out they reveal their provenance. This message has prevailed in tough campaigns financed with ever-larger bankrolls to purchase ever-more-sophisticated appeals to the voter.

Since Shivers led Texans to Dwight Eisenhower in 1952, the rapidity and scope of transition has been impressive. Texas' electoral votes have gone to the Republican nominee in all but three elections during the past half-century. In 1954, Republicans elected a congressman in Dallas County. In 1961, they sponsored a successful U.S. Senate candidate. In 1978, Texans elected their first Republican governor since Reconstruction. Since then, Republicans have won the governor's mansion in 1986, 1994, and 1998. The last Republican elected governor of Texas went on to become president of the United States. In 2002, Republicans captured all statewide offices and control over the legislature for the first time since Reconstruction. Democrats gambled and lost on a ticket featuring an African-American U.S. Senate candidate, a Hispanic gubernatorial candidate, and a white candidate for lieutenant governor. Today's multiracial moderate Democratic Party faces a largely white, conservative Republican Party in a contest for survival for the former and hegemony for the latter. The irony is that just fifty years earlier, white Democrats were the only meaningful participants in Texas politics.

CHAPTER ONE

Portrait of the Politician as a Young Man

MANY, IF NOT MOST, TEXAS NATIVES AND TRANSPLANTS BELIEVE their state is different from, if not better than others. A traveler, however, might be forgiven for noticing little difference. It is almost as though the state's reputation is divorced from the landscape. One of two states to be an independent nation, the largest in land area until 1959, and since 1900 never less than sixth in population, Texas remains an area of contrasts and superlatives memorized from an early age by its schoolchildren. If Texas' history, politics, and social climate resemble those of any other region, it is the South, from which most of the state's white and black population originated and with which it shared strong cultural ties—including a legacy of defeat and racism. Those two legacies in particular contributed to a one-party political system. Democratic dominance of the state and region was as reliable as the misery that was summer—unquestioned as an article of faith, and seemingly unchanging. Yet, change did come to this situation: during the depths of the Great Depression. It sowed the seeds of a two-party state and a two-party South. One of the agents of this change was Allan Shivers. The times and the state made him what he became.[1]

Shivers's great-grandmother, Nancy Shivers, came to Texas from Mississippi in 1846, a year after Texas' annexation. She arrived with a son, Robert, and three daughters—Ella, Phoebe, and Nancy. Her migration differed little from that of many thousands of others from the Deep South, following similar soils, and perhaps family and acquaintances, into Texas. The widow acquired six hundred acres just west of Woodville, in newly formed Tyler County. Although details about their acquisition are not clear, Nancy Shivers owned three slaves: a woman named Dicy and her boy, Louis, and girl, Jenny. While hardly a sufficient number of slaves to place her among Texas' elite, the widow doubtless derived some social status from slave ownership.[2]

With the outbreak of the Civil War in 1861, Nancy Shivers's son, Robert, still in his teens, journeyed east to his home state and joined Company B, 16th Mississippi Infantry. He served for the duration, following his regiment, a part of Gen. Robert E. Lee's Army of Northern Virginia, from battlefield to battlefield. As the Confederacy staggered to eventual defeat, federal forces captured Shivers and held him prisoner until he was paroled in March, 1865. Ignoring the conditions of his parole, Shivers spent the remaining weeks of the war fighting with the Confederate army, surrendering at Appomattox in April. Still a young man, he returned to Texas.

The Shiverses managed to keep their land throughout the war, but defeat resulted in freedom for their slaves. The family farm and personal property were valued at $1,500 in 1870. Robert had purchased his own land, valued at $200, by then. Emancipation likely cut the family's net worth by half, given a conservative estimate of their slaves' prewar value. However, their labor was not lost. East Texas during Reconstruction was not a safe place for freed people to wander about. Staying with one's white folks was often deemed prudent. Dicy and Louis stayed with the Shivers family for at least fifteen years after the war. Daughter Jenny, however, either died or set off on her own sometime in the 1870s.[3]

Robert M. Shivers married his wife, Frances, in 1870. She, too, was a migrant from the Deep South, but a fairly recent arrival from Alabama. She eventually bore Robert six children, five of whom survived to adulthood. Their eldest son, William, became a physician with a practice in Woodville. The only other of their children who made a recorded impression upon the community was Robert Andrew, their third son, born in 1877. As late as 1900, Robert Andrew still worked on the family farm, but he had greater ambitions. He eventually took a job teaching school in the lumber camp at Doucette. In his late twenties, he married and moved to Lufkin—perhaps to satisfy his new wife, Easter, perhaps for better pay. Their son, Robert Allan, was born there on October 5, 1907. Only a few months after the boy's arrival, the family returned to Woodville, taking up residence in a rented home just across from the courthouse.[4]

In 1908, Woodville consisted of a small cluster of buildings and homes around a red brick courthouse. The courthouse was relatively new and a point of pride. So much so, that the county commissioners issued a proclamation in 1906 prohibiting the discharge of firearms within the building. The town's streets were narrow, muddy when wet, and dusty the rest of the time. The Sabine and East Texas Railroad bisected the town and linked it with the wider world. Woodville had no running water or even a sewer system as late as the 1930s. The county provided segregated primary education to grade eight. Tyler County had never been prosperous. Most of its farmers barely made enough to get by, and a third of them did so as tenants. Corn and sweet potatoes were the chief staples of the local diet. Pork was also readily available, as the county was home to twice as many hogs as people. Tyler County did not resemble the cotton kingdom at all. The archetypical southern planter did not dominate local society, but rather a style of entrepreneur more akin to Andrew Carnegie—with both his bad and good points.[5]

Tyler County lay in the thick of some of the largest and last stands of virgin southern yellow pine remaining in Texas. Logging made a few rich and lured many others with the illusory hope of subsistence. The loggers lived in lumber camps, which were really company towns. Logging, sawing, and processing all took place on location. Between two hundred and five hundred laborers manned these operations established in manmade clearings in the great forest. Their pay came in the form of company scrip, typically negotiable only at company stores that charged inflated prices and offered loans at usurious interest rates.[6]

Presiding over most of the logging and milling in the region was Tyler County native John Henry Kirby. Kirby modeled his empire after that of Andrew Carnegie, borrowing in his own way from the "Gospel of Wealth." The lumber millionaire donated freely to local schools and community facilities. His paternalism and philanthropy, which earned him the nickname "The Peon's Pal," concealed a more ruthless side. He controlled local politics and used law enforcement agencies as if they were his own. Vigilant against unionization, Kirby used his power to drive organizers from "a Christian law-abiding community."[7]

In later years, Allan Shivers often referred to the poverty of his upbringing. Of course, poverty is relative, and by the time people cared to record his memories, Shivers was a multimillionaire, making childhood poverty a relative matter indeed. Arguably, he made too much of his family's obscurity. This is common among politicians. Nonetheless, Tyler County was a poor backwater. There is no doubt this influenced Shivers's development. However, the Shivers family was well respected in Woodville, with a consistent income and plainly a cut above the dirt farmers and loggers who made up the community.

Upon returning to Woodville with his wife and infant son, Robert Andrew Shivers continued teaching. He also read law and eventually qualified for the bar. Three years after returning to Tyler County, the couple had a daughter, Maurine. When Robert Allan reached school age, summertime work became a part of his life. He worked in local sawmills, set type at the town's small newspaper, and jerked sodas in the town drugstore. Piety was also an important part of family life. The boy's parents were devout Baptists. His father taught Sunday school and his mother banned alcohol, playing cards, and other instruments of sin from their home. A good switching awaited the lad whenever he skipped out of church early with friends to watch a train pass by town.[8]

By 1920, the family owned a home near the square. Robert Andrew had succeeded in local politics, winning election as county judge—the chief executive of county government in Texas. His son tagged along on the campaign trail and became interested in politics. Judge Shivers worked hard for Progressive Democrat Pat Neff, during his bid for governor in 1920. This meant crossing John Kirby, who backed Neff's opponent, former U.S. senator Joseph Bailey. Neff's Baptist credentials—"never shot a gun, baited a fish hook, used tobacco in any form, not drunk anything stronger than Brazos water"—and Progressivism appealed to the judge. It was the first campaign Robert Allan remembered well in later life.[9]

In 1923, the family moved to Port Arthur, a growing city of forty thousand nearly eighty miles from Woodville. Shivers's official biographers say his parents believed opportunities for their children in the small county seat were too limited. Woodville had no high school, and the family's economic prospects would doubtless improve in the larger city. Port Arthur had become a boomtown after the discovery of oil at nearby Spindletop in 1901. Before the oil boom, the town represented one of several "entrepreneurial errors of enormous magnitude" on the part of its founder, who envisioned it becoming a nexus of rail and sea transport. A small professional and business class thrived in Port Arthur, but most of its citizens were working-class people employed in the petrochemical industry. Fires and explosions posed a constant threat to workers and citizens alike. Three years after the Shivers family moved to town, the Gulf tanker *Venezuela* exploded and burned for hours, causing twenty-nine fatalities.[10]

Robert Allan was sixteen when he graduated from Port Arthur High School in 1924. He wanted to study law and entered the University of Texas (UT) in the fall. The university must have seemed a world away from anything he had yet experienced. Nearly three hundred miles from home, the costs of sustaining and educating the lad proved difficult for the family budget. Despite his highly respectable reputation, Robert Andrew's law practice struggled in its early years. The son dutifully returned home and went to work at the Texas Company refinery, rising from laborer to office manager by the time he was nineteen. He was earning $165 a month by 1928, and had managed to save enough cash to continue his education. Nevertheless, Robert Allan found it difficult to make a decision about his future. Part of him felt the lure of the reliable earnings he was receiving at the refinery. He solicited and received an appointment to either West Point or Annapolis from Rep. John C. Box of Jacksonville. Ultimately, his father and a family friend convinced the young man to return to Austin.[11]

Back at UT, Shivers threw himself into social and political activity. He joined Delta Theta Pi—the "$1.35 law fraternity"—and served on the interfraternity council, as well as participating in the Texas Cowboys spirit group, speaking clubs, and student government. Another activity that helped cement his notoriety on campus was his membership in the "German Club." Whatever its name might suggest, the German Club was *not* about language study. It hosted all-university dances, which were known as "Germans," and Shivers worked as a bouncer and bookkeeper. He also worked part-time selling shoes in a department store. By the fall of 1932, Shivers had become a "Big Man On Campus." He also dropped his first name and began calling himself Allan. He was tall, good-looking, and carefully dressed and groomed. He bought and wore expensive clothes, subsidized with his J. C. Penney employee discount. That spring, he decided to seek the student body presidency.[12]

Student government at UT incubated state leaders. It amounted to a "laboratory" of the state's political future, according to one former student body president who later became a successful politician. It also had an elitist tendency. The best fraternities and sororities dominated all offices and staged expensive election contests. This cabal was known on campus as the "Clique." Elections rarely amounted to anything other than popularity contests. Most students viewed them with pronounced indifference. When members of the Clique won these spectacles, they gained control over both campus publications: the student newspaper, *Daily Texan*, and the yearbook, *Cactus*.[13]

Each year, the back pages of *Cactus* sprouted a section called the "Thorn." The Thorn satirized, made personal attacks against, spread rumors about, and put down students, particularly those in out-groups not affiliated with the Clique. A long-standing tradition, such *Cactus* features as the "Fairy Page" had come under increased criticism by the early 1930s. United States senator Morris Sheppard threatened a libel suit against the yearbook staff in 1931 after the Thorn skewered his daughter. The next year's edition was tamer, but displayed false contrition: "[W]e may thank the stars and the present system of censorship for the mildness of the Thorn."[14] A coalition of out-groups combined in the spring of 1932 to form the "Little Campus" machine. Setting out to defeat the Clique, Little Campus nominated Shivers for student body president. The Clique's candidate was Joe Spurlock. Both campaigns nominated a slate of candidates for the other student offices. University rules limited candidates' spending to $50 each. However, if UT's student government served as a "laboratory" for future Texas politicians, then the distance between the rules and reality reflected state politics. The Clique spent thousands of dollars trying to fend off the upstarts. Aircraft dropped leaflets over the campus. Parades and all-night dances with live music sought to lure support for the sponsor's candidates. Both sides exceeded the spending limit, and both also worked hard to sabotage the opposition. Shivers's supporters created alliances with lesser sororities not involved with the Clique. When questioned about the value of these associations, Shivers replied, "[A] whore's vote is as good as a debutante's in an election." In April, Shivers won the presidency and the Little Campus machine made inroads into the Clique's power elsewhere. Although the Clique retained some power over student publications, Shivers, as president, sat on the publications board and could intervene.[15]

The Clique had been wounded by Shivers's victory, so some recriminations could be anticipated. Its supporters present on the *Cactus* staff in 1933 satirized Shivers as "a Mussolini on a forty acre scale," as "Kingfish," and as a "Ward Boss": "Whether Mr. Shivers won by default, as some say, or whether the good citizenry of the University was caught napping, is beside the point. Mr. Shivers is president. He will not allow you to forget that. His confident step and flashing eye betoken a far advanced case of megalomania." The Clique's wounded pride accounted for some of the bile in the *Cactus*, but Shivers's efforts to perpetuate the Little Campus machine beyond his own tenure as president offended many. The spring, 1933, elections saw Shivers intervene to prevent a recount of votes in the election for editor of the *Daily Texan*. The Little Campus organization's candidate, D. B. Hardeman, led by six votes until an administration committee overruled Shivers and found an additional fifty-six votes for Hardeman's Clique opponent. Little Campus also attempted to control the "University Sweetheart" election in favor of Shivers's girlfriend, Marjorie Sutton.[16]

That same semester, a mysterious publication called the *Blunderbuss* lampooned Shivers and the Little Campus machine. Its author signed himself "Simon Legree," but his identity eventually became known throughout UT. John Patric, who claimed expulsion from three other colleges and had been dismissed from the *Daily Texan* staff for criticizing Shivers, was widely recognized as the culprit. On May 13, 1933, after a campus dance, Patric and Shivers fought on Guadalupe Street, the main thoroughfare west of the UT campus. All accounts have Shivers coming out the victor in the contest. Jake Pickle, then a freshman, but later a Little Campus student body president, claimed Shivers "really worked him over." Some who would later become Shivers's enemies in Texas politics claimed that Little Campus minions held Patric down during the licking. Whatever happened, Shivers and Patric were both arrested. Shivers was fined a dollar plus $10.80 costs by the Austin municipal court for "making a public affray . . . in a . . . public place."[17]

ALLAN SHIVERS RETURNED TO PORT ARTHUR WITH HIS LAW DEGREE LATER that year and set up practice. Barely a year went by before he entered politics. In preparation, he joined various local civic clubs, publicly advocated Gov. Miriam A. Ferguson's $20 million "bread bond" proposal, and sought his father's advice about what office to seek. He told his father that he was interested in the state house of representatives because he thought it would be an easier mark for a first race. "I'd rather get beat for the Senate than win a seat in the House," his father countered. Heeding his father's counsel, Allan filed for the Fourth District senate seat held by three-term incumbent W. R. Cousins. From this first campaign throughout his service in the legislature, Shivers demonstrated adaptability and pragmatism. He also skillfully concealed dissonances with the electorate, and won elections while holding core beliefs fundamentally more conservative that those of the people he represented.[18]

The Fourth District included Jefferson, Orange, Hardin, and Liberty Counties. The Fourth District's wealth and power lay predominantly in Jefferson County, with the large cities of Beaumont and Port Arthur. More than 73 percent of the district's population lived in the county, which, owing to the oil boom, rode out the depression relatively well compared to its neighbors. Unemployment in both cities remained below the national average. The majority of Jefferson County's residents worked in the manufacturing sector. As a result, organized labor represented a potent political force. The other counties were predominantly rural and suffered the devastating effects of the economic downturn in agriculture. In 1935, 84 percent of the Fourth District's farmers were tenants, a factor of misery that was scarcely helped by the slight increase in farm prices after 1929.[19]

Ordinarily, a race against an incumbent would seem exceptionally daunting. However, Cousins had grown out of touch with his constituents. Local labor leaders, a powerful force in Jefferson County, had grown dissatisfied with him. Although labor's support was essential, Shivers had the disadvantages of youth and limited name recognition. Cousin's deprecated Shivers by referring to him as "boy," telling crowds, "Well, he's a good boy, but he's just a boy." The younger man labored to offset these disadvantages by speaking in every town in the district. He tried hard to create in voters' minds a link with the most charmed name in Democratic politics in the period. "I will give to the best of my ability full cooperation to President Roosevelt's effort to bring about a full and complete recovery," he promised.[20]

Both candidates supported collective bargaining and improved workman's compensation. Shivers also promised to support a federal child labor amendment. Cousins balked, claiming such an alteration to the Constitution might unleash threats to "our Southern ideals and schools" from those "who recognize no color lines." Shivers also hedged a bit in his enthusiasm for the New Deal by insisting that the "means adopted" to deal with the depression "are necessarily temporary." Nonetheless, a critical constituency had come to mistrust Cousins and favor his challenger. One area labor leader was convinced "Shivers has a desire to serve the interest of the plain people," and that he had "very liberal views on legislative matters."[21]

Still, much of one-party politics was about personality. Shivers campaigned frenetically in an effort to establish himself with voters. At the same time, he worked to take advantage of his opponent's complacency and exploit whatever publicity he could get. At a Port Arthur rally, Shivers learned of another meeting to be held that same evening in nearby Vidor. When the challenger asked the incumbent whether he planned on attending, Cousins answered that he did not know. As soon as the Port Arthur meeting ended, Shivers sped the twenty miles to Vidor, only to discover that Cousins had not shown. The Jefferson County party chair at first refused to allow him to speak in Cousins's absence. However, as the Vidor rally drew to a close, he relented. Shivers simply told the crowd of his earlier talk with their senator, hoping they would think the overconfident incumbent took them for granted.[22]

Senator Cousins's son, Roy Jr., also present at the Vidor meeting, angrily demanded a chance to rebut Shivers. Speaking to the crowd, the younger Cousins detailed his father's opponent's brush with the law the previous year and called Shivers a "jail-bird." The resulting publicity was not the best kind. As Shivers later told it, when the story "hit the headlines the next morning," he had to do some damage control. That evening, both candidates were present for a rally in Beaumont. Rather than draw lots for the favored last word, Shivers volunteered to speak first.

> Everybody there knew about this incident. So I told them the whole story: that I did not go to jail, but that I did pay a $10 fine, and that I had to fight for what I thought was right. . . .
>
> Then I said that I wanted to say to Senator Cousins that the next time he wanted to charge that I had been in jail, or any other accusation about my character, my reputation or anything else, I wanted him to have guts enough to do it himself, and not send a half-baked kid over to make the accusations for him.

Shivers later credited the controversy with helping him win the election. He carried all four counties in the district, winning 55 percent of the vote.[23]

After entering the state senate, Shivers befriended Alf Roark, a member of the state house for the area. Both were young, eligible bachelors fresh out of college, with a taste for excitement and diversion. They frequented posh nightclubs in Houston. They gambled together on horses. Shivers always found time for a good time in his early days in the legislature. In July, 1935, he even footed the bill for an overnight "fishing, swimming, boating, etc." party for the Fourth District press aboard a rented boat in the Gulf.[24]

Texas state senators still had to make a living because the state stipend for legislators, then as now, was paltry and based on a biennial meeting schedule. Generally, Shivers's Port Arthur law office, which he shared with partner Quentin Keith, took small personal injury cases against employers and insurance companies. They often worked on a contingency basis, taking a third of any winnings as their fee. Shivers also tried his hand at investing in land and mineral rights in an effort to get ahead. Roark and Shivers, together with Liberty lawyer Price Daniel, bought small parcels in oil-rich Liberty County, but their earnings were sparse. "I am sure we will both be able to retire shortly," Shivers quipped to Roark after receiving a royalty check.[25]

As he approached his thirtieth birthday, the boy senator's financial condition potentially threatened his romantic interests. In 1936, he had begun courting Marialice Shary, a graduate of Our Lady of the Lake College in San Antonio and the only daughter of John Shary, millionaire Valley land developer and citrus planter. Of Austrian origins, Shary had come to Texas from Nebraska and built a $55 million fortune. He and his family lived on an extravagantly landscaped

John Shary. Shivers's father-in-law helped pioneer citrus farming in the Rio Grande Valley. Shivers's friends and enemies alike claim his 1937 marriage into the wealthy Shary family contributed to his growing conservatism.

estate near Mission called "Sharyland." The romance was carefully camouflaged. The two saw one another only in the company of friends. When invited to visit Sharyland, Shivers generally brought along Alf Roark. John Shary may have been hostile to a possible match between his daughter and the Port Arthur lawyer. The Sharys were devout Roman Catholics, whereas Shivers was a Baptist. The Sharys were quite wealthy, whereas Shivers was hardly so. In 1937, John Shary at last agreed to bless their union and the couple wed that October, on Shivers's birthday, beginning a forty-seven-year marriage.[26]

Sources both favorable and hostile to Shivers contend that marrying into a wealthy family changed his politics. When John Shary died in 1945, management of Sharyland passed to his daughter and son-in-law. Authorized biographers Sam Kinch and Stuart Long commented that the inheritance "moved [them] solidly into lives of wealth, and this brought more awareness of the federal government's breathing down your neck." Later, Will Wilson — Shivers's lawyer, political ally, and business partner — recalled that the marriage worked a change in the former "personal injury lawyer" and New Dealer. Still others have argued that Shivers's marriage only aided his political transformation. Some insist that Shivers never had an ideology to begin with and was simply an opportunist.[27]

Closer study of Shivers's early career reveals his philosophical tendencies. He had demonstrated an early identification with wealth and privilege, which manifested itself in his dress and manner. He strove to emulate the Clique's swells at the University of Texas, even while working to defeat them politically. He continued this pattern even in working-class Port Arthur, where he would stroll through town wearing spats and carrying a cane. With respect to politics, his rightward tendencies could easily be inferred by his rhetoric. In his first campaign, he proudly touted his support for Franklin D. Roosevelt's New Deal, while also making clear that his support was contingent. Relief measures intended to fight the depression were "necessarily temporary." Finally, the case for an ideological portrait of Shivers can be made from the testimony of some of his allies, who labeled him as unambiguously conservative, even elitist.[28]

Nonetheless, Shivers held his state senate seat for twelve years, in no small part because of his ability to straddle his own views and those of his constituents. In his first term, the young senator from Port Arthur helped sponsor Gov. James V. Allred's pet project: a tax on chain stores. Along with a majority of the legislature, Shivers voted for pensions for the elderly, the impoverished blind, and indigent children. Texas' constitution mandated a balanced budget, and this forced legislators to confront the specter of taxes. Along with the rest of the legislature, he balked at a variety of revenue measures designed to fund these measures. Supporting the liberal Allred's popular chain-store tax offered Shivers some credentials as a progressive force in the state senate.[29]

Shivers's support within his relatively liberal district proved sufficient to protect him from Allred's displeasure when the senator opposed the governor's efforts to end pari-mutuel betting. Another source of tension between Shivers and Governor Allred involved disagreements between the governor's allies in Jefferson County and the senator over local and personal matters. In 1938, the outgoing governor criticized the senator in the midst of his bid for reelection. Allred liked Shivers's opponent, state representative Harry McKee, no better. "I'd have a thundering hard time deciding which of you two to vote for," he told McKee at a political forum in the Hardin County town of Silsbee.[30]

Shivers replied forcefully to Allred's remark, calling it a "typical Allred mugwump statement." He argued that Governor Allred's criticism stemmed from his

Texas Governor James V. Allred (right) and Kansas Governor Walter Huxman, c.a., 1938. Shivers had both personal and political clashes with the liberal Allred.

disagreement with "many of his policies." Claiming the governor wanted a "yes-man," the senator told him to butt out of the Fourth District race. "If Jimmie Allred spent more time attending to his own business, the part of the state government for which he is responsible would not be in such a hell of a mess." The public and acrimonious break with Allred developed from personality conflict as much as ideology. Many years later, Shivers claimed that the governor thought "he was entitled to cast my vote in the senate" because Allred had appointed Shivers's father a district judge in Jefferson County. Shivers, though, was plainly more conservative than Allred and must have felt some freedom to distance himself from the lame-duck governor.[31]

Little separated Shivers and his 1938 opponent. Both supported higher pensions for the elderly, but neither voiced any innovative solutions to the problem of funding them. Allred's original pension plan had never been fully funded, so retirees received roughly fourteen dollars a month. This stretched state finances thin, even as rain leaked into the house chamber of the capitol. Shivers and McKee both had strong records on labor issues. In the most recent legislative session, Shivers had voted with organized labor nine times and never opposed union-supported measures. He had fought against a regressive general sales tax and even opposed legislation banning sit-down strikes.[32]

McKee attempted to put some distance between himself and Shivers by resorting to personal attacks and innuendo. At a Jefferson County political rally, he accused Shivers of having entertained famous fan-dancer Sally Rand in Dallas during the 1936 Texas Centennial Exposition. Neither confirming nor denying the allegations, the incumbent quipped that McKee simply was "jealous he wasn't invited." By keeping to the high road and sticking to the issues, Shivers defeated McKee with little difficulty, garnering 22,259 votes (68 percent) to his opponent's 10,681 (32 percent).[33]

CHAPTER TWO

Turmoil and Transition: Shivers and the Texas Political Scene, 1938–45

AT THE AGE OF THIRTY-ONE, ALLAN SHIVERS HAD WON A SECOND term in the Texas senate. Although personally conservative and married to money, the young politician still represented a prolabor district. His political career began and matured during a tumultuous time for the state's one-party Democratic system. Texas' politics remained peculiarly southern, but the tradition of Democratic loyalty had come under increasing strain. To some Texans, the national party had moved in new and threatening directions. Others embraced the New Deal and its efforts to modernize the state and region. A struggle developed between these two camps, which drew in all participants in the state's politics. Shivers worked hard to appear neutral, even though his personal views and friendship network indicated sympathies with the anti–New Deal faction. Throughout the late 1930s and into the 1940s, the intraparty war grew in intensity across a series of smaller battles. The young state senator hovered at the periphery. By careful observation, he strengthened his political skills in this period and prepared for statewide office.

Political scientist V. O. Key Jr. argued that the region's one-party politics prevented genuine debate of economic and class issues. Rather than competing public-spending priorities and debate over taxation to fund these, southern Democratic politics centered on personality and faction. Political elites distracted voters from poor public services and regressive taxation by exploiting side issues that enabled them to keep power. The "fearful specter of Negro rule" loomed as the chief distraction used to convince whites to stay within the one-party system. In this system, the "haves" nearly always won. They then used the state government to legislate and tax according to their own interests. Nationally, southerners formed a powerful and cohesive bloc within the Democratic Party and obstructed federal efforts to alter the regional political system. As a result, Key observed, "the South as a whole . . . developed no system or practice of political organization or leadership adequate to cope with its problems."[1]

Key's analysis, written in 1949, was based on an in-depth study of individual southern states' political tendencies. He recognized that the New Deal, World War II, and demographic changes threatened the one-party system, perhaps bringing on a new two-party politics. Key expected these tensions to develop more quickly in states on the fringe of the Deep South, which had a "higher degree of freedom" from the race issue. Texas' urban and industrial growth during the 1940s brought about "the vague outlines of a politics . . . in which irrelevancies are pushed into the background and people divide broadly along liberal and conservative lines." An emergent "modified class politics" characterized by bitter party factionalism presaged the dawn of a two-party era. However, Key also pointed out that economic elites would struggle against anything that threatened their dominance over the state Democratic Party. They did so through the old method of distracting the electorate from real economic and class concerns. This made state politics during the 1940s a risky business for those with higher ambitions.[2]

Texas' one-party system lacked a strong "machine" according to Key's analysis, but behind the scenes a machine of sorts had developed: the Texas Establishment. Historian George Green described the Establishment as "a loosely knit plutocracy comprised mainly of Anglo businessmen, oilmen, bankers and lawyers." Politicians backed by the Establishment worked to keep Texas' state services minimal, its taxes regressive, its minorities in their place, and its labor unions weak. These leaders spoke the rhetoric of states' rights and struggled against the growing federal government of the New Deal era. As the 1930s closed, the Establishment increasingly asserted itself, and the resulting struggles with more liberal party elements eventually forced all to choose sides.[3]

Shivers's reelection in 1938 coincided with a decided anti–New Deal turn in Texas Democratic politics. When Gov. James Allred, a Roosevelt administration ally, declined to seek a third term, thirteen candidates entered the race to replace him. Most political observers expected a runoff. Political novice W. Lee O'Daniel of Fort Worth won a majority in the July primary, shocking seasoned political observers. A transplanted midwesterner, O'Daniel managed a flour milling company. He was a former Republican who had never paid a Texas poll tax. As a promotion for his company's Hillbilly brand flour, O'Daniel hosted a daily radio program featuring country and western music along with patriotic and religious homilies. Thousands listened each noon, assuring him greater name recognition than even veteran politicians. His platform in the race had been the Ten Commandments and the Golden Rule. When other candidates asked for specifics, O'Daniel promised "less Johnson grass and politicians, more smokestacks and

Governor W. Lee "Pappy" O'Daniel enjoys fried chicken and a glass of milk. O'Daniel carefully cultivated his "country boy" image in both his political campaigns and daily radio show. His 1938 election shocked veteran politicians, including Shivers. In 1941, O'Daniel won election to the U.S. Senate.

businessmen." He also promised increased old-age pensions and an end to the poll tax and capital punishment. All could be accomplished, he told voters, without increased taxes.[4]

Once in office, O'Daniel proved to be anything but progressive. The increased pensions quickly pushed state finances into the red. Texas was broke, so the new governor turned to the business lobby for advice on revenue measures that could be used to fund the pensions. With their coaching and support, O'Daniel proposed a "transaction tax" of 1.6 percent on most business transactions. Legislators balked at the thinly disguised sales tax. Governor O'Daniel then sought a constitutional amendment authorizing a sales tax, while proposing a freeze on the already low severance taxes on natural resources. The state house rejected the amendment, leading to a budget crisis. Rather than compromise, the governor resorted to a scorched earth approach to state appropriations. He cut hospital beds, moneys for state wards, and slashed the highway budget by half. Still, public enthusiasm for O'Daniel did not wane. He continued to broadcast

Allan and Marialice Shivers welcome a visit from Governor and Mrs. O'Daniel, 1940. O'Daniel, with his back to the camera, holds baby John. The governor visited legislators in their homes to gain support for his regressive tax schemes. O'Daniel's policies and appointments strengthened conservatives' hold over state Democratic politics.

daily from the governor's mansion and mobilized public opinion against the legislators. In the 1940 primaries, O'Daniel again won without a runoff, but half of the house members who had voted against his sales tax went down to defeat in their bid for reelection.[5]

As war in Europe and Asia threatened the United States, O'Daniel used the sense of crisis to attack organized labor. During the 1941 legislative session, he urged action against "labor leader racketeers" who threatened American preparedness. He also asked the legislature for legislation banning violence or threats of violence by picketing strikers. The governor's proposal did not specify penalties for threats or violent acts by management or strikebreakers. It was intended to have a chilling effect upon the right to strike. The "anti-violence" measure passed and merged with the governor's wider campaign against so-called fifth-column elements within the Lone Star State. During the 1940 campaign, O'Daniel warned President Roosevelt of the dangers posed to Texas by subversives. He also told his daily listeners to report any suspicious activity to the governor's office. Fearful writers replied in the hundreds as the governor deliberately fed mass hysteria.[6]

The governor's obsession with labor and fifth-column threats fed his desire for a bigger stage. His chance came when U.S. senator Morris Sheppard died in April. Required to appoint an interim replacement pending a special election, O'Daniel did not want to select someone who might later be a viable opponent. He therefore appointed Sam Houston's youngest son, by then an octogenarian, as interim senator. Senator Andrew Jackson Houston obligingly dropped dead six weeks later. Without an incumbent to threaten his chances for election, Governor O'Daniel ran against a field of twenty-eight other candidates. Several notables stood between the governor and the U.S. Senate, but Rep. Lyndon B. Johnson, with Roosevelt's backing, was the strongest challenger. In the June special election, O'Daniel edged Johnson by thirteen hundred votes amid accusations of fraud.[7]

Like most Austin insiders, Senator Shivers initially did not know quite what to make of Governor O'Daniel. He had scoffed when his own father predicted O'Daniel's election. Just as the flour salesman's ascent to the governor's mansion indicated a rightward shift in state politics, the Port Arthur senator increasingly demonstrated his own conservative ideology in the changed climate. His differences with O'Daniel's agenda reflected his own district's political makeup rather than deeply held personal principles. Shivers parted company with the governor over the "transaction tax." When O'Daniel excoriated legislative opponents on the air, the senator discovered quickly the media's power to mobilize voters. Letters streamed in criticizing his opposition to the transaction tax. "[Y]ou know O'Daniels [*sic*] carried this State 30 to 1," one angry Fourth District resident wrote. "You ought to be ashamed of yourself the way you are bucking him." Ironically, Shivers sat on the senate committee that killed the only alternative to the governor's bill: increased severance taxes. While he clearly did not wish to alienate his constituents with a sales levy, there is no evidence that he supported higher taxes on Texas' high-rolling oil and gas industry.[8]

Shivers did go along with some of Governor O'Daniel's controversial political appointees. He presided over the nominating committee that reviewed all gubernatorial appointments. The governor repeatedly pushed anti–New Deal appointees upon a reluctant state senate. In 1939, O'Daniel selected James M. West, a Houston millionaire, to sit on the state highway commission, only to see him rejected by the senate. Two years later, he appointed West Texas rancher J. Evetts Haley to the state livestock sanitary commission, only to see the appointment fail. Both men had belonged to the Jeffersonian Democrats, a far-right organization established to defeat Franklin Roosevelt in the 1936 presidential election. Shivers's committee reported favorably on both men. Because the final senate votes on both West and Haley were taken during executive session, individual votes were not recorded. However, it seems unlikely the two would have cleared Shivers's committee without his support.[9]

Organized labor represented the Fourth District's best-organized and most-cohesive constituency. Shivers's response to O'Daniel's antilabor program indicates emergent ideological dissonance with the unions. During the 1939 session, Senator Shivers voted with labor on only one of four occasions. When O'Daniel's antiviolence legislation came to the state senate in 1941, Shivers voted for it, inviting its use against him in the 1942 primaries. For the remainder of the 1941 session, he supported labor's position on four of seven bills. In 1942, Shivers easily defeated his predecessor and 1934 opponent, W. R. Cousins, in the summer primary. Cousins campaigned against the younger man primarily upon his vote for the antiviolence bill. Still, labor stuck with Allan Shivers, who won a third term.[10]

When O'Daniel ran for the U.S. Senate in 1941, Allan Shivers supported Lyndon Johnson. However, Shivers's support cannot be taken necessarily as an ideological endorsement. Rather, the senator's support reflected his developing personal relationship with Representative Johnson. The following year, when O'Daniel sought a full term in Washington, Shivers sided with him against former governor James Allred. Johnson allowed Allred the use of his political network and passed on a list of his allies in Southeast Texas, including Shivers. Allred, knowing he could not expect the Fourth District senator's support, crossed Shivers's name off the list provided by Johnson. Shivers may have prevailed upon his father-in-law to deny Allred financial backing in his race against O'Daniel. A direct appeal to John Shary from Allred's wife ended up in his son-in-law's personal papers, and the former governor's financial records indicate no aid ever came from the Valley millionaire. Shivers's position in 1942 might have stemmed from his personal animosity toward Allred, but it also indicates a possible greater ideological affinity with Senator O'Daniel.[11]

Shivers and O'Daniel differed greatly in personality and style, although the former later admitted having learned a great deal about politics from the latter. O'Daniel's ability to appeal to "personal desires and personal emotions" demonstrated to Shivers the power of "the psychological approach to almost everyone's desire for love of mother, home, and country." O'Daniel's rhetoric repeatedly convinced ordinary Texans that he understood them, even as he gutted public services and protected the interests of the wealthy. As governor, O'Daniel created and used political capital by direct appeal to the public, using the mass media to enhance the power of a relatively weak office. Had O'Daniel been more politically astute, he might have worked harder to control the state Democratic Party and thereby wield even greater power. Shivers's own political style included O'Daniel's rhetorical and media savvy, but added to it control over the party machinery.[12]

RISING DOUBTS ABOUT THE NEW DEAL AND THE NATIONAL DEMOCRATIC Party's future influenced Texas' actions on the national scene. Vice President John Nance Garner's 1940 bid for the Democratic presidential nomination dramatically illustrated the growing divisions among Texas Democrats. The former Uvalde congressman and U.S. House Speaker had served as FDR's running mate in 1932 and 1936, even though he heartily disliked the vice presidency's limitations. Like many conservative Democrats, particularly southerners, the vice president grew hostile toward the New Deal after 1935. Protections for labor unions, as well as legislation providing workers a guaranteed minimum wage and capping the number of hours worked violated traditional regional patterns of deference and interfered with private enterprise. After 1936, black voters' growing influence led northern Democratic politicians to press for a federal antilynching law. Possible federal action against lynching alarmed regional leaders and resulted in a Senate filibuster. Roosevelt's failed attempt to pack the Supreme Court in 1937 alienated still more legislators. During the 1938 summer Democratic primaries, the president worked against his intraparty foes. The purge failed, and most of the targeted southern conservatives returned to Washington even more deeply embittered. Garner himself grew so angry over the court-packing scheme that he actively worked to subvert it. This caused a nasty break with Roosevelt, and the vice president all but deserted Washington for his South Texas ranch for the remainder of his term.[13]

In 1940, Roosevelt feigned disinterest in a third term, while trying to engineer a "draft" by the national convention. His behavior frustrated supporters and would-be nominees alike. Speaker Sam Rayburn, U.S. senators Morris Sheppard and Tom Connally, and Texas' party leadership worked to win the nomination for Vice President Garner. They planned to seize the Texas delegation and offer Garner as a favorite son at the national convention. Garner's chances looked good with national polls showing him the frontrunner in a race without Roosevelt. Neither Rayburn, Sheppard, nor Connally acted out of any animus toward FDR, but rather out of collegial loyalty to Garner. In order to take a pro-Garner slate to the national convention, his allies needed to win control of Texas' state Democratic convention in May.[14]

The convention nearly erupted into a brawl as the two sides argued bitterly. Led by former San Antonio congressman and mayor Maury Maverick, former governor James Ferguson, and Rep. Lyndon Johnson, those favoring Roosevelt succumbed to their rivals—but not before extracting a significant concession. Although Garner won Texas' delegation, the convention passed a resolution praising the New Deal and the Roosevelt administration. The unity measure did not please the more-determined conservatives present. At the national meeting, however, sentiment for Roosevelt easily overwhelmed the other candidates. Rayburn and most other Garner supporters easily fell into line behind the president, though some resented his choice of Agriculture Secretary Henry A. Wallace as running mate. Texas Democratic chair E. B. Germany, a Dallas steel millionaire, and some wealthy oil barons washed their hands of the national party and openly supported Republican nominee Wendell Willkie.[15]

Allan Shivers's political philosophy and career trajectory contributed to his own growing discomfort with the New Deal. Although he had spoken in favor of Roosevelt's court-packing plan, the young senator became progressively disillusioned. Like many other politicians, Shivers kept a "speech file" from which he gleaned ideas for his talks. While not a window into his soul, its contents demonstrate his ideological orientation during the late 1930s and 1940s. He kept for future reference an address by Sen. Tom Connally during the successful filibuster against federal antilynching legislation. Shivers was so struck by Connally's effort that he wrote him a congratulatory note saying, "We need more men in Legislative Halls who have the courage of their convictions." He also collected speeches from Wendell Willkie—such as "We the People, a foundation for a political platform for recovery" and "The Faith That Is America"—as well as much more venomous attacks upon the New Deal by state party leader E. B. Germany and Frank Gannett, publisher and founder of the Committee for Constitutional Government.[16]

Shivers also kept a "joke file" full of gems used to introduce speeches. The following example speaks to his ideological inclinations during the period:

> There was a Northern man around here the other day and he said to the old man, who is a Confederate veteran, "I guess you are a Democrat." The old man allowed that he was and proud of it. The Northern man asked, "Did you vote for Roosevelt the first time?" Simpkins [the old man] said he sure did. He asked him if he voted for Roosevelt the second time and the old man said that he did. "Would you vote for him a third time?" he was asked. Simpkins drew himself up proudly and said, "I sure would vote for him a third time," and then he kinder slumped and said, "But I want to tell you something. If you darn Yankees don't quit voting for him you are going to ruin this country."

Shivers jotted a note to his secretary on the clipping that read: "You'll appreciate this joke." Her reply playfully suggested: "I think this was intended for you." Senator Shivers plainly had misgivings about the New Deal and a third term for FDR, but he nonetheless supported the president in 1940. Years later, Shivers described himself as a "Wilsonian liberal" who had favored the early New Deal, but later saw Roosevelt as a "sick man" who allowed the Democratic Party to drift from its roots.[17]

TEXAS DEMOCRATIC STRIFE ALSO INFLUENCED A SERIES OF CONTROVERSIES at the University of Texas that culminated in 1944 with the firing of the school's president. The university had been a periodic target of politicians as far back as Gov. James Ferguson's tenure (1915–17). Indeed, a clash with the University of Texas contributed to Ferguson's impeachment and removal from office. During the late 1930s, a Texas house committee investigated possible communist influence within the university's Economics Department and a student political organization. Alleged communist activities at the campus drew the attention of U.S. representative Martin Dies's House Un-American Activities Committee in the early 1940s. Both bodies saw charges of communism as an excuse to harass faculty and students with liberal and New Deal sympathies. During the 1930s, Gov. James Allred had appointed a relatively liberal and tolerant board of regents that worked to safeguard academic freedom. However, from 1939–44, Allred's appointees gradually rotated off the board and were replaced by those of Governors O'Daniel and Coke Stevenson.[18]

O'Daniel and Stevenson chose regents based upon ideology, specifically seeking ultraconservative anti–New Deal businessmen for service on the board. The new crop of regents worried that many professors were "too radical" and disapproved of academicians commenting upon public issues. In 1941, after the last of Allred's appointees had departed, the regents zealously attacked academic freedom. They abolished the position of university public relations director without warning or a hearing for its occupant. When four UT economics professors spoke in favor of New Deal labor protections to a Dallas newspaper, a kangaroo court of regents dismissed the men. Although it failed to do away with tenure completely, the board weakened it significantly. When the English Department's textbook committee placed John Dos Passos's *U.S.A.* trilogy on the supplemental list, regents banned the work as "obscene" and "perverted." The regents dismissed President Homer Rainey on November 1, 1944, after he addressed a faculty meeting and condemned the censorship. University students went on strike and eight thousand marched to the capitol and governor's mansion. The controversy led to the American Association of University Professors censuring the university's administration. Regent Lutcher Stark summed up the board's dismissal of Rainey rather clearly: "The president of the University of Texas occupies the same position to the Board of Regents as a general manager of a corporation does to its Board of Directors."[19]

Away at war, Shivers had little directly to do with events leading to Rainey's dismissal. However, as a state senator, he demonstrated the same attitude toward academic freedom as Stark and the conservative regents. In 1937, he intervened to prevent publication of a master's thesis on Port Arthur's city government that he found objectionable. Shivers contacted university officials who had the student

Coke Stevenson, governor 1941–1947. Stevenson proved even more conservative than O'Daniel. Shivers backed his successful bids for lieutenant governor and governor. However, in 1948, Shivers supported Lyndon Johnson against Stevenson in their controversial U.S. Senate contest.

"eliminate several features" to prevent "anything being published which is derogatory to any individual or group." Then, in 1943, just before Shivers shipped out to Europe, former classmate A. W. Walker Jr. asked the senator to intervene on behalf of a fired law school professor. Walker explained that Prof. George Stumberg had applied for leave only to have regents take his request as a resignation. Shivers's response seemed sympathetic to the professor, even downright tolerant of Stumberg's known liberal sympathies: "He has a lot of peculiar ways, but who doesn't?" However, after looking into the matter, the senator came down squarely on the side of the regents. Stumberg, it turned out, had defended the four economics professors fired in 1942, failed to follow proper procedure in seeking leave, and capped it all by being "impolitic in his persistence" when disagreeing with the regents. "After all," Shivers explained, "a person cannot cuss out the boss every morning before breakfast and expect to keep his job. I think Stumberg . . . an excellent professor of law . . . although I have always thought he was probably too theoretical as well as hot tempered."[20]

Allan Shivers's actions in the case of the objectionable thesis demonstrated his willingness to use power to squelch criticism. To a point, he had shown this same tendency during his student government days. Coming at a time during which university professors were being hauled before legislative investigating committees, it also clarified his sense that state officials had the right to interfere in minute university processes. In the Stumberg matter, the senator initially appeared quite sympathetic, as though he liked the law professor and thought the man had been unfairly treated. However, his views quickly changed after he apparently heard the regents' side of the story. Whatever transpired between Stumberg and the board, Shivers's comments indicate that he shared the regents' proprietary view of the university. These two small pieces of the wider UT struggle clearly indicate that Shivers's sympathies lay with the right wing in state politics. Moreover, his conservatism was not merely economic, but also social. The graduate student and the law professor had both forgotten themselves and their place.

TEXAS' DEMOCRATIC POLITICS SUFFERED ANOTHER PRESIDENTIAL ELECTION year upheaval in 1944. With Franklin Roosevelt unchallenged for the Democratic nomination, fear that he might seek a fourth term led some conservative Democrats to hatch a scheme to prevent his reelection. Texas money helped fund the movement. The idea received particularly positive attention in the South, with two main variants emerging. Outside of Texas, discontented Democrats concentrated on a third-party candidacy for Virginia senator Harry Byrd, an outspoken Democratic critic of the New Deal. In Texas, Anti–New Deal forces planned to seize control of the state Democratic convention, nominate an anti-FDR delegation to the national convention, and, more importantly, select a slate of "independent" presidential electors pledged to no candidate. If Roosevelt won the general election in a state with independent electors, the electors could circumvent the popular vote. If enough states went for Byrd or chose the independent-elector strategy, the election might end up in the House of Representatives. There, with each state receiving a single vote for president, the South could extract concessions on everything from civil rights to labor relations from the party most willing to meet its terms.[21]

The anti–New Dealers organized at the precinct and county level as a first step toward implementing their strategy. The May precinct conventions generally were sparsely attended affairs, and the ongoing war further held down attendance. With strong organization and ample money, New Deal opponents won at the precinct and county levels, particularly in urban areas. They dominated the state convention in Waco, where observers noted a powerful oil and gas industry presence. The conventioneers chose independent electors pledged to vote against the nominee unless the party restored the old two-thirds rule for presidential nominations and condemned the recent *Smith v. Allwright* Supreme Court decision, which had invalidated the white primary. The national convention nominated Roosevelt for a fourth term, and predictably refused to condemn *Smith* or return to the two-thirds rule. In presidential election years, Texas Democrats held two state conventions. The first, in May, selected national convention delegates and electors, while the second, in September, ratified the results of the summer primary and wrote the party platform. The New Dealers resolved to take control of the September convention and reverse their May defeat. When they succeeded—after a close vote, fistfights, and swearing matches—Roosevelt supporters replaced the independent electors with ones loyal to the president. Thwarted, anti–New Deal forces formed a third party, the Texas Regulars, to oppose Roosevelt and Republican nominee Thomas Dewey in November. Roosevelt thrashed the Republicans and the Regulars, winning 71 percent of the vote.[22]

Although the Texas Regulars conflict arose while Shivers was at war in Europe, it helped create the political environment in which he had to operate upon his return. No record exists of his position on the intraparty battles of 1944. However, he built close business and political relationships with Regulars and their sympathizers before and after that contentious campaign. He also sympathized later in his career with key portions of the Regulars' agenda. Independent oilmen Arch Rowan and Hugh Roy Cullen maintained ties with Shivers. Rowan later allowed the politician to use his personal aircraft for political purposes and Cullen helped fund some of Shivers's statewide campaigns. Representatives of big oil, such as Humble Oil lawyer Clint Small and Socony-Vacuum attorney W. A. Weinert served with Shivers in the state senate. Oveta Culp Hobby, publisher of the *Houston Post*, backed the Regulars and Shivers throughout his career. The Texas Regulars' opposition to labor unions, the direction of the national Democratic Party, civil rights, and federal "rule by regimentation" all found their way into Shivers's rhetoric in subsequent years.[23]

THE WAR YEARS TRANSFORMED TEXAS AND THE SOUTH AND HELPED exacerbate Democratic Party tensions, setting the stage for intraparty clashes to come. Texas became an urban state, wealthier than ever before, with growing middle-class and unionized-labor constituencies. New urbanites demanded improved public services and strained against a political system oriented toward county seat and small town. African Americans and Tejano citizens began to press against white supremacy. The war provoked questions about the nature of freedom in the United States and led to greater federal interest in the well-being of racial minorities. Like other southern conservatives, the Texas Establishment struggled to control the effect of these trends upon state politics. When Allan

Shivers returned from the war, he faced the implications of these developments for his political career.

In 1940, 54.6 percent of Texans lived in rural areas compared to 45.4 percent in cities with more than ten thousand inhabitants. World War II drove the urban population to nearly 60 percent and triggered a downward spiral in the state's rural population that still continues. The increased urbanization mirrored trends throughout the South, but Texas' citification was well advanced relative to the rest of the region in 1940. Texans' migration to the cities dramatically outpaced that of other southerners during the war. Wartime industrialization fueled the move to town, and while regional industrial capacity doubled in the war years, the value of Texas' manufacturing sector quadrupled. Farms decreased in number, but grew in size, value, and output. Federal money contributed to the southern boom. The national government spent roughly $4.75 billion in the region, with Texas receiving a significant share owing to its powerful congressional delegation. More than a million soldiers trained at fifteen Texas army bases and forty air bases, war contracts helped lift the state out of economic depression, and the new prosperity hinted at even better days to come.[24]

Wartime economic growth also strengthened organized labor's presence in Texas. Union membership more than tripled in the state from 1939–53, again reflecting wider regional changes. Unions brought or forced higher wages and better working conditions, but labor still faced long odds against capital and management. Nevertheless, politically savvy union leaders and rank-and-file members increasingly played a role in Democratic politics, particularly in localities that had witnessed industrial growth. The Texas Gulf Coast, including Beaumont–Port Arthur in Shivers's Fourth District, saw organized labor accrue even greater political influence. Texas' growing middle class took advantage of government veterans' programs promoting small business, education, and vocational training. These "climbers" took new prominence in major cities, but also smaller towns and county seats. Regionally, middle-class couples took to conspicuous consumption, civic activism, and frequently identified with their social betters.[25]

World War II had a destabilizing effect on segregation policies in Texas and the rest of the South. The war against Nazism's racist ideology highlighted the incongruity of segregation with American ideals. African Americans pointedly spoke of the "Double V"—"victory at home and abroad"—and their aspirations for equality grew as the war's end drew closer. Federal actions and policies made practical and symbolic inroads into the racial caste system. The Fair Employment Practices Commission (FEPC) was created in 1940 to investigate employment discrimination in war work. Although weak, the FEPC infuriated many southern whites, who thought the commission threatened regional racial and class norms.

Four years later, the U.S. Supreme Court ended a twenty-year legal battle and overturned the white primary in Texas. Southern state leaders recoiled at the decision Mississippi's Rep. John Rankin called a "communistic drive . . . to destroy white supremacy in the South." War work boosted the skill level of many African Americans and improved their economic lot through better, if still segregated, employment. The federal government paid the families of black servicemen the same living stipends provided to white soldiers' families. As a result, the economic hold of the white community over blacks weakened for the duration. Federal regulation of transportation to conserve vital war materials also led to the temporary integration of some rail and bus service in the South.[26]

Texas whites reacted quite negatively to these developments. Governor Coke Stevenson, a staunch segregationist, warned the FEPC not to undermine the racial hierarchy. Commission officials replied that since Texas law did not mandate employment discrimination, their agency did not threaten segregation by promoting fair hiring. Stevenson thundered against the Supreme Court's attack on the white primary. Even modest black economic gains angered whites. A Houstonian bemoaned paying equal stipends to black military families because "the greater number of nigger women have left the servant occupation for the more abundant life." Another Texan, traveling on an interstate train, was "knocked cold" at the sight of "a black negro, perhaps a close ally of our National negro party" sharing his sleeping car on the Texas and Pacific Railroad. Some African Americans grew emboldened and ignored segregation in urban public transport. A white visitor to Beaumont in 1942 observed, "some Negroes are now violating [segregation] laws with impudence." Dallas police officials proposed arming city bus drivers to enforce segregation rules.[27]

Whites lashed out violently when confronted with these challenges. In 1942, Texarkana whites lynched a black man for having raped a white woman, despite questionable evidence as to his guilt. When U.S. Attorney General Francis Biddle asked Governor Stevenson to take action against the mob, explaining that Axis propaganda had seized upon the event, the governor responded that he had already publicly spoken about the matter and refused to do more. Moreover, he blamed "certain members of the Negro race" who "from time to time furnish the setting for mob violence by the outrageous crimes they commit." Stevenson did even less when Beaumont erupted in a race riot in June, 1943. Responding to a false claim that a black man had raped a white woman, some four thousand to five thousand whites invaded the black section of town, burning, looting, and beating residents. Three died and hundreds were injured before martial law restored order. Stevenson refused to postpone a trip out of state to handle the matter and left the president pro tempore of the state senate to serve as acting governor. Wartime dislocation and job competition exacerbated racial tensions across the country that spring and summer. Beaumont, in Shivers's Fourth District, had experienced the same dramatic growth and racial unrest as another southern city plagued by rioting that year: Mobile, Alabama.[28]

Texas' largest minority group, citizens of Mexican descent and Mexican citizens residing in the state, also saw its situation altered by the war. Ambiguity permeated relations between Anglos and Tejanos, giving segregation and racism in Texas a bifurcated quality. For census purposes, Tejanos were "white" and could vote, although political bosses tightly controlled their votes in some regions. Nonetheless, Hispanics in much of the state encountered segregation similar to that faced by black Texans. Intermarriage occurred with some frequency, but the acceptability of such unions often depended upon social class. Some Anglos, most notably Gov. Coke Stevenson, demonstrated an acceptance of Tejanos unheard of with African Americans. In 1943, the Mexican government retaliated against Texas' application of Jim Crow laws to its citizens by halting the flow of *braceros* (guest workers) to the state's agricultural regions. With bigotry threatening to impede the war effort, the Texas legislature passed the Caucasian Race Resolution that summer, putting the state on record as supporting voluntary integration and condemning the mistreatment of Mexican citizens and Tejanos alike. Stevenson himself lauded "the high integrity, the initiative, and public spirit" of Hispanics. He felt genuine, if reserved, warmth for Tejanos and Mexicans and cooperated with federal efforts to restart the flow of war workers over the border.[29]

At the request of the U.S. State Department, Texas established the Good Neighbor Commission (GNC) to assist in conflict resolution and investigate discrimination. Stevenson not only backed the biracial commission, he also supported antidiscrimination legislation. "Meskins is pretty good folks," the governor explained. "If it was niggers it'd be different." Although he appeared oblivious to the contradiction, Stevenson inadvertently shook segregation's foundations. By 1945, with the war drawing to a close, Stevenson and GNC members pressed to have the commission made permanent. The Forty-ninth Legislature agreed, and Sen. Allan Shivers, just back from overseas, voted with the majority. However, the legislators balked at taking more meaningful action against discrimination. When San Antonio senator J. Franklin Spears proposed criminalizing discrimination against Hispanics, East Texas senators, recognizing the potential threat to segregation for blacks, submitted amendments that emasculated the measure. Shivers voted against Spears's original bill, but supported a meaningless substitute.[30]

The Stevenson administration's dual policy toward Texas' two minorities troubled many whites. East Texas' legislators had stonewalled efforts to protect Hispanics with black aspirations clearly in mind. Big city newspapers also condemned legislative efforts to end anti-Hispanic discrimination, recognizing the threat to all segregation. Both African-American and Hispanic Texans recognized

Governor Stevenson speaks to shipyard workers in Port Arthur. State Senator Allan Shivers stands at right; middle left is State Representative DeWitt Kennard, and at far left is shipbuilder Bruno Schulz.

the significance of the state's wartime concessions. The Dallas chapter of the National Association for the Advancement of Colored People (NAACP) praised the GNC and suggested that Governor Stevenson not forget black Texans. Even some Tejano correspondents thanked the governor for his aid while at the same time reminding him of the plight of Texas blacks. When Stevenson blasted the FEPC, its chair pointed out the irony of "your excellency's expressed concern" about discrimination toward Tejanos.[31]

Thousands of minority veterans returned from the war determined to submit no longer. Dr. Hector P. Garcia and other Tejano activists formed the American G.I. Forum to challenge segregation in South Texas. Although it predated the war, the League of United Latin American Citizens (LULAC) stepped up its activities after 1945. Across the South, the NAACP saw an increase in membership and activity through the war years and afterward. Following its successful legal challenge to the white primary in Texas, NAACP lawyers filed suit against the University of Texas seeking integration of its law school in 1945. After the 1944 *Smith v. Allwright* decision, public opinion polls showed some divergent attitudes among Texans about the future of Jim Crow. However, whites generally appeared just as determined to reassert their dominance with the close of hostilities. The white struggle to control Texas' minorities became ever more prominent in state politics in succeeding years. As a child of East Texas married into Valley aristocracy, Allan Shivers must have felt the pull of this issue quite keenly.[32]

WORLD WAR II CHANGED TEXAS SIGNIFICANTLY AND ACCELERATED CHANGE throughout the South. The bonds that held the Democratic Party together in the Lone Star State had frayed. For a time, it appeared that conservative forces hostile to the direction of the national party had been held at bay. Some had already begun voting Republican in presidential years while working to strengthen control over the state party. Economic and social forces unleashed by the war brought new controversies and new intraparty battles. Major Allan Shivers returned from the service in early 1945. He served with distinction in the military governments established in Italy and France and was awarded the Bronze Star. He also returned with larger ambitions than the state senate. Up until 1945, Shivers had carefully avoided manifesting his own ideology for fear of angering his constituents. He had managed to sidestep playing any public role in Texas' Democratic Party skirmishes. In the years ahead, if Shivers wished to stay in politics, he would not be able to conceal his colors.[33]

CHAPTER THREE

"That All Depends upon God and Allan Shivers"

1945–49

TEXAS DEMOCRATS' INTERNECINE BLOODLETTING DURING THE EARLY 1940s badly strained party unity and opened fissures that widened afterward. Allan Shivers, meanwhile, had kept his sympathies carefully hidden. Active duty overseas also sheltered him from some of the intraparty warfare. The Port Arthur senator returned from war with ambitions for statewide office and won the lieutenant governorship in 1946. Shivers expanded the power of Texas' most powerful elected office. No longer representing a relatively liberal bastion in southeast Texas, Shivers enjoyed greater freedom to act on his own conservative views. The immediate postwar years brought upheaval and change to both Texas and the South. Conservative Democrats grew more disenchanted with the national party. Shivers's own party loyalty weakened during the two and one-half years he presided over the Texas senate. Like many other southern Democrats, he worked hard to hold at bay the changes that were pressing upon his state and region.

Shivers had been back in Texas only three months when the *Beaumont Journal* touted him as a candidate for lieutenant governor in the 1946 elections. He renewed his contacts with wealthy and powerful friends he would need to sponsor a statewide race. Along with a group of state senators, he dined with construction tycoon Herman Brown, who bankrolled LBJ and other politicians. He hunted conservative millionaire W. S. Schreiner's ranch. Maynard Robinson, a lawyer friend from San Antonio, suggested Shivers run for either attorney general or lieutenant governor. Robinson argued that the senator could count on a second base in the Rio Grande Valley in addition to his own district. His associations with John Shary would surely enlist support from the Valley's machine politicians.[1]

Before running for state office, however, the state senator needed a statewide reputation. Given the more conservative direction of Texas politics after the war, appeals designed for his constituents in southeast Texas might not work elsewhere. With postwar strikes and shortages sweeping the nation in 1945–46, unions presented a tempting target as they tried to consolidate gains made during the war. Across the South, conservative politicians took advantage of voter frustration to bash labor. Shivers launched his first attack on organized labor even before the war had ended.[2]

In early 1945, John L. Lewis and other national labor leaders proposed that workers receive royalties on their produce. Shortly thereafter, Senator Shivers offered a resolution condemning the suggestion, which passed on a voice vote. Jefferson County government and business leaders praised his attack on "labor dictators" and U.S. senator W. Lee O'Daniel had it entered into the *Congressional Record.* Responding to labor strife in his district later that year, Shivers told fifteen aggrieved Jefferson County taxpayers to blame union bosses and the federal government for their problems. Organized labor needed more regulation, he argued, since "it was a business comparable to that of the largest industry." Concern over local workers' autonomy clothed Shivers's offense at unions' interference in local affairs. "Certainly, the laboring man in Port Arthur should not be answerable to some Union official in Washington, New York or Chicago, with an absolute right to control whether our local citizens work," he wrote. Nonetheless, Shivers did not sever all ties. Late in the 1945 session, he voted against a house bill that would have banned the closed shop. Still, local union members would remember Senate Resolution 46.[3]

The high point of the session for Shivers had come in April. During an executive session, the state senate drafted the Port Arthur politician as its preferred candidate for lieutenant governor in the coming year's elections. After feigning disinterest, he agreed to run. The senators kept their poll secret until after the candidate's formal announcement. Before then, however, Jefferson County newspapers speculated about his ambitions. Condemning extremes right and left, he announced for lieutenant governor on March 10, 1946. The *Port Arthur News* praised Shivers's announcement. "He is liberal without being radical," the *News* gushed, unaware of the rightward shift in the senator's views since 1934.[4]

Texas' 1946 Democratic primaries proved contentious and ugly. Resentments still boiling after the 1944 intraparty battles contributed to the tension. The liberal-loyalists had defeated the Texas Regulars then, but postwar Texas had grown more prosperous, more urbanized, and more conservative. The Congress of Industrial Organizations's (CIO) Operation Dixie recruitment drive and a rash of strikes in the state and across the South contributed to the ferment. Finally, racial issues rose to greater prominence in 1946 than in previous years. As a lawsuit challenging segregation at the University of Texas law school moved through the courts, black voters prepared to participate in the first Democratic primaries since *Smith v. Allwright* had banned the white primary. Many whites saw these developments as evidence of "agitators among the negro race." Across the South, the immediate postwar years brimmed with uncertainty and unease.[5]

A particularly nasty gubernatorial race pitted former UT president Homer Rainey against four more conservative candidates. Lieutenant Governor John Lee Smith appeared to be the frontrunner among the conservatives to face Rainey in a runoff, but he squandered his lead early in the campaign. The conservatives turned most of their fire upon Rainey, whom they vilified as an atheist, a race mixer, and a tool of the unions. Conservative railroad commissioner Beauford Jester

Beauford Jester, governor 1947–1949. Though conservative, Jester tried to conciliate divisions within the state Democratic party. He opposed Truman's nomination in 1948, but backed him against Republicans and Dixiecrats in the general election.

eventually bested the other conservatives and defeated Rainey in the runoff. Shivers paid close attention to the governor's race, but carefully avoided being sucked into it. As a state senator, he may have had some interest in Smith's campaign, and he may have disliked Rainey. However, he took some advice from a staffer to heart: "It's going to be Rainey against the field—so be careful what you say about Rainey, and if you can't say anything good, *just don't say.*" Though hardly as brutal as the gubernatorial contest, Shivers's own race was far from gentlemanly.[6]

The Texas senate's candidate faced only two major opponents: state representative Joe Ed Winfree of Houston and Fort Worth radio personality Boyce House. House had statewide name recognition and media presence, while Winfree was generally regarded as the more liberal of the candidates and relied upon a base in Houston and southeastern Texas. If Shivers had expected a fairly easy and statesmanlike move to higher office, the fight he faced must have been a rude shock.[7]

Boyce House tried to outflank Shivers on the right, forcing the more experienced politician on the defensive. The political newcomer accused Shivers of being a tool of the CIO. He also portrayed the senator as being too cozy with African Americans. One house broadside featured a clipping from the *Dallas Express* praising Shivers for his "liberal progressive principles." Allowed to vote in the Democratic primary for the first time ever, black voters found themselves courted and held at arm's length by both candidates. Shivers's own supporters attempted to link House to African-American voters, even as their candidate spoke in favor of "a first-class university" for black Texans. Shivers claimed that his most dangerous opponent spread "offensive rumors" and aroused "racial hatred."[8]

The crowded field in the lieutenant governor's contest insured a runoff. In the July 28 first primary balloting, Shivers won 47 percent of the vote to House's 37 percent. A significant number of Texas political pundits had expected House to lead Shivers into the runoff, but unanticipated developments helped cripple House's campaign between July 26 and the August voting. The Fort Worth radio personality's rhetoric grew more erratic and extreme, allowing Shivers a chance to appear moderate while being quite conservative, and thereby attract voters who had supported more liberal but defeated candidates. A number of powerful conservatives took a second look at Shivers as House seemed to lose control of the race. West Texas rancher and right-wing extremist J. Evetts Haley liked House personally, but supported Shivers because he thought the senator was stronger "on fundamentals." Conservative Dallas millionaires V. A. Collins and his son, Carr, "repented" of their support for House and came out for Shivers in the runoff.[9]

In mid-August, House accused the senator of being owned by the CIO and of being a Texas Regular at the same campaign forum. That same evening, he called Fort Worth police and reported that he had seen a prowler. House accused

Shivers of sending the mysterious stranger to spy upon his opponent and steal some of House's speeches. The Fort Worth police department responded to the radio personality's accusations by dispatching an officer to watch his residence. The officer was instructed to ignore anything else House might have to say.[10]

A highly publicized quarrel with Port Arthur union members harmed Shivers at home, but offered a chance to gain positive attention statewide. The distance between Shivers and his former labor supporters came sharply into focus at his Port Arthur precinct's postprimary meeting. Attendees met to determine the precinct's delegation to the Jefferson County convention. The precinct chair had included the senator's name even though he was unable to attend the meeting. An oil worker and CIO member, W. S. Povall, moved that Shivers's name be struck from the delegate list. A "chorus in favor" of the motion resulted and the precinct dropped the senator's name. In theory, Shivers was ineligible because he would not be present to sign the party loyalty pledge as a delegate. Nevertheless, the slight appeared calculated.[11]

Shivers, attending as a proxy delegate, entered the county convention hall to a "tremendous ovation." Blaming the incident on "radical, loudmouthed CIO leaders," the candidate for lieutenant governor warned against "minority control of our party," adding, "I do not believe our government or our officials should be controlled by radicals." Sinister forces conspired against him, Shivers maintained, despite Povall's assertions that the motion had been made in "ignorance of political machinery." Shivers told Jefferson County Democrats: "I do not know the man who made the motion to strike [me]. He has said he made the motion in ignorance, but I do not think any paid CIO organizer is ignorant." The precinct fracas made open enmity Shivers's standard approach to labor afterward. It also likely strengthened him in his runoff against House.[12]

Shivers won the runoff by a margin of 56 percent to 44 percent. Thirty-one percent of those who voted for the Port Arthur senator came from Texas' ten largest urban counties. He won all of those except for his opponent's home county, Tarrant. Just under 29 percent of House's votes came from the major urban areas. His lopsided win in Tarrant County helped inflate the measure of House's support among urban Texans. Between them, the urban counties accounted for 30 percent of the statewide vote in the second primary. The hotly contested gubernatorial runoff did not have a marked effect upon voters' choices in the lieutenant governor race. Statewide, Rainey supporters plainly tended more toward Shivers, perhaps owing to his senate reputation. Those who voted for Jester were only narrowly more likely to support Shivers. Since neither Shivers nor House made the governor's race an issue in the campaign, these choices would appear to be based primarily upon voters' own perceptions of the candidates. There were regional variations in the candidates' support as well. House did very well in West and

Central Texas, particularly areas within easy broadcast range of Fort Worth radio station WBAP. Shivers, however, piled up large majorities in South and East Texas.[13]

In his first statewide race, Allan Shivers demonstrated methods that would characterize his later campaigns. First, he effectively played upon Texans' mistrust of unions, a common trait in the South generally. The unions and their leaders represented an intruding outside presence that aimed to supplant local authority and norms. In later campaigns, Shivers often portrayed himself as a special target of organized labor. He also spoke of himself as representing law and order and the common good against outsiders bent upon accumulation of power.[14]

Second, Shivers employed a fairly sophisticated racial rhetoric that avoided outright race baiting in favor of more carefully phrased white supremacy. In this manner, he avoided the kind of demagoguery that might put off an increasingly middle-class but no less racist white electorate. He called for a statewide effort to equalize segregation so as to prevent federal moves against the institution. At the same time, he asserted that segregation was the preferred lifestyle of both races, repeating a cherished white myth. He never forgot that the majority of his audience was white. His racism was paternalistic, which meant he felt an obligation to protect and "be good" to blacks. This changed later, however, when such paternal attention met resistance. When that occurred, Shivers—like most whites—looked upon African Americans as they would an "ungrateful child."[15]

A month after Shivers's nomination, Mack H. Hannah—a longtime family friend, black businessman, and supporter—wrote the presumptive lieutenant governor and urged that he not forget those African Americans who had voted for him. He asked Shivers to work hard against any effort to return to a white primary by a legislative end-run around *Smith v. Allwright.* The white politician refused to commit himself, but he did pay his black friend the ultimate paternalist compliment: "I have known you and your family since I was a small boy, and I do not hesitate to say that if all the Negroes were of the type that you and your family have been, we would have no trouble with racial prejudice."[16]

"TEXAS DEMOCRACY IS ON THE RIGHT ROAD AGAIN," A SUPPORTER EXULTED after Shivers's victory in the August, 1946, runoff. "It looks like more of the same in the Governor's chair, with some improvement in the Lieutenant Governor's office," *Texas CIO Notes* commented, finding mere relief in Shivers's victory. The presumptive lieutenant governor represented a bit of an unknown quantity. Some regarded him as a liberal or a moderate. Others correctly saw him as a conservative, including those who knew him well. A Valley business acquaintance predicted that Shivers and Jester would "lead the nation in returning to constitutional government, turning away from . . . radicalism and socialism."[17]

Postwar Texas faced serious problems. The transportation, education, and public health infrastructure had strained under the load of wartime expansion. Its Byzantine tax system could not supply sufficient funds to pay for the state's minimal public services. Black and Hispanic Texans pressed against the constraints of second-class citizenship. The state's higher education system faced a legal showdown over segregation with little chance of winning cheaply. Labor and management relations were marred by strikes and economic disruption. Shivers became a powerful player in statewide politics as lieutenant governor, influencing Texas' response to these issues. He also accumulated considerable power for himself while pursuing a more plainly conservative agenda than many had expected.

Texas' state constitution dates from 1876 and represents a cumbersome and outdated monument to white Southern memories of Reconstruction. It established a plural executive branch, spreading executive power across seven offices. The offices of the comptroller, attorney general, and lieutenant governor were viewed as particularly powerful and made excellent stepping-stones to the governor's mansion. The comptroller controls tax collection and certifies that state budgets are balanced before they become law. The attorney general represents the state in civil litigation and gives advisory opinions that carry the force of law. The lieutenant governor presides over the state senate and succeeds the governor in the event of death, resignation, or removal from office.[18]

As the senate president, the lieutenant governor appoints committees and assigns bills to committees. Bills need not go to a panel with appropriate jurisdiction. The lieutenant governor might consign an objectionable bill to a committee likely to kill the measure. The lieutenant governor also controls parliamentary procedure and senate rules. The senate's calendar system amplifies this power. Legislators typically hope to avoid controversial bills and will seek to have other measures considered out of calendar order. This requires a two-thirds vote of the body, but before a vote can take place, a senator desiring such action must first gain recognition from the presiding officer. Senators thus work hard throughout each session to accumulate the goodwill of the lieutenant governor in order to gain recognition at crucial moments during floor debates.[19]

Shivers forged strong alliances with important conservatives heading critical committees, but he used the stick as well as the carrot to control the body. If a committee charged to take a particular action failed to do so, Shivers would reassign legislation. "Shivers would really raise hell with you if you promised him something and did not deliver," recalled Corsicana senator James Taylor. When crossed, the lieutenant governor could be "vindictive," and he always knew "where the pressure points were." Even when operating with an iron hand, he displayed a remarkable knack for staying "aloof and pure and above the fray." He preferred to work through others, with the result that one sensed his involvement but rarely saw evidence of it.[20]

The state senate frequently met in executive session to allow for anonymity and secrecy when deciding important matters such as executive appointments. Generally, however, the press was given a reason for the convening of an executive session. Shivers expanded the use of executive sessions in a manner that alarmed some. In one 1949 case, he insisted that executive sessions could be held "any time [the senate] wishes" without offering a reason. A *Corpus Christi Caller-Times* editorial labeled his attitude toward open government "cavalier." Once, when an appropriation for a cancer research center in Houston teetered between life and death in the senate, the press asked Sen. James Taylor about its chances. He broke into a "big slow grin" and replied, "That all depends upon God and Allan Shivers."[21]

The lieutenant governor's conduct on major issues during the 1947 legislative session demonstrated both his ideological orientation and his thorough grasp of power. Early in the 1947 session, a ballot reform measure fell to Shivers's control over committees and procedure. Texas voters used numbered ballots that could easily be traced. Texas law required a "negative ballot," on which voters indicated their selection by marking through the names of the candidates they opposed, leaving the name of the candidate they favored untouched. Numbered ballots allowed for retaliation by county machines. This practice invited fraud. Conservative forces in the state Democratic Party lobbied hard to retain the old system. Not only did the lieutenant governor successfully maneuver against the bill, he also stopped senate consideration of a house ballot-reform measure.[22]

Shivers's new power coincided with increasing pressure from Texas' racial minorities on the issue of segregation. Federal and Mexican government pressure during World War II forced state leaders to carefully examine the treatment of Tejano residents and Mexican citizens working in the state. Through the *bracero* program, federal authorities had sought Mexican workers to relieve wartime agricultural labor shortages. The U.S. government guaranteed standardized wages, a cap on the number of hours worked, and decent working conditions. Governor Coke Stevenson established the Good Neighbor Commission to investigate labor abuses and racism. Under committee director Pauline Kibbe, the GNC became a permanent state agency and aggressively investigated the racial climate along the border.[23]

By 1947, wartime resolve had passed and the legislature prepared to reexamine the GNC's status. Kibbe had published a book—*Latin Americans in Texas*, based on her experiences and research in 1946—which drew praise from academics and activists, but angered some South Texas politicians and businessmen. Agribusinessmen in particular had grown tired of the forty- to sixty-cent hourly wage required for *braceros* and increasingly turned to illegal laborers, whom they paid a quarter an hour. Voluntary integration efforts also broke down with the outbreak of peace. Renewed protests from the Mexican government, combined with additional fact-finding efforts by Kibbe and the commission, brought calls for her ouster.[24]

Kibbe's boss, GNC chairman R. E. Smith, began negotiations with Lieutenant Governor Shivers in May, 1947, with an eye toward preserving the commission and sacrificing its director. The pressure on Kibbe increased as the summer progressed. In July, Smith forbade her from speaking to the press. He also ordered her to destroy a report viewed as too favorable to CIO organizing efforts in the Valley. Rumors of a plot against Kibbe spread throughout South Texas. In early September, she resigned along with several of her staff. Sympathetic politicians blamed Shivers and Edinburg senator Rogers Kelley for engineering the pressure campaign. Shivers denied it, but did point out that Kibbe's "political outlook" kept her out of step with the state senate. He also denied the outgoing GNC director's contention of widespread discrimination and misery in the Valley. After all, the lieutenant governor averred, he employed three hundred to four hundred "Mexicans," of whom half were "wetbacks" and "practically all" received more than twenty-five cents an hour.[25]

Shivers, as the senate's presiding officer, also helped push a number of harsh antilabor measures through the Fiftieth Legislature. In April, the legislature sent bills to Governor Jester banning the closed shop, automatic deduction of union dues from wages without worker consent, and secondary boycotts and strikes. Additionally, the Fiftieth Legislature severely limited picketing, requiring fifty feet between individual picketers. Unions also found themselves subjected to state antitrust laws. These measures coursed through the state senate with little difficulty. The right-to-work bill passed on a voice vote with no negative voices heard, and the ban on secondary boycotts sailed through "without a word of debate."[26]

The 1947 session's emphasis on union busting reflected the times and also Texas conservatives' long-building displeasure with the New Deal and Fair Deal. This economic emphasis indicated that even the end of the white primary had failed to shake whites' confidence in the continued viability of segregation. In 1948, civil rights "came of age" as a national political issue, which made for more friction between conservative southern Democrats and the national party. Responding to racial violence across the South in 1946, President Harry S. Truman created a presidential commission on civil rights that urged federal action against voting restrictions and segregation. Conservative Texas Democrats, some of whom had been working against national party nominees since 1936, saw a chance to wedge southern whites from the Democratic fold or, alternatively, force the national party to back down on civil rights.[27]

On February 2, 1948, Truman proposed a civil rights program to the nation that included a federal antilynching law, a ban on the poll tax, a permanent Fair Employment Practices Commission, and promised executive action against segregation in the armed forces and by carriers of interstate travelers. "The Federal Government," Truman asserted, "has a clear duty to see that the Constitutional guarantees on individual liberties and equal protection under the laws are not denied or abridged anywhere in the Union." Given southern whites' traditional position within the Democratic Party, Truman appeared to be gambling with his own future. However, presidential adviser Clark Clifford had told Truman that southern white opinion "can be safely ignored" when considered against the likely gain in black and liberal votes. Nonetheless, a southern third-party challenge seemed probable. Though disapproving of Truman's civil rights plan, most Texas politicians saw little gain in supporting a Deep South revolt against the president. Instead, powerful Texans attempted to prevent his renomination.[28]

The struggle against Truman united an assortment of big city bosses, union leaders, disenchanted liberals, and southern whites. Governor Jester offered a measured condemnation of the president's civil rights message and sought to draft Gen. Dwight D. Eisenhower to carry the Democratic standard. When intraparty efforts to stop Truman's nomination flopped, Jester found himself very much "on the spot." Although conservative backers and constituent mail pressed him to ally with the emerging States' Rights Democrats (Dixiecrats) and their nominee, Gov. Strom Thurmond of South Carolina, Jester eventually fell into line behind Truman. His conciliatory approach to the administration angered many, including former lieutenant governor John Lee Smith, who compared him to Benedict Arnold and condemned his "complete surrender." Other Jester critics saw Lt. Gov. Allan Shivers as a potential challenger to the governor in the summer primaries. Shivers refused comment, thus keeping his options open.[29]

In the end, Shivers decided not to challenge the governor. Instead, he sought a second term as lieutenant governor. He tried hard to avoid involvement in the swirl of a controversial election year. Although Governor Jester took center stage in responding to Truman's civil rights initiative, citizens also made their opinions known to Shivers. Mail about Truman's proposals came in steadily enough for him to devise a form letter with which to reply. In response to criticism of the president, the lieutenant governor assured correspondents "the views which you have expressed . . . coincide almost in every detail with mine." He claimed that southern and Texas whites "have too long followed a policy that almost disfranchises us in national politics." The problem, Shivers explained, stemmed from Republican indifference toward the South and Democrats taking the South for granted. Shivers's views were reasoned and measured. He made it plain he opposed Truman's program, but did not belabor the point.[30]

Loyalist Democrats who favored Truman and Texans considering support for the Dixiecrats both sought some sort of commitment from the lieutenant governor. Springtime preprimary organizing efforts, barbecues, and public meetings buzzed with questions about what politician supported what faction. "I haven't attended any of them and don't intend to," Shivers wrote a friend. "I think I'll have a Shivers barbecue, take up a collection, pass the hat and do my own fundraising, campaigning." He was not alone. Other significant Texas political figures worked just as hard to keep out of the emerging controversy. Sam Rayburn, outgoing U.S. senator O'Daniel, and others steered clear of springtime political events that might associate them with one or another Democratic faction. Although a supporter of Lyndon Johnson's U.S. Senate candidacy, Shivers kept quiet about his preference in LBJ's tough race against former governor Coke Stevenson. In a sense, these evasions proved unnecessary. Shivers received only token opposition in the Democratic primary, which he easily swept aside.[31]

Shivers's private sympathies in the period have been characterized as "Dix-

Jester, behind podium at right, takes the oath at his first inaugural, January 21, 1947. Lieutenant Governor Allan Shivers sits to the right of the podium. As lieutenant governor, Shivers enjoyed greater power over the legislative process than did the governor.

iecrat." Early in 1948, he agreed with a correspondent that Truman's civil rights program had rendered him a "dead duck" in the coming presidential race and tried to conceal his hostility with indifference. Reenergizing his campaign through vigorous travel and speaking, Truman crossed Texas during a September whistle-stop tour. The trip proved an enormous success, drawing nearly a million Texans to see the president, including two hundred thousand in San Antonio alone. When Truman rolled into Austin, Shivers was conspicuously absent from the gathering of top state officials. Despite the misgivings of many top Democrats and his advocacy of civil rights, Truman carried Texas with 1,322,000 votes to Republican Thomas Dewey's 304,000 and Dixiecrat Strom Thurmond's 114,000. Ironically, Truman's greatest margin of victory was in a state whose governor and lieutenant governor had written him off.[32]

Truman's unexpected victory left Texas Democrats little choice but to patch up their relations with the national party. Governor Jester declined his invitation to the inauguration and sent the lieutenant governor in his stead. January 20, 1949, dawned clear and cold in Washington, and the lieutenant governor rode in the back of an open car in the inaugural parade. The overcoat he had borrowed from Lyndon Johnson offered scant protection from the chill wind. As he rode past Truman's reviewing stand late in the afternoon, the crowd laughed at the sign on the car: "Lieutenant Governor Shivers."[33]

THE LIEUTENANT GOVERNOR RETURNED FROM WASHINGTON AND PLUNGED into the work of the Fifty-first Legislature. During the 1949 session, Shivers presided over a state senate considering significant civil rights and education measures. He also thought ahead to his next step in statewide politics. Texas governors had adhered to a two-term tradition, and all observers expected Beauford Jester to retire from politics. Shivers seemed a likely prospect for the 1950 gubernatorial race. His future success depended upon legislative achievements. Lieutenant Governor Shivers met the challenge with leadership that was at times visionary, and at others, business as usual.

Harry Truman's reelection prodded Texas' reluctant leadership into action to rectify some of segregation's worst abuses in hopes of preventing federal intervention. Repeal of the one-dollar poll tax occupied the legislature intermittently throughout the session. It eventually required a constitutional amendment, which could not be submitted to voters until a two-thirds majority of both houses approved it. The Texas senate, led by its presiding officer, fought hard to retain voting restrictions, leading to a clash with the more liberal Texas house. Edinburg senator Rogers Kelley proposed an amendment to eliminate the tax but retain the state's restrictive residency requirement. It survived in committee, but then was ignored until April. East Texas senator Wardlow Lane offered an amendment that required a minimum $1.50 "registration fee" and included a local option to increase the fee. This transparent shell game actually would have increased the cost of voting. Nevertheless, it was driven through the chamber by conservative votes and rulings from the chair. Shivers managed to avoid responsibility by leaving the senate during the final vote. In the end, the state senate stood firm against real reform, opting to send voters an amendment repealing the poll tax and replacing it with Lane's registration fee. They rejected it in November.[34]

Hoping to "forestall" a federal antilynching statute, Governor Jester asked for a state bill directly aimed at ending the practice as early as 1948. Jester saw the measure's value as primarily symbolic. Passage would help "modernize" Texas and "take the wind out of the sails of northern Democrats and Republicans." The bill passed from house to senate rather quickly, but then "bogged down" in the upper house. Senate conservatives such as Wardlow Lane and Seguin's R. A. Weinert apparently worked to kill the bill. Reported favorably out of committee in March, the antilynching measure did not reach the floor until the last week of the session in June. Worried about its chances, Jester lobbied Shivers and the bill's senate sponsor, Hill Hudson of Pecos, to press for a vote. The measure passed the senate by a 20–8 margin on the last day of the regular session. Shivers's support no doubt helped move the legislation. Signed by Jester, the Texas antilynching statute preceded those of other southern states by twenty years.[35]

Significant in its own right, but also linked to questions of civil rights and modernization, education reform dominated the 1949 session. Two years earlier, Governor Jester had appointed a select committee to study the state's public education needs. Headed by Paris senator A. M. Aikin and Rocksprings representative Claud Gilmer, the committee reported to Jester in 1948. The panel tried to convince him to call a special session to consider their reforms. With a tax increase and other unpleasant choices likely, the governor chose to wait for the regular legislative session. When the Fifty-first Legislature took up the proposals, it divided them into three separate pieces of legislation, increasing the chances that most of the proposals would survive.[36]

Senate Bill (SB) 115 contained the most controversial elements of the plan. It centralized textbook adoption, consolidated many rural districts, established the Texas Education Agency, and made the state commissioner of education an appointive position. The most significant reform, contained in SB 116, was financial. The bill created a minimum foundation program that set minimum teacher salaries and established a matching-funds system by which state money augmented local district budgets. Senate Bill 117 arranged for funds transfers within the state government to facilitate the foundation program.[37]

The senate debate proved rancorous, particularly with respect to SB 115. Consolidation provoked howls at the Gilmer-Aikin Committee's "undemocratic" methods. Textbook standardization threatened local autonomy. The argument over an appointed commissioner of education led to the most fireworks. In effect, SB 115 would remove the elected state superintendent, L. A. Woods. Woods had earned the enmity of members of the Gilmer-Aikin Committee as well as conservative politicians, including Governor Jester. He had supported Homer Rainey in 1946, and openly supported greater spending for black schools and teachers. One select committee member even referred to Woods as a "burnt offering on the Gilmer-Aikin altar" intended to attract conservative support for reform.[38]

The lieutenant governor played an important role in SB 115's eventual passage by managing the calendar in such a manner that it forced consideration of the bill early in the session. This prevented senators delaying consideration of this most controversial of the Gilmer-Aikin reforms. Shivers skillfully outflanked a filibuster against the bill by keeping the senate in session until it collapsed, rather than allowing breaks for weary opponents. Early on the morning of February 16, SB 115 passed by a vote of 16–8. The other two Gilmer-Aikin bills passed with less drama by early June.[39]

According to historian Numan Bartley, Gilmer-Aikin set the standard for similar southern school reform during the period. Though generally intended to prop up segregation and owing their funding to regressive consumer taxes, these measures "laid the basis for conspicuous improvements in public education." Still, some of the Gilmer-Aikin reforms represented "meaningless tinkering." Critics correctly point out that despite the landmark legislation, Texas' schools lagged far behind the national averages in funding and academics. Foundation funding doubled state expenditures on education, but the formulas used to calculate state payments to local districts often rewarded rich school districts with low local property tax rates at the expense of poorer districts with considerably higher ones. Gilmer-Aikin evolved out of a broad consensus favoring improvement of Texas' public education system, but it did so in a segregated society. Segregation and its preservation remained a subtext throughout the adoption process. The funding inequities inherent in the legislation led to legal challenges that continued into the 1980s.[40]

As the session drew to a close, Shivers demonstrated his power over the senate and the legislative process by spearheading efforts to have Beaumont's Lamar College elevated to a four-year institution. The measure had passed the house, but owing to Gilmer-Aikin's dramatic increase in school funding, a tax increase loomed. Obtaining more funds for a purely local project appeared unlikely. Conservative senators appeared determined to kill the legislation through parliamentary maneuver. Ostensibly the brainchild of Jefferson County legislators, the appropriation did not stand a chance without Shivers's support. The lieutenant governor forcefully drove the bill to the governor's desk. Governor Jester, though unconvinced of the need for another four-year school, chose not to challenge the Lamar appropriation, fearing Shivers's ability to hamstring other, more important, legislation. As Jester aide Weldon Hart put it: "Brother Shivers can operate in reverse as well as forward gear."[41]

While capable of determined heavy-handedness on behalf of local pork, the lieutenant governor also demonstrated foresight and leadership in the late session. He orchestrated the introduction of several constitutional amendments that would modernize Texas' government and its organic law. Enabling legislation for both the Legislative Budget Board and Legislative Council, which conducted research on budget and proposed legislation for the legislature, passed. A constitutional change that would have increased the terms of state officials to four years failed, but amendments calling for annual sessions and salaries for Texas' underpaid, part-time legislators passed both houses and were placed on the ballot in November. Both went down to defeat, killed by poor turnout and strong opposition from major lobbies interested in preserving the status quo.[42]

SHIVERS'S ACTIONS DURING THE 1949 LEGISLATIVE SESSION CANNOT BE separated from the speculation that surrounded his political future. Some legislators had marked Shivers for future advancement as early as 1946. Observers also noted that his likely opponent to replace Governor Jester would be Attorney General Price Daniel. The lieutenant governor denied his position represented a "political stepping stone," but he kept quiet the next year when some conservatives touted him as a more doctrinaire alternative to Jester. Still, the picture had been complicated somewhat by the end of the 1949 session. Shivers's heavy-handed control of the senate had alienated some, making him "probably the least popular politician in the state." Railroad Commissioner Olin Culberson made some noise about the gubernatorial race and questioned Shivers's fiscal conservatism.[43]

April polling indicated strong name recognition for Shivers statewide. Forty-four percent of likely voters had heard of him, second only to state school superintendent L. A. Woods among possible 1950 gubernatorial candidates. Reassuring news came blended with bad tidings. San Antonio political boss Owen Kilday seemed to favor Culberson, and Attorney General Daniel was working to build his name recognition by tackling the emerging issue of offshore oil rights. Public relations consultant Ken Harper warned Shivers of a "two fisted campaign on hot issues" in 1950. The lieutenant governor attracted more unfavorable attention when he left Austin at the height of the Gilmer-Aikin debate and journeyed to Washington, D.C., for a series of meetings with important federal contacts, including Speaker Sam Rayburn, Sen. Lyndon Johnson, and U.S. attorney general Tom Clark. It was rumored that Shivers had gone to the capital to press for Jester's possible appointment as ambassador to Mexico. The news media gave credibility to the rumor, although the evidence indicates that Shivers went to Washington to discuss offshore oil. Denials from both the lieutenant governor and Jester did little to dispel accusations of a cynical plot to advance Shivers into the governor's mansion by moving the governor to Mexico City.[44]

The 1948 election and the following legislative session had deeply stressed Texas' Democratic Party, wearying officeholders and the public alike. Governor Jester invited legislators to a buffet at the governor's mansion to celebrate the session's conclusion. Though tired, he still managed to throw a good party. Lieutenant Governor Shivers was there, but he left the next day with his family for their Woodville farm. At a staff party on July 10, Jester and his family relaxed at Lake Travis, taking time for yachting and an impromptu softball game. That evening, Jester caught the 11:15 overnight to Galveston via Houston alone. As he boarded the train, he asked the porter to wake him at 7:30 A.M. Sometime in the small hours of the morning, Beauford Jester suffered a heart attack and died in his sleep.[45]

The first person to reach Allan Shivers was a reporter from the *Houston Press*—at 8:15 in the morning on July 11. A scramble ensued to arrange an inauguration ceremony. The new governor decided to have the swearing-in right there on the farm. A crowd of twenty-five hundred gathered from the surrounding area and elsewhere for the afternoon event. An informal picnic was held afterward. He determined rather quickly to keep Jester's competent staff for the remainder of the term. Newspaper commentators were quick to note the contrast between the expansive and gregarious Jester and the stately, reserved, and calculating Shivers. While many questions loomed as to how he would perform in office, most observers recognized that his position for the 1950 gubernatorial race had been greatly strengthened.[46]

CHAPTER FOUR

Ascent and Election in His Own Right
1949–50

MANY YEARS LATER, PRICE DANIEL RECALLED HIS FEELINGS UPON hearing of Jester's death: "I figured I hadn't been living right." Shivers's ascension presented problems for Daniel's planned race for governor. The sudden shift in political fortunes required both to rethink their positions. While Shivers had likely planned to run for governor in 1950, his plans had not factored in incumbency. It offered some advantages, but precious few guarantees. Between July, 1949, and September, 1950, Shivers fought not just for the Democratic gubernatorial nomination, but for control over the party machinery itself. He succeeded through superb political intelligence and organization. A special legislative session allowed him to press a moderate reform agenda and appeal to rank-and-file Texas voters. However, he remained true to his conservative allies in his opposition to civil rights and his antifederal position in the developing controversy over offshore oil.[1]

Three months after becoming governor, Allan Shivers commissioned Austin public relations man J. J. "Jake" Pickle to do a detailed political reconnaissance of the state. Pickle was no stranger to politics. He, too, had been president of the University of Texas student body. He worked on Lyndon Johnson's National Youth Administration staff and had assisted Johnson with his early political campaigns. After World War II, Pickle helped form the Austin-based public relations firm of Syers, Pickle, and Winn, which mainly catered to a political clientele. After accepting the governor's commission, Pickle met with "leading citizens" in each county seat and large town in an effort to create a statewide network of key Shivers supporters.

Pickle's forays into the hinterland revealed problems for the governor. Some believed Shivers's long service in the state senate had made him a pawn of special interests. Although his wealth may have given him greater independence than other lawmakers, his money aroused as much suspicion as his lengthy political career. Other observers worried over the "Dewey factor," suggesting that Shivers looked good but lacked substance.[2]

One opponent admitted that "women were fascinated by his good looks," a fact that worried some of the politicians who faced Shivers. Once, in an early race, an opponent accused Shivers of wearing a toupee. A friendly source described him as a "consummate candidate" with a good memory for faces and names. However, he was also "aloof" and a bit of an elitist. He was never fully comfortable with working crowds, plainly preferring the company of the well heeled. Audiences found him "articulate" and "impeccably dressed," even "regal." "If a man could be beautiful," liberal legislator Edgar Berlin recalled some years later, "he was a beautiful man."[3]

Pickle reported that he had encountered "valid criticism" that the governor seemed "too stiff, too unbending, too good-looking, too polished, too smooth, too much reserved." Shivers's ideological transformation from his early days in the state senate did not play well either. It appeared that "too many oilmen, too many big businessmen, too much upper-crust" surrounded the new governor. The taint of elitism fed East Texas rumors that Shivers owned as many as twenty-one cars. Pickle advised him to "take the lead for one or two liberal things." One could, he suggested, oppose the poll tax or call for better eleemosynary institutions or old-age pensions and "make no one especially mad." The governor might even get away with mild criticism of special interests if he chose his words carefully. Lastly, the veteran political observer told his client that religion might pose a problem. Shivers's wife was Catholic and this caused worries in some quarters. "You hear it all the time," Pickle explained, but cautioned against responding directly to such criticism. A "Little Red Arrow Character and religious speech" before an audience of his fellow Baptists would blunt any simmering prejudice.[4]

Normally easy-going and jocular gubernatorial aide Weldon Hart, who had known Shivers since his student days, also offered some plain words of advice. He urged his boss to exhibit a kinder, gentler side. The "personally cold, calculating, ruthless, and inordinately ambitious" image Shivers projected had to change. Such advice ran counter to the increasing pressure the governor felt from Democratic Party conservatives. Hints of varying subtlety reached Shivers from the right in late 1949 and early 1950. Former railroad commissioner Olin Culberson appeared primed to challenge him. Attorney General Price Daniel had worked to stake out an irreconcilable position on state-federal relations and offshore oil. Ed Burris, president of the Texas Manufacturers' Association (TMA) told the governor to cut state spending and quit speaking of tax increases to meet a likely budget shortfall. Otherwise, Burris warned, Culberson might "wean away" conservative support. Business leaders wanted the state budget cut as much as 15 percent to avoid a tax increase.[5]

With a special legislative session unavoidable, Shivers prepared Texans for a tax increase, but Weldon Hart thought he lost the "preliminary skirmishes" on the budget in the press. Conservative friends told the governor that his political future depended on the economy and corralling the "extravagant and wasteful" Fifty-first Legislature. Oil and banking interests made noises about supporting a Culberson candidacy. Some had even come to see Shivers as a "little left of center" in his politics. Oilman and Dixiecrat Arch Rowan, an important political ally, bluntly told the governor that conservatives wondered if they could trust him. Shivers replied that he was "about fed up" with the pressures upon him. He insisted that he had to balance ideological purity with political reality. Tied to the expensive Gilmer-Aikin reforms, the Lamar College appropriation, and, by his own silence, with Jester's support of Truman, Shivers's political base trembled beneath him.[6]

THE GREAT DEPRESSION HAD PROVEN TEXAS' BIENNIAL BUDGETING SYSTEM to be a disabling anachronism. Population growth in the 1940s strained the system still further. Entering 1950, the state faced a $26 million revenue shortfall due to declining oil prices. Shivers called a special session to alleviate the cash crisis and protect key state services. He had the power not only to call a special session, but also the constitutional authority to dictate its agenda. In introducing that legislative agenda, Shivers would have to make the speech of his political life. The only way open to preserving programs and balancing the budget appeared to be increased taxes. Knowing he had to sell this solution, he turned to Weldon Hart to craft the address. Hart clearly and dramatically contrasted the issues: "Texas, the proud Lone Star State—first in oil—forty-eighth in mental hospitals. First in cotton—worst in tuberculosis. First in raising goats—last in caring for state wards." This clever appeal to the humanity and vanity of Texans went down in history as the "Goat Speech." With it, Shivers outflanked his conservative critics, while at the same time moving to calm them.[7]

As governor, Shivers demonstrated a remarkable ability to bend the business lobby to his will. This clout stemmed from his credibility as a wealthy businessman. He spoke the businessmen's language and understood where to apply pressure or appeal to their self-interest. After calling major business leaders to the governor's mansion, Shivers reassured them of his conservative principles, but just as determinedly insisted that state services be maintained at current levels. Polls indicated that most Texans favored either an increase in the business franchise tax or direct taxes on mineral extraction to meet the budget gap. The governor pointedly told lobbyists that failure to back his plan would strengthen the "wild taxers in the House." Shivers intended to ask for an increase in the hodgepodge of consumer taxes enacted during the depression. Although some complained about the governor's "cracking the whip," the business lobby and legislators complied. Many hoped to use the special session to push favored projects, but the lawmakers knew no other business could be conducted until they fulfilled the purpose of the called session. The budget crisis was resolved largely on the backs of consumers, and business acquired renewed faith in Allan Shivers.[8]

THE SHIVERS ADMINISTRATION'S FIRST YEAR ALSO WITNESSED STRUGGLES with the state's minority population as it challenged segregation. Like many white Texans, the governor held paternalistic attitudes toward African Americans and Tejanos. Postwar demands for equality from minority activists hardened his belief in segregation. This element of his personality became policy. In the early skirmishes of the civil rights movement in Texas, Shivers made plain his determination to obstruct progress. Until his departure from office in 1957, Shivers's conservatism and segregationist views were inseparable. Each fueled and strengthened the other.

During the autumn of 1949, the NAACP attacked segregation in Texas' state parks. No statutory separation existed; blacks simply were excluded by custom. With neither an existing statute nor separate facilities, the state parks board faced likely defeat in court. Moreover, the board refused a suggestion from the state attorney general's office recommending the creation of separate facilities in a remote area of Tyler State Park to calm East Texas blacks. If the case ever reached the U.S. Supreme Court, Shivers aide William McGill told the governor, "they'll get it—swimming pools and all." By year's end, the suit had expanded from fourteen parks to the entire system. When Shivers's special session agenda had been completed, the legislature took up the matter of forestalling integration. The board estimated the cost of park equalization at nearly $1 million. McGill bluntly told the governor the issue "must be faced realistically," but worried that a federal court order would bring a "rather serious situation."[9]

Shivers took the attitude of "let them sue-and-be-damned" and told the parks board not to "take any steps which might appease the court." However, he hoped to avoid an actual showdown with the federal court system over parks. It made little sense for the governor to ask the legislators for more money to improve parks that might well be integrated anyway. This would likely offend budget hawks. Shivers recognized the political value in standing firm, but he also wanted to allow himself some maneuver room. This could be accomplished by championing fiscal responsibility and segregation at the same time.[10]

Instead of asking for money, the parks board requested a formal segregation statute to cover the parks. Legislation sponsored by Sen. Warren McDonald of Tyler segregated the parks, but also created a study committee to determine the costs of facilities equalization. The bill passed the senate with ease, but debate raged in the house. Laredo representative Abraham Kazen Jr. condemned segregation for weakening "national unity." Glowering at his colleagues, Kazen thundered, "I saw the blood of Negro-Americans, Anglo-Americans, Latin-Americans, and German-Americans blended and trickle down the slopes of a hill in Italy." The chamber erupted with applause from the gallery and floor, after which the house voted 86–22 to segregate. The governor signed the bill in late February. In 1952, a court order resulted in the integration of Texas' state and city parks.[11]

White Texas' relations with Tejanos also presented thorny problems for Governor Shivers. A member of the Valley's landed gentry, Allan Shivers had worked to weaken the investigative efforts of the Good Neighbor Commission during the Fiftieth Legislature. Legislative pressure in turn had purged controversial GNC executive secretary Pauline Kibbe, who was succeeded by former State Department diplomat Tom Sutherland, a Texan who had helped engineer the agency's creation. Sutherland proved a disappointment to conservative interests, continuing the activism present under Kibbe. The GNC particularly angered leading South Texas whites after becoming involved in the Felix Longoria affair of 1949.[12]

Longoria had been killed during fighting on the Philippines island of Luzon in 1945. Nearly four years later, his remains were returned to his family in Three Rivers, south of San Antonio. The Longorias attempted to arrange for the Rice Funeral Home to handle his burial, but were "discouraged" from doing so because "white people object[ed]." Dr. Hector Garcia, head of the Corpus Christi–based American G.I. Forum, went to the press hoping to stir up public outrage against discrimination. State and local officials engaged in denials and damage control as the story spread nationally, but the controversy took on an added dimension when Sen. Lyndon B. Johnson's office intervened. Johnson adviser John B. Connally contacted the GNC's Sutherland to gain more background information to pass on to the senator. Senator Johnson condemned the funeral home's refusal to handle Longoria's body and arranged for the soldier's interment in Arlington National Cemetery. State representative J. F. Gray of Three Rivers howled for an investigation of the whole affair, particularly the GNC's cooperation with Johnson. Legislators "browbeat" members of the Longoria family as they testified before the committee and eventually exonerated Three Rivers's white community of discrimination. A bill to terminate the Good Neighbor Commission, championed by Gray, died when Governor Jester agreed to move out GNC chairman R. E. Smith and, eventually, Executive Secretary Sutherland.[13]

Shivers doubtless wanted Sutherland out as well, since the Truman administration was contemplating investigating migrant labor conditions in Texas. Like many of the Valley's white elite, the governor did not want the GNC assisting a federal inquiry. However, his political position after becoming governor remained tenuous, requiring Shivers to act warily. When R. E. Smith stepped down as GNC chairman in September, 1949, Governor Shivers replaced him with Fort Worth Dixiecrat Neville Penrose, who approached his position much less aggressively than had Smith. Penrose found the commission's investigative duties "aggravating" and "irritating." Moreover, he regarded legitimate press criticisms of Texas' migratory labor practices as communist propaganda. In January, 1950, the GNC's investigative responsibilities passed to the Human Relations Council (HRC), chaired by Smith with Sutherland as executive secretary. Penrose continued to run the GNC, which concerned itself primarily with goodwill between the Texas and Mexican governments. The Good Neighbor Commission kept its state funding. The HRC was bankrolled entirely by Smith, whose zeal diminished as his resources drained away. Shivers argued that the new arrangement allowed for a more vigorous investigation of "isolated incidents" of discrimination because the HRC's reliance on Smith's money freed it from control by the legislature. By the end of 1951, the HRC had disappeared.[14]

This bureaucratic sleight of hand may have saved Shivers from a potentially embarrassing state agency, but it did not prevent critics outside state government from airing their concerns. The Mexican government placed several Texas counties on its blacklist in 1949. Meanwhile, the *bracero* program tottered on the verge of collapse as increasing numbers of Texas farmers rejected *braceros* in favor of illegal laborers. With the war over and illegal labor streaming into the state, few fretted over the Mexican government's protests. Still, the Shivers administration and the GNC periodically investigated discrimination in an effort to demonstrate goodwill to Mexican leaders. In 1948, a federal district court ordered an end to the segregation of Hispanic schoolchildren in Texas in *Delgado v. Bastrop I.S.D.* In early 1950, Shivers and Penrose investigated compliance with the decision, but the results of their probe remained confidential. The Shivers administration neither publicized nor acted against violations of the federal court order.[15]

Meanwhile, Hispanic leaders pressed for stronger statements against discrimination. Shivers demurred, instead relying upon Tom Sutherland to mute protests. Dr. Hector Garcia of the American G.I. Forum complained, "our Governor is pushing off . . . his responsibilities" on the weakened GNC and HRC. The Corpus Christi activist bluntly reminded Shivers that Tejanos had not "forgotten" his tepid response to the Longoria affair. In early 1950, a Gonzales restaurant refused to serve Garcia's wife and a party of her friends. The G.I. Forum and Spanish-language press responded by hammering the governor for not having "taken any steps to remedy" such overt discrimination. Corpus Christi's *La Verdad* accused Shivers of "passing the buck" when he promised there would be an investigation.[16]

With a possible conservative challenge for the gubernatorial nomination looming, Shivers could not afford to make an enemy of Garcia. Tejanos could vote and, as voters, could not be ignored completely. Two days of "almost continuous long-distance telephone conversations" between Sutherland and the Corpus Christi physician led to a meeting between Shivers and Garcia in early March. Garcia sought an official condemnation of discrimination by Shivers. Sutherland advised the governor's office to ask Garcia to draft such a statement and make every effort "to approximate" the views expressed in it in the final draft. Shivers adviser Bill McGill warned the governor that too bold a statement might open the governor up to similar demands from black Texans. Nevertheless, Shivers accepted the draft antidiscrimination statement proposed by the G.I. Forum's leaders. The meeting sufficiently mollified Garcia that he endorsed Shivers in the summer primary. However, it also resulted in suggestions that Shivers meet with black leaders having the "right attitude." The governor failed even to toy with the idea, leading some to theorize that he was "anti-negro."[17]

Leaders of the NAACP nonetheless attempted to take advantage of Shivers's meeting with Garcia. They presented the governor with a laundry list of potential reforms that did not alter segregation, but certainly threatened to make it more expensive. Providing black state inspectors for black state barbers and placing black policemen and state troopers in predominantly black areas topped the list. In addition, the civil rights organization suggested a separate board for Texas State University for Negroes and a black elevator in the state capitol. That April, a state Democratic Party fundraising dinner demonstrated the place of African Americans in Allan Shivers's Texas. Vice President Alben Barkley was to be the guest of honor at the state Jefferson-Jackson Day celebration. Conservative party leaders planned to seat black Democrats at separate tables. Liberals, however, asked for mixed seating. Rather than risk the disruption of liberals ignoring the seating chart and mixing anyway, the conservatives excluded blacks altogether. Invitations were prepared using a colorblind roster and African Americans who inadvertently received one were turned away at the door. The dispute drew no attention from Vice President Barkely's visit, but it still resulted in unwanted bad publicity.[18]

Less than two months later, on June 5, NAACP lawyers won a critical victory over segregation in Texas before the U.S. Supreme Court when, in *Sweatt v. Painter*, the high court ordered the UT law school to integrate. Texas' makeshift black law school failed the constitutional standard of substantial equality under *Plessy v. Ferguson*, according to Chief Justice Fred M. Vinson. University president Theophilus S. Painter responded with an announcement of his intention to "observe the law" rather than resist integration. Achieving substantial equality seemed too expensive a goal given the state budget crisis earlier in the year. Although Governor Shivers was strangely silent about the *Sweatt* decision in his public comments, other southern governors vented. Georgia's Eugene Talmadge proclaimed that "the line had been drawn" and called the decision "a dagger ready to be plunged into the very heart of southern tradition."[19]

GOVERNOR SHIVERS KEPT QUIET ABOUT *SWEATT* FOR TWO REASONS. FIRST, it was not unexpected in Austin. As early as 1949, top state leaders had acquiesced in the admission of black students to the UT medical school in Galveston. The state caved in when confronted with the costs of establishing an equal black medical school. Second, that same day the Supreme Court also ruled against Texas in a case involving state ownership of offshore lands potentially rich with petroleum. The "Tidelands Controversy," as the dispute was known, became a central political issue in postwar Texas before 1954.[20]

Properly defined, the tidelands encompass that portion of the shoreline between the high and low tide marks. State control over this strip of land was never questioned. In the debate over offshore oil, the term *tidelands* applied to underwater lands in the Gulf of Mexico out to Texas' traditional boundaries. This partially calculated misnomer helped fuel the emotions attached to the issue. Federal courts generally recognized a three-mile limit of state authority over "marginal seas." However, Texas' traditional boundaries arguably extended 10.3 miles into the Gulf. Spain had claimed marginal seas out that far, and Mexico did the same. After the Texas Revolution, the Republic also asserted the 10.3-mile limit. When annexed, Texas' claim received federal recognition, which was confirmed in 1848 by the Treaty of Guadalupe-Hidalgo, which ended the Mexican War. The 1845 annexation agreement also stipulated that Texas retained ownership of its public lands, a unique arrangement between a state and the federal government.[21]

The federal government largely ignored the question of state control over marginal waters until 1937, when Interior Secretary Harold Ickes and his boss, President Roosevelt, began to question Texas' claim. A congressional joint resolution claiming federal control failed to clear the House of Representatives, in no small part due to the machinations of Texas' powerful congressional delegation. California's leasing within the three-mile limit prompted this heightened federal interest. Reacting to these developments, the Texas legislature asserted state ownership of three Spanish leagues in 1939. Two years later, the state used an old legal principle that based seaward boundaries on the range of a cannon shot. Texas claimed the continental shelf from the low tide mark outward twenty-seven miles. State senator Allan Shivers of Port Arthur sponsored both pieces of legislation.[22]

The tidelands question lay dormant during World War II. As has been seen, the war years widened the gulf between oil interests and the national Democratic Party. This was particularly true in Texas. The petroleum industry's hostility did not make national Democrats more conciliatory. On September 28, 1945, not even a month after the war's end, President Truman issued an executive order declaring federal ownership of the continental shelf. The following year, Truman ordered Attorney General Tom Clark to sue California to gain court endorsement of federal ownership. Clark's legal attack left open the possibility of future suits. Advising President Truman to stand fast against state claims of federal aggrandizement, former interior secretary Ickes insisted that the dispute involved little in the way of high principle. "This is a question of oil," Ickes told Truman. The administration proceeded on this same understanding without apparent concern about potential political damage.[23]

In June, 1947, six U.S. Supreme Court justices found for the federal government, arguing in *United States v. California* that the United States had rights "transcending those of a mere property owner." National security concerns justified federal control, if not ownership, of resources underneath the marginal seas. Although Attorney General Clark reassured Texans that the California suit was "nothing to get excited about," the reaction from Texas officials verged on hysteria. The Texas School Land Board (TSLB), made up of Governor Jester, Land Commissioner Bascom Giles, and Attorney General Daniel, condemned the decision. Daniel and Giles labored to exceed each other in their criticisms. Daniel claimed *United States v. California* represented the greatest "blow . . . against . . . property rights of a state since the Civil War." Giles went so far as to suggest that Texas secede from the Union. Both men coveted Jester's job, and Daniel in particular saw the Tidelands Controversy as his ticket to the governor's mansion. Tom Clark responded with a warning against any further shrill rhetoric aimed at him or the administration. Lieutenant Governor Shivers remained largely silent.[24]

Three months later, Jester established the Statewide Tidelands Committee (STC) to work with the TSLB in coordinating Texas' defense of its offshore oil rights. The official line held that Texas was defending its tidelands in an effort to protect "the interests of the public schools." Lurking behind the scenes, the oil industry financed the struggle—information that elected officials tried to obscure. The governor's office made a point of searching out early contributions of "dimes and pennies" from Texas schoolchildren. These should come "spontaneously and *without apparent inspiration from official sources.*" Only then could an STC treasurer be chosen and industry funds accepted. Oil industry leaders hoped for state control, since Texas levied a royalty of just 12.5 percent and federal royalties ranged as high as 25 percent. The industry's technological limitations in undersea drilling at the time did not prevent it from looking to the long term. A significant portion of the STC mission involved fomenting popular indignation against the federal government; oil dollars funded this effort. As the year's end drew near, the TSLB issued leases for 2.65 million acres, some for tracts as far as twenty-seven miles out. This provocative move prompted the Truman administration's eventual decision to sue Texas.[25]

The administration, however, held off taking any action until after the 1948 elections. Harry Truman's bold civil rights proposals earlier that year prevented too much focus on tidelands oil by Texas voters. A March, 1948, opinion poll showed Texans worried most about the cost of living, followed by racial equality. The tidelands issue ranked a distant sixth. When it became clear that Truman would be the Democratic nominee, Governor Jester took a conciliatory tone toward the president. For his part, Truman acknowledged Texas' distinctive claims to the tidelands during his September whistle-stop campaign through the state. Presidential aides even researched differences between Texas' claims and those of other states. Truman easily won Texas that November, which prompted state officials to allow themselves some optimism. Their euphoria was short-lived. On December 21, 1948, Attorney General Clark filed suit against Texas, asking for a declaratory judgment as to ownership and demanding the payment of all proceeds from state leasing to the federal treasury retroactive to June, 1947.[26]

News of the federal suit infuriated and shocked Texas politicians. Jester declined an invitation to the January, 1949, inaugural ceremonies. Administration officials, particularly Tom Clark, became objects of public scorn in Texas. The Houston Chamber of Commerce called Clark an "erstwhile Texan" determined to "nationalize all interior lands and resources." Clark dismissed such charges as "preposterous" and hinted that Texas officials, especially Price Daniel had provoked the crisis. When Louisiana and Texas both leased into the Gulf beyond their traditional limits, the federal government responded. Years later, a Truman administration official told Sam Rayburn that Texas' decision to lease in 1947 had provoked the suit. Even after suing his native state, Attorney General Clark wrote a Texas colleague that it was "still not too late" to bring the state and federal governments together in some sort of compromise.[27]

Despite the federal lawsuit, two potential ways out remained. Congress could pass quitclaim legislation with which the federal government would drop its assertion of ownership. President Truman took a hard-line position in favor of federal ownership. Even if a quitclaim bill passed, the president would veto it, and an override seemed unlikely. The best hope was compromise. The tidelands issue made nationally minded members of Texas' powerful congressional delegation uncomfortable; they wished to be rid of it. Texas' junior senator, Lyndon Johnson, tried to avoid all contact with the matter, privately viewing it as "nothing but fluff." House Speaker Sam Rayburn and senior senator Tom Connally wanted a resolution before the 1952 elections. Representative John Lyle proposed an even division of profits and control of the tidelands by a special commission made up of federal and state appointees. Lyle's proposal was based on geologists' assertions that most continental shelf oil was beyond Texas' three-league boundary. The TSLB, goaded by Price Daniel, insisted that "there can be no compromise." Nevertheless, an alternative compromise floated by Rayburn and Johnson offered more promise. It proposed that oil revenues from lands out to the traditional boundaries be divided with states receiving 67.5 percent and the federal government 32.5 percent. Revenues earned from drilling beyond the traditional limits would also be divided, but with the percentages reversed. Semantic troubles remained, but the outlook for compromise looked promising. Clark thought the plan a good one so long as Texas recognized the nation's "paramount rights"; Governor Jester understood federal officials' interest in "saving face" and suggested an "agreement for an *exchange of interests*." Even the ordinarily standoffish land commissioner, Bascom Giles, warmed to the idea.[28]

Throughout 1947–49, Allan Shivers sought an end to the tidelands clash. As lieutenant governor, he did not sit on the school land board with Jester, Giles, and Daniel, and so was not under any immediate obligation to follow them in their denunciation of the federal government. Shivers correctly perceived Daniel's effort to monopolize the issue. The lieutenant governor had long cultivated relationships in Washington, traveling there frequently and "talking around." He owed many of his contacts to his friendship with Lyndon Johnson. In a remarkable departure from most state officials, Shivers endorsed a compromise. He also questioned whether or not Texas stood a chance against the federal government in court. Land Commissioner Bascom Giles attacked his stance while both Jester and Daniel remained quiet. Despite the criticism, Shivers journeyed to Washington in May, 1949, in hopes of aiding a possible compromise. "I was the only one they could talk to," he recalled years later.[29]

Shivers's ascent to the governor's mansion two months later forced him to rethink his position. For all practical purposes, Daniel sabotaged compromise by convincing the TSLB to reject the Johnson-Rayburn alternative. When he became governor, Shivers inherited Jester's TSLB seat. Now, saddled with the responsibility to safeguard school lands, he could no longer afford to dissent. Daniel had portrayed all previous talk of compromise, especially that by Shivers, as "a deliberate effort . . . to cast reflection upon my handling of the lawsuit and to blame the necessity of a compromise thereon." While the two men undoubtedly disliked each other, there had to be unity on the tidelands matter. Governor Shivers needed to deprive his strongest opponent of his most powerful weapon and work to unite the state Democratic Party around himself in time for the 1950 primary.[30]

THE GOVERNOR'S SUCCESS AT COURTING TEXAS DEMOCRATIC FACTIONS remained in doubt throughout the spring of 1950. In April, Olin Culberson, the conservative favorite in the gubernatorial race, withdrew after a mild heart attack. Attorney General Price Daniel sought reelection rather than challenge Shivers. A rumored campaign by former governor and senator W. Lee O'Daniel bedeviled

Shivers until late May, when O'Daniel quashed the idea. The brief O'Daniel surge cut the governor's approval to 67 percent. After O'Daniel disavowed having any ambitions, Shivers's public approval rebounded to 76 percent. Polls indicated the success of the governor's careful political positioning. East Texas voters who disliked him viewed him as either a New Deal liberal or corporate stooge. Nonetheless, even though his approval rating was lowest in the east, it still stood at a strong 64 percent in the region. In the end, only former Baylor University law professor Caso March challenged Shivers. Driving around the state in a car decked out with steer heads and foxtails, March called for a tax on natural gas extraction to fund the Gilmer-Aikin school reforms and told voters that Shivers was "for the big 'uns and I am for the little 'uns." Despite the support of organized labor and South Texas political boss George Parr, March failed to receive even a quarter of Shivers's total vote, losing 829,730 to 195,997.[31]

Despite his resounding victory, Shivers did not control the state party machinery. Throughout the 1940s, the State Democratic Executive Committee (SDEC) had operated independently of the governor's office. The bitter intraparty bickering of the forties revolved around conflicting attitudes toward the national party and its ideological direction, with the SDEC often in the thick of the fight. Party conventions at the precinct, county, and state level produced divisive conflict between competing political factions. Texas' difficulties mirrored those experienced by other southern state parties, particularly in the wake of the 1948 Dixiecrat revolt. In 1950, Shivers planned to bring peace inside the party. While strongly conservative and allied with former Texas Regulars and Dixiecrats, he reached out to amenable liberals in the name of party unity. The Texas Democratic Party would be unified around the governor himself.[32]

Governor Shivers planned a takeover of the SDEC at the September state party convention in Mineral Wells. He turned to Jake Pickle to choreograph the meeting. Party conventions meeting in each state senate district chose the SDEC. That meant Pickle would have to control the state convention and override local choices for the executive committee. This "hatchet work," as Pickle called it, required manipulation of the convention process. The governor reassured liberals of his devotion to a united party, while at the same time Pickle lined up support among conservatives and collected proxies from distant delegations unable to attend the convention. With control of the convention assured, the next move would be Shivers's. "[T]he governor would look over the people nominated in the district caucuses and if he saw someone on there who was personally obnoxious, he would say 'Knock 'em off,'" Pickle recalled.[33]

The first test of Pickle's strategy came during a debate over the seating of contested delegations from Brazoria, Dallas, Harris, and Tarrant Counties. County conventions had produced rival slates of delegates, and the state convention had to determine which ones to seat. Pickle had lined up the conservative delegations behind the governor, even though some included former Regulars and Dixiecrats. Shivers supported this move, so long as the conservatives remained loyal. Asked what loyalty meant in this context, the governor's response concealed more than it explained. "Loyalty is kinda like virtue," he told reporters. "You're either loyal or you are not loyal." Among the 202 delegates in Harris County's conservative delegation, eighty-nine had bolted the party in 1944 and seventy-two had supposedly never cast a Democratic ballot. Still, Jake Pickle's steamroller ensured their recognition. The convention voted 1620–440 to seat the conservative delegations.[34]

Liberal delegates divided on this critical vote. Some, such as San Antonio state senator Woodville Rogers, backed the governor's agenda in the name of unity. Others offered resistance, but with meager results. When Pickle attempted to vote Walker County by proxy, Minnie Fisher Cunningham challenged him. The convention as a whole backed Cunningham, but the clash mattered little. South Texas machine politicians, often allied with the liberals, split their proxies. Laredo's Abraham Kazen voted his proxies with Shivers, whereas George Parr used his to oppose the governor. With or without proxies, Pickle had the votes and carried the fight. Shivers thus got a state party leadership made in his own image.[35]

The 1950 convention baffled party liberals. Having avoided public involvement in earlier party squabbles, Shivers had at last shown his colors. It took some time for the shock to wear off. When it did, even liberals who had been supportive of Shivers struggled to understand what had happened. "So far as anybody knew, [Shivers] had been and was thought to be a good Democrat," Temple lawyer Byron Skelton remembered. Shivers had ordered Skelton's brother off the SDEC. Dickinson banker and liberal activist Walter Hall wrote Skelton and expressed surprise at Shivers's action, considering Skelton's previous support for the governor. It took nearly a month for Skelton to answer Hall, during which time he had sorted out Mineral Wells in his own mind. "I believe everybody was out trying to polish the apple in order to court the favor of the Governor," he opined. Currying Shivers's favor did no good, however. Pickle had "used every trick in the book" to engineer the governor's "completely ruthless" takeover of the party. Skelton noted Shivers's insistence upon a roll-call vote on the contested delegations. With the outcome never in doubt, Skelton theorized, the only reason the governor pressed for the long, drawn-out vote was to demonstrate his own power and embarrass his opponents.[36]

Shivers supporters insisted that the SDEC purge did not reflect ideological considerations. Indeed, critics from the Deep South who were even more conservative complained that Texas appeared on the "middle road" and saw Shivers's leadership as "neither hot nor cold." The 1950 party platform hinted at future points of contention, but also contained some straws for liberals to grasp. The document contained bland praise for the Good Neighbor Commission and expressed hope for continued improvement of relations between Tejanos and Anglos. Arguing that outsiders and minority groups caused whatever strife existed between whites and blacks, the platform promised "to keep in mind the *Texas* constitutional requirement of separate, but equal facilities for our colored citizens." Restrained but clear declarations of states' rights and Texas' claim to offshore oil reassured conservatives. Liberals received a guarantee of party loyalty from Shivers for his remaining public life. The platform itself praised "his unquestioned loyalty to the Democratic Party."[37]

Some Texas liberals sensed that the governor's power play had a larger ideological purpose. Maury Maverick warned President Truman that Shivers "will give you public support, but no fighting support." Shivers thought himself "well set in Washington," which actually weakened the president's position in Texas. "The state machinery is oiled against the Administration and the national machinery still fully accepts [this]," the former congressman complained. "The point is," Maverick added, "this State can be lost, as any other state." Henri Warren, a veteran of Truman's World War I artillery unit living in Texas, saw Dixiecrats ascendant in Shivers's state Democratic Party. If the Democratic National Committee failed to act, Warren explained, the 1950 SDEC would choose presidential electors in 1952. Byron Skelton urged the president to intervene on behalf of Texans loyal to the national party, adding that any talk of loyalty by Shivers's SDEC was "lip service." The White House brushed off the warnings. Governor Shivers controlled the state party. He had pledged himself to party loyalty. As far as the president's advisers were concerned, the party battles in Texas had ended. Shivers, however, had allied himself with Truman haters with whom he had long been close. Loyalists recognized this and saw a break coming. All Shivers needed was an issue.[38]

CHAPTER FIVE

Maneuvers, Intrigues, and Party Leadership 1951–52

Although Shivers's 1950 "Goat Speech" had advocated "one or two liberal" state programs, it led only to stopgap solutions. Spending increases in 1949–50, combined with declining petroleum prices, brought another budget imbalance, resulting in the need for a new financial remedy in 1951. State comptroller Robert S. Calvert warned that maintaining 1950 spending levels would require an additional $50 million in revenue for 1951–53. Rural constituencies clamored for the construction of new farm-to-market roads, further straining the budget. Despite doubling education spending—rocketing Texas from thirty-eighth nationally to thirty-sixth—the landmark Gilmer-Aikin reforms did not fully satisfy public-school reformers. At least as important from Shivers's perspective, representatives of important business lobbies, including the Texas Manufacturer's Association and the mineral industry, pushed as they had a year earlier for no additional taxes.[1]

The events of 1951–52 demonstrate just how "southern" Texas politics remained even after the remarkable modernization the state had experienced since 1933. Despite apparent moves toward a bipartisan system, it remains significant that changes came on the terms of the state Democratic organization and the governor. The conduct of politics continued to emphasize personalities at the expense of issues. Yet, when issues did surface, they typically distracted voters from bread-and-butter concerns and instead served the interests of more conservative politicians. Shivers followed the typical southern model of low and regressive taxation, minimal state services, and a purely economic justification for those incremental improvements in state programs that emerged. Allan Shivers's Democratic Party allowed a first-ever Republican primary, but sought to control it through cross-filing. The Democrats did so to benefit the political aspirations of

Allan Shivers in western garb. Like many Texans, Shivers liked to revel in the state's western image. However, Texas politics and race relations remained decidedly southern. As governor, Shivers worked to keep one-party Democratic control over state politics, even while courting national Republicans.

Dwight Eisenhower against a presumably more liberal presidential nominee from their own party. Shivers bitterly fought tax reform intended to more equitably raise revenues and assure their reliable flow. He deliberately picked fights with the national Democratic leadership. He worked to incite Texans against a federal government bent upon racial integration and stealing their offshore oil. Shivers also began skillfully blending these views with his anti–New Deal/Fair Deal attitudes.

In 1950, the governor had lined up the lobbies behind modest improvements in state health and education spending. A key to his success with Texas' powerful lobbyists was his ability to go directly to the business interests that paid them. He was one of and at one with Texas' business elite. Business leaders believed Shivers's portrayal of himself as their closest friend in government and were convinced that he alone could keep reform and taxes under control. In governing and politicking, his personal philosophy reflected the years he had spent in a variety of businesses. Governor Shivers's business interests stretched across state and included land, mercantile, media, insurance, and agricultural holdings from the Valley northward into East Texas. The governor presided over his holdings partially with the aid of his gubernatorial staff. Moreover, he micromanaged day-to-day life in Sharyland to the point of following news of the sexual liaisons of the school district staff. With a good business mind and the capacity to work on many projects at once, he had a seamless grasp of power and money. Without question, Shivers sympathized with and felt most comfortable among the best-off Texans. He might have employed the "common touch" for political advantage, but never comfortably. In 1951, the renewed budget crisis found him in a stronger political position than he had been in the previous year.[2]

Shivers, intent on avoiding the drastic spending cuts consistently advocated by business leaders in trying economic times, also planned to prevent efforts to improve the state's regressive tax structure. The modest increases he proposed in oil, gas, and sulfur severance taxes brought no complaints from the mineral industry, in which small independent producers stood to lose more than big businesses. The centerpiece of Shivers's solution to the continuing budget mess remained higher "sin" taxes combined with a new gasoline sales tax. A number of legislators balked at the continued effort to balance the state budget on the backs of consumers and demanded that the oil and gas industry in particular bear more of a burden. Ordinarily, higher taxes on business stood no chance in the Texas legislature. However, the interests of the Farm Bureau and liquor lobby converged with proposals for a more progressive state tax code. The result was Shivers's first major legislative defeat—along with indications of a new break within the Texas Democratic Party.

Although most Texans lived in urban areas, malapportionment gave rural legislators and the Farm Bureau great power in Austin. They demanded increased spending on rural roads regardless of the dire budget picture. Governor Shivers planned to end a $15 million yearly guarantee for farm-to-market roads in the 1951–52 biennium. He also planned to halt revenue sharing on existing gasoline taxes—money the counties often used to pay off road bonds. Such a move would force localities to raise funds directly from local taxpayers. The governor's proposal drew fire from farmers, their lobbyists, and county officials. The legislative coalition Shivers had formed to support the measure unraveled when two important rural legislators, Dolph Briscoe of Uvalde and Clyde Whiteside of Seymour, reneged on their pledge to back the governor's roads bill. Despite the best efforts of Shivers's other legislative allies, the state house killed his bill, leaving the road funds uncut. Now the house had to raise the money, prompting liberal legislators to propose a "gas gathering" tax on all natural gas flowing out of the state through pipelines.[3]

The gas-gathering tax was both a reaction to regressive taxation and a blow against large outside corporations. The demand for natural gas had increased nationwide because consumers saw it as a cheaper, cleaner alternative to other fuels. Unlike Shivers's increased severance taxes, however, the gathering tax would fall hardest upon major producers owning pipelines. Representative Jim Sewell of Navarro County proposed the tax and several "green" and relatively liberal legislators coalesced around him. Sewell's proposal called for a one-cent-per-thousand-cubic-feet levy. With 7 billion cubic feet leaving Texas each year through pipelines, the tax promised yearly revenues of $25.5 million — easily covering the budget shortfall for each year of the biennium.[4]

The House Revenue and Taxation Committee killed the tax, but it found new life in the Agriculture Committee. Sewell's bill reserved half of the gas-gathering revenues for rural roads, but awarded a quarter each to education and cities for street construction. The gas-gathering proposal was so attractive to cities, counties, educators, farmers, and taxpayers that Shivers found himself outflanked. The gas-gathering tax passed the house, but the governor's men succeeded in killing it in the state senate. As a result, each legislative chamber passed its own budget and tax scheme. When time ran out on the regular session, Shivers called for a special session and the gas-gathering tax again sprang to life.[5]

The governor derived some tactical advantage in the special session because the legislators' already meager pay fell to just five dollars a day. They thus usually hurried to get out of Austin and back to making a living. On this occasion, however, twenty-two determined supporters of the gas-gathering tax moved into a run-down former fraternity house at 1700 San Jacinto. The "Gas House Gang," as they became known, fell in behind the liberal leadership of Jim Sewell and D. B. Hardeman of Denison, but reflected an alliance of liberal and rural interests. Conservative rural legislators like Dolph Briscoe mixed with urban liberals like San Antonio's Maury Maverick Jr. and Port Arthur's Edgar Berlin. The Farm Bureau fed the Gang, allowing for longer resistance to the governor's roads plan. Meanwhile, the liquor lobby, hoping to stop increased "sin" taxes if the gathering tax failed, supplied free booze. When morale grew low, Hardeman would recite from *Henry V* as the happy few drank. Although the Gas House Gang did not appear to be animated primarily by hostility to Shivers, the governor sent his aide Weldon Hart to the "People's Headquarters" to investigate. Hart reported there were variations in the temperament of Gang members, but he also noted their shared determination.[6]

The Gang ultimately handed the governor an embittering defeat, forcing him to back down on the rural roads measure and sign a gas-gathering tax of .0045 of a cent per thousand cubic feet. Moreover, Shivers, who was furious with Briscoe for deserting him early in the fight, had shown legislators of all stripes that, as D. B. Hardeman put it, "you could do business with Allan." Failure to reciprocate a favor or to follow through on a promise ended any future hope of doing business with the governor. When Shivers later sought sponsors for legislation, he shunned Briscoe. The governor also moved ruthlessly to decapitate the Gas House Gang's leadership. He pushed Sewell aside with a district court judgeship in Navarro County. By influencing redistricting, Shivers knocked out other Gang members. The gas-gathering tax fight made it plain that the governor's relations with the liberal wing of the party had deteriorated.[7]

LIBERAL DETERMINATION TO BLOCK SHIVERS ON TAXES GREW MORE INTENSE amid questions about his party regularity. An elaborate election code revision, House Bill (HB) 6, wound its way through the legislature alongside the gas-gathering tax and rural roads bills. The revision strengthened antifraud provisions and the attorney general's powers over elections. Shivers's own public endorsement of HB 6 centered on these arguments. The whole matter of election revision scarcely received any media attention. The bill passed the house by an overwhelming margin, 113–13, with support from several liberals who at the same time were tenaciously fighting the governor on taxes: Berlin, Hardeman, Maverick, and Sewell. In the senate, HB 6 became a magnet for amendments, the most controversial of which allowed candidates to cross-file in both political parties for the November general election. Senators passed the bill as amended, which served as a wake-up call for house liberals. They tried to fight the new measure, but succeeded only in slowing its final passage, 79–50, thus sending electoral reform with cross-filing to the governor for his approval.[8]

Supporters of the national Democratic Party reacted to cross-filing with a shudder. However, another elections measure had also passed during that session which brought the issue into sharper focus. Early in the session, Edward Dicker, the representative from Dallas County's Park Cities and the house's only Republican, proposed legislation requiring Republican precinct and county conventions beginning in 1952. A curious alliance of liberal and conservative Democrats combined with Dicker to pass the measure. Some liberals had long argued for a two-party system to give voice to those not part of the conservative establishment. Conservative Democrats supported a more formalized GOP nominating process because of a likely presidential run by retired general Dwight D. Eisenhower. Ironically, Dicker recalled, "the forces that called themselves Republicans were really the ones that were working against me." With cross-filing, conservative Democrats could support Eisenhower in the GOP primary and then vote for the Democratic slate running as Republicans in the general election.[9]

Only Shivers could stop cross-filing, but the rationale for HB 6's other provisions provided political cover for signing the measure. Henry Zweifel, the

Republican state chairman, and prominent Temple Democrat Byron Skelton pleaded for a veto. Shivers turned a deaf ear, however, and signed election reform with cross-filing into law on June 7. The governor thereby smudged party lines in Texas beyond recognition. All of the statewide Democratic officeholders save for Agriculture Commissioner John White eventually announced their intention to run on both tickets in the November, 1952, general election. Gubernatorial aide Bill McGill commented that White "finds himself out in a cold, cold world, having been more or less aligned with the Federal administration." Down-ballot liberals and other party stalwarts accused Shivers of "destroying" the state Democratic Party. The extent of the governor's involvement in the cross-filing scheme remains hard to trace, but McGill clearly understood that Shivers was intent on further isolating liberals. Cross-filing would blunt the potential competitive effect of the Republican primary and further strengthen Shivers's and his allies' hold on the state political scene.[10]

Although their position remained weak with respect to Shivers, some Republicans greeted with optimism developments that might enable them to create a viable party in Texas. The Republican Party had always been an alien institution in Texas. Its presence was a product of the Civil War and Reconstruction. African Americans were the party's largest constituency into the 1890s, with some white support from native Unionists and Northern migrants. In 1870–74, Edmund Davis served as Texas' first (and for more than a century only) Republican governor. The Democrats responded by sweeping Davis from power and cementing in the collective memory a false and self-serving image of the GOP governor as a dictator. The Republican Party remained powerful locally for a time, particularly when fused with protest parties such as the Greenbackers, Prohibitionists, and Populists. Disfranchisement measures enacted in 1903 and 1905 drove most poor whites and African Americans from the political process and reduced the state Republican Party to the status of patronage broker. Until the 1930s, white Texas Republicans tended to be either migrants from states with two-party systems or ethnic voters with long-time allegiance to the party.[11]

From 1921 until he died in 1950, the Texas Republican Party had been the personal fiefdom of state chairman R. A. Creager of San Antonio. A Texas German, his party allegiance was almost congenital. Creager actually tried to *discourage* people from joining the party. When Valley millionaire Lloyd Bentsen Sr. migrated to Texas from North Dakota, the Republican chairman urged him to become a Democrat for the good of the state. During the 1930s and 1940s, the state Republican Party steadfastly supported the isolationist, anti–New Deal views of Ohio senator Robert Taft. Winning Texas did not matter to Creager. He hoped merely to wait out Democrats Roosevelt and Truman and control patronage when a Republican finally made it back into the White House. Houston oilman

Jerry Cullinan called Creager the "Japanese Gardener" because the Texas GOP was like a bonsai under his control, unable to grow. A like-minded party leader, Henry Zweifel of Fort Worth, succeeded Creager as chairman in 1950.[12]

Both Creager and Zweifel had to contend with an increasing number of defections from Democratic ranks throughout the late 1930s into the early 1950s. Some broke with the Democratic Party in response to Franklin Roosevelt's court-packing effort in 1937. Others remained Democrats until FDR ran for a third term in 1940. More joined the party after World War II, as Texas grew more urbanized and affluent. An increasing number of Texans began voting Republican for president, but still kept close contacts with the state Democratic Party. The converted, however, itching to make Texas a two-party state, grew restive under Creager's and Zweifel's leadership. An Eisenhower candidacy promised to attract more voters to the Republican Party in Texas. Presidential Republicans would eventually become down-ballot Republicans, some reasoned. Others realized that Shivers's backing of cross-filing had ensured that the GOP would not become viable in local Texas politics until sometime in the distant future.[13]

SHIVERS'S RELATIONS WITH THE NATIONAL DEMOCRATIC PARTY WORSENED palpably in 1951. The state's 1950 defeat before the U.S. Supreme Court had not only led to desperate efforts at compromise, but intensified a campaign on the part of state leaders and their oil company patrons to fuel public anger and fear over the loss of the tidelands. The effort to stoke public concerns proved fruitful. By late 1949, well before the Supreme Court issued its negative decision, opinion polls showed the tidelands leading a list of public anxieties that included such hot-button issues as the rising cost of living, racial equality, employment, education, and housing. The governor took advantage of public opinion to demonstrate his own inward hostility toward the Truman administration and national party throughout 1951. In mid-April, when Douglas McGrath, chairman of the Democratic National Committee (DNC), visited Austin, Shivers was not on hand to greet him.[14]

Jake Pickle quickly notified Sen. Lyndon Johnson of Shivers's snub of McGrath. "Many of the governor's friends are still wondering why he was not here instead of . . . Woodville," Pickle wrote, promising to keep the senator posted on Shivers's activities. Johnson recognized Shivers's power and, though wary of him, primarily hoped to corral and pacify him. McGrath's visit had followed Truman's highly publicized firing of Gen. Douglas MacArthur. MacArthur's dismissal gave Shivers another chance to distance himself from Truman by backing an invitation to the general to address a joint session of the Texas legislature. Convinced the general's appearance would promote a "forthright debate" of foreign policy, the governor endured some modest criticism. MacArthur's June visit generated "no enthusiasm" in official Austin, according to Pickle, who told Johnson "it is safe to report . . . that the town is not going wild in any sense."[15]

The next month, in the aftermath of the cross-filing bill, Pickle first warned that the governor might bolt the party the following year. When Shivers summoned his "hatchet man" to offer him the job of running the 1952 state party conventions, Pickle had coyly responded that he no longer did political work for anyone but Senator Johnson. The governor explained that it was his intention to "be damned sure I am in charge of that Convention" and hinted that he planned to prevent a Truman reelection bid. Moreover, he opposed any effort to nominate Sam Rayburn, whom he disliked and thought was too close to the president. Shivers also expressed his regard for and willingness to work with LBJ. Pickle worried that their conversation portended "a rough and bloody affair"—of which he wanted no part. Johnson speculated that the governor's bluster represented an opening volley in a race against Tom Connally for the U.S. Senate. If the news worried Johnson, he gave no indication of it.[16]

After the 1950 Mineral Wells convention, some Texas liberals recognized that "we were in trouble with Allan." They worked hard to convince Rayburn that the governor could not be trusted, only to have Lyndon Johnson come along behind them and reassure the old man of his reliability. The conflicting information had Rayburn "in a complete dither" throughout 1951. When harried by too much information, the speaker tended to lean on LBJ, whom some liberals accused of "playing footsy with Allan." The liberal-loyalist leadership began organizing in advance for the 1952 conventions, forming the Loyal Democrats of Texas (LDT) that summer. Some liberals thought the very purpose of the LDT, which was led by Austin attorney Fagan Dickson and Maury Maverick Sr., seemed exaggerated. Former San Antonio legislator Woodville Rogers refused to believe Shivers planned anything other than party loyalty. "Allan's not gonna bolt the party," Rogers insisted in disbelief. "The Democratic party is his god. He's a member of the Church." In July, 1951, Dickson, who was busy forming the LDT, tried to strengthen his ties to Shivers by asking the governor to appoint his wife to the State Parks and Wildlife Commission. It appears to have been difficult for even those most mistrusting of Shivers to imagine what lay ahead.[17]

More disturbing news came from outside Texas in late July and early August. Senator Karl Mundt (R–South Dakota) suggested a southern-conservative and Republican alliance against President Truman. Mundt argued that civil rights and Truman's national health insurance and aid to education proposals offered a basis for agreement between the GOP and dissident southern Democrats. Under Mundt's scheme, Rayburn would be permitted to remain House Speaker, while the Republicans would nominate a southerner to serve as vice president or select several for cabinet positions. As unlikely as the Mundt Plan seemed, the South

Dakotan's specific praise of Shivers's support of cross-filing shook Texas Democratic loyalists.[18]

The precise nature of Shivers's future plans were not yet clear, but the mechanics of a battle for control of the state Democratic Party had already been set in motion. Those closest to the governor knew he opposed Harry Truman and that he particularly detested the party loyalty espoused by more nationally minded Texas Democrats such as Rayburn. Even former Dixiecrat presidential candidate Strom Thurmond recognized and complemented Shivers's hostility toward the national party and leadership. In mid-November, Rayburn's own words drove the wedge deeper. At the Southern Governors Conference in Hot Springs, Arkansas, the House Speaker ignored the unspoken agreement about the meeting being a nonpolitical affair and delivered a ringing endorsement of Truman's presidency. The lone Republican present, Maryland governor Theodore McKeldin, stalked out. The Democrats remained behind, including four who had participated in the 1948 Dixiecrat revolt. Another conference speaker, *Arkansas Gazette* editor Harry Ashmore, further strained comity by urging voluntary progress on civil rights as the only means to forestall tougher federal action. However, it was Rayburn's words that most upset the governors. "Methinks he protesteth his virtue too much," Shivers quipped.[19]

Governor James F. Byrnes of South Carolina blamed the speaker's rant on their host, Arkansas governor Sidney McMath, a liberal Truman supporter. According to the *Dallas Morning News*'s Allen Duckworth, Byrnes pulled Shivers aside and "gave him an earful" about the speaker and the need to defeat the president. Shivers agreed: Rayburn had angered him also, Truman had to go, and Sid McMath had done a poor job of planning the conference. Despite the fireworks, the Hot Springs conference failed to live up to the media's expectations. "I think it was a good conference," Alabama's Gordon Persons later wrote Shivers, "particularly so since all of the Governors showed discretion in not letting some of the newspaper people start us in a riot."[20]

Although the Southern governors did not riot, those who were displeased with the national administration commiserated and plotted. An anguished attendee cornered James Byrnes and told him the South needed a "Moses to lead us out of the wilderness—a man like you." The South Carolinian saw Shivers standing nearby and pointed his way, as if to say, "there's your man." Governor Shivers used the conference to make plain his support of "most anybody else" for the Democratic presidential nomination in 1952. He suggested both Eisenhower and Georgia senator Richard Russell as strong potential standard-bearers. When asked about a southern third party, Shivers insisted that any regional effort should remain within the two-party system. Nevertheless, some thought even these complaints were too tentative.[21]

A *Houston Post* editorial assured readers that the governor needed to be "cryptic" in his public comments, but that he kept political faith with Byrnes and Virginia senator Harry F. Byrd. Although Shivers never came out and said he would bolt the party if Truman were nominated, the *Post* reminded readers that the governor had not sworn to support the party nominee regardless of who it was. Following the conference, members of the Texas delegation returned the way they had come: aboard the private plane of Forth Worth oilman and Dixiecrat organizer Arch Rowan. Meanwhile, the LDTs, who had warned Truman of trouble in Texas, now had their suspicions seemingly confirmed.[22]

TWO POSSIBLE POLITICAL CAREER PATHS LAY OPEN TO ALLAN SHIVERS in 1951. One was to seek reelection as governor; the other was to campaign for higher office. Press speculation about a Shivers race for the U.S. Senate abounded throughout the year. The incumbent, Sen. Tom Connally, had been a New Deal stalwart, head of the Foreign Relations Committee, and national in his political viewpoint. Despite his close connections to both Roosevelt and Truman, Connally had faithfully served Big Oil—from the Connally Hot Oil Act of 1935, to his stout defense of the oil depletion allowance. Nevertheless, his tenacious party loyalty and ties to Truman's unpopular foreign policy irritated many of his long-time supporters. Oil industry lobbyist Clint Small informed Shivers that he could count on oil's backing if he decided to challenge the incumbent. Texas Power and Light president John Carpenter passed along word of his own support. Truman, Rayburn, and Johnson saw Shivers's antiadministration posturing as preparation for just such a race. Although the governor did briefly consider challenging Connally, he kept it to himself.[23]

Precisely why Shivers opted to stay in Austin is a matter of conjecture. Ever attentive to political developments, FBI agents in Texas received information from a "normally very reliable" and "very much inside" Dallas source that Shivers had decided to run and even assembled financial backing in late 1951 and early 1952. His plans fell apart, according to bureau sources, when Connally's people let Shivers know the incumbent possessed incriminating photos of the governor. The photographs reportedly showed a much younger Shivers partying with Sam Maceo, Galveston's late organized crime boss. Less lurid reasons have also been suggested. Weldon Hart claimed the governor liked the "stability of life in the mansion," especially with his children already in school or nearing school age. John was eleven going on twelve, and Bud would turn six and Cissy five in 1952. Moreover, Marialice Shivers had never liked elections or the dislocation politics brought to her household. Just as important, a political revolution was brewing in the state and there was a widespread perception that only Allan Shivers could pull it off. All of these things no doubt informed the governor's decision to defer a U.S. Senate race.[24]

Attorney General Price Daniel had hoped Shivers would seek a promotion. Above all other ambitions, Daniel wished to be governor. He had grown frustrated waiting on Shivers to make up his mind in 1951. Daniel considered running for governor in 1952 regardless of Shivers's plans, but Temple attorney and loyal Democrat Byron Skelton advised him to wait for Shivers to announce his intentions. Daniel floated rumors of a U.S. Senate bid, hoping to force the governor to declare first. Shivers, however, did not rise to the bait. One afternoon in late 1951, Daniel encountered Shivers outside the capitol and confronted the governor about the uncertainty of his plans. He insisted that Shivers alone could beat Connally. Years later, Shivers recalled that Daniel had nearly cried as he "begged me to let him run for Governor." The governor demurred, however, saying that Texas needed Daniel in Washington to fight for the tidelands.[25]

Age and geography—both men began their careers in southeast Texas—made Daniel and Shivers rivals. The governor did not like the attorney general, blamed him for losing the tidelands case, and saw him as not "quite his match." Their personalities differed greatly. Shivers had come up from almost nothing, whereas Daniel rose to public office as a small-town aristocrat. They had risen through the political ranks and had been involved in business deals together. Daniel, recalled D. B. Hardeman, was "a bit of a prude about the manly excesses of life," whereas the more "charismatic" Shivers viewed them with "more raw-blooded, red-blooded" relish. Another liberal antagonist, Maury Maverick Jr., preferred Shivers to Daniel because although the governor might "kick the shit out of you," he did so up front. Daniel, on the other hand, would "invoke Jesus and God and then slip around and stick a knife in you." Others pointed to the way Shivers baited his rival as proof that he had a malicious streak when dealing with Daniel. John Osorio said Shivers disliked what he perceived to be Daniel's hypocritical streak. Hardeman related a story about Shivers traveling at night with his state-trooper driver in the country outside Fort Worth. Seeing a small building with a weakly shining neon sign that read "Hotel," the governor suggested a bit of mischief. "I'll bet that's a whorehouse over there," Shivers reportedly joked. "Do you know what we ought to do? We ought to go over there and register . . . in the name of Price Daniel, and then get the blotter Xeroxed or photographed and send it to Price. He'd drop dead."[26]

Shivers's decision to run for governor reflected his growing role in the clash over the tidelands. Although Shivers had long nursed disagreements with the national Democratic Party, he needed a strong emotional issue to justify a possible bolt in 1952. In 1950 and 1951, state money had been directed toward the Texas Property Defense Association (TPDA), a lobbying group that defended Texas' claim to the tidelands. The TPDA tried to stoke fires of concern across the nation, hoping to attract support for Texas' position by appealing to wider fears of federal power. As part of this grassroots appeal, Shivers wrote several columns that appeared in newspapers in places as diverse as McCall, Idaho; Mechanicsburg, Pennsylvania; and Walsenburg, Colorado. The TPDA funneled campaign funds from Texas to politicians elsewhere who might be sympathetic to the state's tidelands dilemma. The association provided funding for George Smathers's race against Claude Pepper for a U.S. Senate seat in Florida and worked to arrange opposition to Alabama senators John Sparkman and Lister Hill.[27]

Such efforts were intended to gain sufficient support for quitclaim legislation to override a Truman veto, or build a bloc of sympathetic congressmen and senators in the event a Republican won the presidency in 1952. According to Weldon Hart, when federal ownership supporters in Congress "hit upon the infallible bait" in the summer of 1951, it marked the "beginning of the end" of the quitclaim effort. They proposed that tidelands' oil revenues be earmarked for federal aid to education and divided amongst all the states. This effectively outflanked state ownership advocates and no quitclaim measure came to a vote for the remainder of the Eighty-second Congress.[28]

Hart in particular recognized that the tidelands struggle would provide an excuse for making a break from the national Democratic Party during the 1952 election cycle: "It occurs to me that this might be a pretty good time to stage a tidelands campaign in Texas — not altogether for the sake of the tidelands. More than anything else, this issue epitomizes the quarrel between the national administration and the State of Texas. . . . Any campaign that created sympathy for the state's side of the tidelands fight would almost automatically create good will for the proponents of that side. By the same token, it would further stimulate dissatisfaction with the present administration." The propaganda bombardment to which the people of Texas had already been subjected thus came down to this: Where the Regulars and Dixiecrats had failed, their political heir had the power to succeed.[29]

On December 7, 1951, the governor met with Arch Rowan, Lamar Fleming Jr., Tom Sealy, J. E. Price, and former state senator Clint Small. Rowan and Fleming had spearheaded the Dixiecrat movement in Texas in 1948. The other men had all expressed sympathy with the Mundt Plan. Between them, they agreed to stay within the two-party system. They also agreed to prepare a political revolt. "If we say we're going to support the nominee — no matter who they are — we might as well send a letter to the convention instead of a delegation," Shivers told them. The men plotted to lead Texas into the Republican column if an acceptable Democratic nominee did not emerge. Since at this point Harry Truman, the sitting president, was the presumptive nominee, it was simply a matter of time before a break with the Democratic Party occurred. A favorite-son candidacy for the "youngish, aggressive" Shivers drew praise from as far away as Florida. Conservative Fort Worth congressman Wingate Lucas called the Texas governor a "logical successor" to Truman. By January, 1952, the Shivers organization in Dallas, Houston, Austin, and Wichita Falls was working in tandem with local anti-Truman groups. Weldon Hart told *Newsweek* and *Time*, whose editors were eagerly awaiting the opportunity to run cover stories on the photogenic insurgent, "it was a little early yet" to break the story. Shivers's approval was all that was needed to start the New York presses rolling.[30]

As the year's end drew near, a young lawyer attached to the state attorney general's office received an unusual request. Shivers's secretary of state, John Ben Shepperd, contacted John Osorio and relayed orders, presumably from the governor, to research the legal scope and strength of the state Democratic loyalty pledge. Forty-six years later, Osorio recalled being "naïve" about the implications of this unusual assignment. After quietly looking into the legal points, he presented his findings before a receptive State Democratic Executive Committee in April, 1952. The young attorney's performance so impressed Shivers that he asked Osorio to join his staff. The two men maintained a close working relationship for the remainder of Shivers's political career and beyond. Osorio's research assignment strongly implied that Shivers had already decided the course he would follow in the event of a collision between his political interests and those of the national party.[31]

NATIONAL POLITICS PROVED TO BE AS COMPLEX AS THOSE IN TEXAS. President Truman remained constitutionally eligible to run for reelection in 1952. Although he had toyed with the idea of retirement as early as 1950, even going so far as to draft and file away a statement, his inability to entice Illinois governor Adlai Stevenson into the presidential field led him to consider running again. The war in Korea, a strike by steelworkers, and alleged White House corruption caused the president's public-approval rating to plummet farther than it had in 1946–47, previously the nadir of his presidency. After losing the March, 1952, New Hampshire primary to Tennessee senator Estes Kefauver, Truman announced that he would retire at the end of his term.[32]

Word of Truman's impending retirement came as a mixed blessing in Austin. Weldon Hart, worried that the president's departure "deprives us of our best weapon—the enthusiastic desire to get rid of him," told Shivers that a continued fight against "*Trumanism*" presented other problems. It was easy to be "*positively negative*" about Truman, but now the situation would force Shivers to dissent in generalities. Shivers's allies, Hart continued, must "revamp" their program and "avoid meeting the opposition on ground of its own choosing, i.e., the party pledge." A little "wholesome demagoguery" on unity offered the governor a chance to change the terms of the debate by "diverting attention . . . from the party pledge." If Shivers wanted to outflank the issue of party loyalty, Hart advised, he should insist the national Democratic Party to respond to Texas' concerns. Accordingly, in his response to Truman's departure from the race, Shivers told Texans he wanted more than the president's retirement. "The fight against Mr. Truman, as an individual and a symbol, has been won. The fight must continue," he insisted, "for candidates and platform planks acceptable to Texas."[33]

The Democratic field included two southern senators, the liberal Kefauver and Georgia's Richard Russell. Russell was the only Democratic candidate who met Shivers's litmus tests on the tidelands, civil rights, and big government. He enjoyed the support of Texas' junior senator, Lyndon Johnson. When Truman announced his retirement, Russell asked the Texan for his support, vowing in return to support LBJ for vice president should his own presidential candidacy fail. The relationship between Johnson and Russell was primarily personal; the Georgian was a political mentor. It had little to do with ideological agreement, but in some ways was a pragmatic arrangement whereby Johnson learned what it took to advance in the Senate. Governor Shivers's support of Russell reflected kindred political philosophies. Still, Shivers did not plan to seek a Texas delegation pledged to the Georgia senator. The coming primary season might bring a challenger from the left, so endorsing Russell early might actually weaken Shivers.[34]

The governor, as has been explained, relied upon the public's perception of him as a moderate, coolheaded leader to advance into statewide office. Liberal elements in the state Democratic Party had given him their support, doubtless thinking him preferable to other, more plainly conservative, opponents. However, developments in 1950–51 seemed to fracture the governor's consensus. Weldon Hart warned of possible problems keeping the minority voters Shivers had attracted since 1946. Tejano voters saw Shivers as "reasonably sympathetic," but also supported President Truman's civil rights initiatives. Many did not see the point of their governor's repeated condemnations of the president, causing Hart to opine that "there is little or no use talking to the Latinos now about supporting us in the precinct, county and state conventions." An open endorsement of Russell might harm the governor's standing still further, Hart cautioned. His contacts in the Tejano leadership seemed to offer Shivers a choice: remain loyal to the national party and its civil rights stands or lose their support. At first, the governor had coyly avoided dealing with the Tejanos' civil rights aspirations. However, from 1952 on, he tacitly obstructed them. As for protecting, let alone even building, a base among black Texans, the governor appears never to have considered the idea.[35]

Although Richard Russell met with the governor's approval, the chances of his securing the nomination were slim. Long a New Deal critic, he had also sternly opposed Truman's Fair Deal and civil rights efforts. In short, Russell did not stand a chance—and Shivers no doubt knew it. Feigning efforts to influence the nomination process, he prepared Texas for what lay ahead. On April 18, Shivers spoke before the SDEC. His speech had no conciliatory content and sounded like a secession proclamation. Devoting substantial attention to the question of party loyalty, Shivers took the next step toward bolting from the party.

> Our First Political Loyalty is to the Free and Independent Democratic Party of Texas as the unshackled guardian for more than a century of true Texas traditions of Democratic government and as the protector and promoter of the best interests of our commonwealth, its people and its principles.
>
> We repudiate as alien to our heritage and foreign to our freedom those self-appointed and self-seeking serfs of a corrupt national political machine who under the self-styled label of "loyal" presently seek to prostitute the power and pillage the opportunity of Our Texas Democratic Party to aid in recapturing and redeeming the National Democratic Party from left-wing domination and machine control. I scorn the suggestion that "loyalty" demands an abject, contemptible, and unconditional surrender in advance to the whims or the dictates of any absentee overlords of the national party. The self-governing and self-respecting Democratic Party of Texas, which nurtured the still small light of the Party of Jefferson and Jackson for fifty years during which it was extinguished in darkness in the North and East, does not slink and cower, hat in hand, to anybody's back door to make a blind trade of our heritage for a handout.

Shivers at last had come clean about his own political metamorphosis. However, it was not he and Texas that not changed, but rather the Democratic Party. In rejecting the party of Truman, he affirmed his "unswerving and unshaken loyalty" to the "true and historic Democratic party."[36]

After blasting Truman and the national party, Shivers demanded platform language reflecting the concerns of Texas' "true and historic Democratic party." First, he called for a tidelands state-ownership plank in the national platform. "Tolerance and brotherly love cannot be imposed by law or enforced by coercion," Shivers lectured. This meant that "hate-breeding and trouble-making" civil rights and fair employment initiatives must cease and be replaced by voluntary efforts at "harmony and brotherhood." To stop the "tentacles of creeping socialism," he insisted that the federal government reduce spending in all "non-essential, non-defense" areas and lower taxes. Lastly, the governor wanted all communist influence purged from the national government, so that a "spiritual reawakening" and "moral regeneration" might take place in Washington.[37]

In addition to these impossible demands, Shivers proposed that Texans send an uninstructed delegation to the National Democratic Convention in Chicago that summer. No likely Democratic nominee or dark horse could meet the conditions necessary to gain Shivers's endorsement. The governor's vision of a "true" Democratic Party had died in 1936, along with the two-thirds rule, so he could not have failed to recognize the clash ahead. His laundry list of demands prevented any reconciliation and capped a long fight that had been going on in Texas Democratic circles since the late 1930s. Where the Jeffersonian Democrats, the Garnerites, the Regulars, and Dixiecrats had all failed, Shivers appeared poised to succeed. Believing that he possessed both the power and the right issue with which to wedge Texans from the national Democratic ticket, Shivers warned, "the Democratic Party of Texas is to be dealt with in 1952."[38]

CHAPTER SIX

Vote Texan, Vote Ike

1952

AFTER NEW BRAUNFELS, IT APPEARED CLEAR THAT SHIVERS HAD no intention of mending the rift in the state Democratic Party and that he was planning to wage war against the national party. Weldon Hart, Shivers's chief political adviser, spoke as though a clash could not be prevented. Fagan Dixon telephoned Bexar County loyalist organizer Kathleen Voigt and instructed her to reserve meeting space, fearing loyalists might "have to walk" at the May state convention. From Washington, a concerned Lyndon Johnson tried to mend relations between Governor Shivers and Sam Rayburn. Rayburn did not necessarily want the loyalist group to prevail, but he also did not trust Shivers to control the Texas delegation. Johnson, through Weldon Hart, informed the governor that Rayburn, who would preside over the national convention, might refuse to seat a Shivers-dominated delegation unless he toned down his rhetoric. Rayburn was willing to accept an uninstructed delegation, but he would not allow Shivers to be seated until he took the party pledge. Johnson promised to keep trying to soften Rayburn's stance, but added that it was "essential" Shivers take the symbolic pledge.[1]

Much of the organizing necessary to capture the state convention scheduled in May began in January. Shivers's key allies received instructions through a "Convention Organization Guide" drafted by Weldon Hart and John Van Cronkhite, a former lieutenant of Leander Perez, a key Louisiana Dixiecrat. It instructed operatives on tactics for controlling precinct conventions, including when and what to move, resolve, and vote on. The Shivers organization flowed downward all the way to precinct level following the intricate network established by Jake Pickle in late 1949 and early 1950. With no backing from Washington and no organizational strategy, the Loyal Democrats of Texas were in disarray. They expected a beating from the governor's forces in May. However, as Austin journalist Stuart Long confided to Hart, the loyalists expected to regain control at the September convention—just as they had in 1944 and 1948.[2]

Locally, Shivers's minions moved efficiently and ruthlessly, at times resorting to heavy-handed tactics to seize precinct and then county conventions. Precinct meetings rarely attracted many voters, making a takeover relatively simple. It was a matter of organization and turnout. A precinct boss declared for either side must get his or her voters to the meeting, preferably early. This presented a problem for wageworkers, the voters most likely to be organized against the governor. Whichever side got to the meeting first with the most began the precinct convention promptly at 7:30 P.M., perhaps after setting a clock five or ten minutes fast. Sometimes meeting places that had been agreed upon in advance might be moved on short notice. Once assembled, voters took the loyalty pledge, elected a temporary chair and secretary, and began the meeting. If handled correctly, the meeting could convene, elect officers, and select a delegation to the county convention in half an hour. If the steamroller encountered opposition, parliamentary procedure could be manipulated to achieve the desired result. If things got a little heated and words were exchanged, the defeated faction would—if well organized—leave and form a rump convention. A week or two later, the whole process would begin again at the county convention, sometimes with two or more delegations from a precinct claiming legitimacy. The county convention would then rule on which ones to admit.[3]

The county conventions, held in early May, predictably favored Shivers's faction. The governor's machine managed to control 1,009 of the state's 1,152 precincts. Shivers forces carried Dallas, Houston, Fort Worth, and El Paso, along with most of the smaller cities. In each case, the loyalists bolted and held rump conventions. The governor quickly made plain his intention to make a clean sweep of the loyalists. "I'm tired of a lot of ultra-intellectual parlor pinks and so-called liberal crackpots running the Democratic Party," he declared. Of the major cities, only San Antonio's Bexar County convention fell to the loyalists. There, forces supportive of the national party, led by Maury Maverick Sr., defeated Shivers's allies. When Texas Democrats descended on San Antonio for the state convention on May 27, the battle lines had been clearly drawn. The delegates quickly discovered they could not agree on anything—not even a temporary roll. Determining the legitimacy of competing delegations took considerable time. When the State Democratic Executive Committee issued a report on convention organization, Maverick dissented with a minority report that called for all delegates to pledge support to the national party's presidential nominee. Shivers's handpicked state chair, J. E. Wheat, ruled Maverick's report out of order. Shouting above the crowd, Maverick told his followers: "Let us go. It's time for us to walk out into the rain."[4]

The loyalists exchanged taunts and a few punches with their opponents as they pressed out of the hall and into a steady light rain. They walked several blocks to La Villita, a Works Progress Administration replica of a Mexican village, and crowded into cramped facilities. Once Maverick called them to order, he led delegates in the party pledge. "I will support the nominees of the Democratic party in Texas," he began, then in an aside, "even if it's Shivers." After that, the assembled loyalists pledged support to "the nominees of the national convention." Speaking to the rump convention, Maverick dubbed those assembled in the "official" convention "Shivercrats." The moniker stuck. Meanwhile, at their convention, the Shivercrats approved an uncommitted delegation for the Chicago national convention and refused to take the party pledge. As they had in 1950, a smattering of liberals—including Woodville Rogers and former Austin mayor Tom Miller—remained loyal to the governor. Conservative sentiments and personal loyalty to Shivers characterized most of the convention delegates. They passed resolutions condemning the Truman administration and its heresies. The Shivercrats' delegate slate included Fort Worth oilman Arch Rowan and Houston's E. E. Townes, prominent supporters of the Dixiecrat movement in 1948. The loyalists sent an integrated delegation that included Dr. Hector Garcia and black minister G. J. Sutton to challenge the Shivercrats in Chicago.[5]

Despite being routed at the precinct, county, and state conventions, anti-Shivers forces fielded a challenger to the governor in the summer Democratic primary after Sam Rayburn gave the rebels his tacit blessing. Texas unions, Dickinson banker Walter G. Hall, and liberal oilman J. R. Parten pooled modest funds and urged Ralph W. Yarborough to run against Shivers. Born in East Texas, Yarborough had served as assistant attorney general under James V. Allred, saw combat in World War II, and served as a district judge in Travis County. Strongly loyalist in his sentiments, the Austin judge's ambitions apparently worried the governor. Before Yarborough's announcement, one Shivers staffer suggested elevating him to the state supreme court to prevent his opposing Shivers's secretary of state, John Ben Shepperd, for attorney general. Shivers bluntly told Yarborough that he had already rounded up most of the available campaign cash for Shepperd, thus making a race for attorney general futile. Yarborough, who claimed that Shivers had "threatened" him during their talk, willingly accepted when the loyalists asked him to run against the governor.[6]

Yarborough's campaign languished early on, low on funds and largely ignored. Shivers compounded his opponent's problems by refusing to run on state issues, thus hurting Yarborough's effort to draw him into meaningful debate. The governor's backers closely monitored Yarborough's campaign, noting that the challenger sought out black voters by attending a "Juneteenth" celebration in Austin. Instead of running against Yarborough, Shivers ran against the national party and his opponent's financial backers, especially Parten. The governor claimed that Parten had tried to intimidate him by promising to mount a "strong and well-financed opposition." Parten reacted angrily to the charge, which seemed plainly ridiculous when one realized that Shivers controlled most of the campaign financial sources.[7]

Moreover, in the event Yarborough's candidacy became threatening, the governor's staff prepared harsh attacks against him. One staffer suggested that Yarborough be publicly tied to "socialist" Maury Maverick and wealthy loyalist Lillian Collier, whose Brazos Valley cotton plantation permitted an alleged African-American branch of CIO farm workers. A proposed press release that suggested the LDT represented a "reunion of yesterday's and today's CIO-pinko workers" would have injected an ugly rhetoric into the race. Whether on Shivers's orders or in recognition of Yarborough's weakness, this harsh attack was never allowed to pollute the debate. Yarborough did not stand a chance in 1952, and Shivers hated to "demagogue" unnecessarily. One prominent loyalist later admitted that it would have been "practically impossible" to run a strong race against the governor in 1952.[8]

As the July primary drew nearer, Yarborough gained some momentum from questions about Shivers's party loyalty. However, the final vote tally showed that the governor had soundly defeated the challenger, winning 224 of 245 counties. Still, Yarborough had increased his name recognition and managed to permanently endear himself to Texas liberals. He picked up 488,000 votes (36 percent of the total) and won twenty-one counties, doing especially well in East, Central, and West Central Texas. The urban-rural distribution of Yarborough votes was roughly even. Although Texas' cities had a higher concentration of labor and liberal voters than did the countryside, Yarborough had attracted rural voters concerned with both the ongoing drought and Shivers's party loyalty. Although Shivers had easily bested his challenger, he still needed credible evidence that he was a good Democrat. He hoped to obtain it by leading the state delegation to the Democratic national convention—which he did in the midst of the primary campaign. Meanwhile, Maury Maverick and the LDT intended to stop him in Chicago.[9]

TEXAS SENT TWO DELEGATIONS TO THE NATIONAL PARTY CONVENTION in July. Shivers assailed the LDT as "Trumanites" who admitted "in black and white that they are for federal ownership of our Tidelands." The governor's handlers urged him, "ostensibly at least," to appear to actively govern the state during his race against Yarborough. Both Hart and VanCronkhite told him he would need to store up good press because of the bad press sure to follow the convention. Loyalist forces, meanwhile, worked to prevent the Shivercrats from being seated at the national meeting. They prepared a booklet for conventioneers that explained Shivers's relationship to earlier disruptions in Texas and the South in 1936, 1940,

1944, and 1948. While the governor had not actively participated in those battles, he certainly had befriended principals in past controversies and held many of their views. The loyalists called their pamphlet *The Texas Story* and urged Democrats from across the nation to rally to their aid.[10]

Speaker Rayburn's condition for seating Shivers's delegation remained unchanged. Rayburn intended to demand that Shivers take the pledge. Three other delegations—those from Virginia, South Carolina, and Louisiana—had already refused to do so. South Carolina and Louisiana had both supported the Dixiecrats in 1948. The Shivercrats negotiated with Rayburn even as they investigated the possibility of filing a legal challenge if barred from the convention. Throughout the convention's critical early days, Shivers remained in contact with his allies in Texas, including already-declared Eisenhower supporters like Houston oilman Roy Cullen. Rayburn received contradictory advice about even bothering to negotiate with Shivers. Lyndon Johnson argued that the governor could be trusted, whereas LDT secretary Creekmore Fath, an Austin lawyer, urged the speaker to recognize Maury Maverick's delegation. Fath was talking to Rayburn when Shivers came calling. Speaker Rayburn and Shivers quickly adjourned to an adjoining room and met privately for a few minutes. When they reemerged, Shivers bade all who were present goodnight and went on his way. After the governor left, Rayburn announced he would seat the Shivercrats because Shivers had given his solemn word to support the Democratic nominee.[11]

"The Promise," of all the disputed incidents in Shivers's career, remains among the most problematic. Only Rayburn and Shivers ever knew what transpired between them that evening. Whether or not Allan Shivers actually promised Rayburn anything can never be known or confirmed. It seems unlikely anything short of a categorical pledge would have satisfied the speaker, given his wariness of the governor. Then again, if Rayburn, and by extension Johnson, wished to isolate Texas liberals, any bargain with Shivers might have served their interests. Yet another possibility exists: Shivers promised one thing and Rayburn took it to mean something else. The governor's eventual failure to fulfill Rayburn's expectations resulted in a complete break between the two and assured there would be a vendetta on the speaker's part. "He lied to me," Rayburn huffed when Shivers eventually renounced the party nominee. "You don't lie to me. . . . I don't want the son of a bitch at my funeral." According to his biographers, Rayburn struck Shivers's name from every book in his private library.[12]

When Shivers later defected, Johnson and Rayburn were both "beside themselves" in response to the betrayal, giving every indication of total surprise. The governor's staff suggested he redefine the issues surrounding the Promise. Maurice Acers advised his boss to urge voters to split the ticket in November because it "would permit you to remain a Democrat." Because of Shivers's "Honorable

Means" assurances to Rayburn, the Democratic nominee would appear on the Texas ballot, but it did not "morally or legally" bind the governor to support him. To accomplish this spin on the Promise, Acers suggested that the Shivercrat line be "planted" in Texas' obliging major newspapers. Taken together, the intensity of Rayburn's anger, Shivers's undisguised disdain for the speaker's party loyalty, and Acers's memo indicate some deception on the governor's part.[13]

Loyal Democrats of Texas representatives at the Chicago convention felt thoroughly betrayed. Furious at Democratic National Committee chairman Frank McKinney and other national party leaders to whom they had turned for help, Maury Maverick told President Truman: "McKinney treated us like dogs." Unable to imagine Shivers backing the party's eventual nominee, Adlai Stevenson, Loyal Democrats warned the administration of the governor's imminent defection. "The True Democrats of Texas have been humiliated and enfeebled," wrote Dallas lawyer William D. Kimbrough in August. Even as Shivers moved "every pebble and cowchip" to win Texas for Eisenhower, Kimbrough murmured "the prayer that someday the National Party will stop throwing us to the wolves." Following the convention, Shivers insisted that he might yet support Stevenson, depending upon his answers on a number of issues. Abilene attorney Dallas Scarborough told Truman, "don't let Stevenson agree to anything" when he meets with Shivers.[14]

The national party's treatment of Texas' loyalists in Chicago represented part of a strategy to avoid a 1948-style meltdown. It had the desired effect in the South. State parties generally endorsed the Stevenson-Sparkman ticket, but individual southern Democratic leaders quietly participated in efforts to assist Eisenhower. In South Carolina, Gov. James Byrnes signed the "South Carolinians for Eisenhower" petition intended to get the Republican nominee on South Carolina's ballot. However, Byrnes insisted his signature should not be considered an indication that he supported Eisenhower for president. Former Dixiecrat presidential nominee Strom Thurmond also endorsed Ike, as did Louisiana governor Robert Kennon and Plaquemines Parish boss Leander Perez. Throughout the region, as in Texas, conservative Democratic elements that had long chafed under the New Deal and Fair Deal labored on the Republican's behalf while remaining nominally Democrat. National Democratic Party leaders made little response.[15]

The Truman administration and national party leadership, completely misunderstanding the depth of resentment in the region, looked for Stevenson to sweep the South in November. The South had remained essentially solid in 1948, despite the Dixiecrat revolt. Surely, they reasoned, conditions in 1952 were no match for the dangerous political situation four years earlier. To some extent, Rayburn and Johnson's coddling of Shivers contributed to the DNC's failure to appreciate the current situation's severity. Yet, even seasoned White House adviser Clark Clifford deluded himself concerning the loyalty of Texas' Democratic leadership. After a February meeting with Democratic National Committeeman Wright Morrow, himself an important figure among Texas' Dixiecrats, Clifford convinced himself and likely Truman that the "south cannot get anywhere by leaving the Democratic Party." Indeed, Clifford refused to see reality right up to election night, predicting that Texas and the rest of the South save for Virginia and Maryland would support Stevenson. The president told worried Texas loyalists that the governor's forces represented the minority in their state.[16]

THANKS TO THE 1951 LAW AUTHORIZING A REPUBLICAN PRIMARY IN TEXAS, state Republicans had also been waging a bitter struggle for the future of their party that summer. State GOP chairman Henry Zweifel tried to protect his organization for Ohio senator Robert Taft against the "one-day Republicans" he loathed. Eisenhower supporters Jack Porter and Alvin Lane reassured the one-day Republicans that they could sign the pledge in good conscience, because cross-filing would allow Democratic nominees for all state positions to appear on the GOP ballot in November. Across the South, in places such as Georgia and Louisiana, "Old Guard" state chairmen found themselves besieged by Eisenhower's troops. In Texas, Republican precinct meetings had been even more sparsely attended than the Democratic ones, making them easy pickings for the well-organized Eisenhower forces. To ensure Ike's supporters got the idea, Oveta Hobby's *Houston Post*, a nominally Democratic newspaper, put out over four hundred thousand "primers" on precinct hijacking tactics similar to those the Shivercrats had used.[17]

The Old Guard's bitter opposition to recent Republican converts erupted into a floor fight at the GOP's Mineral Wells state convention. Republicans for Taft insisted that the Eisenhower delegates were merely unreliable Democrats and independents. Some of them were put off by Ike's preferred mantle of hero called to service by a popular crusade. The financial and political incest between the general's Texas backers and the Texas Democratic machine galled Old Guard partisans. Hugh Roy Cullen unabashedly poured money into the pockets of both Republicans and conservative state Democrats while lecturing Eisenhower on the failings of southern Republicans. "The carpetbagger Republicans of the South who have been in control of the Republican Party since the Civil War are apparently for Taft," the oilman remarked, "and we should be happy about this because people of the South refuse to go along with these kind of people."[18]

Cullen's sentiments justified the anxieties of the long-suffering Texas Old Guard. Zweifel and his allies feared a sellout. Porter and other new Republicans strongly desired a two-party state. They believed that presidential Republicanism represented a wedge with which to develop the Texas Republican Party. Election results since 1944 demonstrated steady growth in ticket splitting, but some Texas

Republicans estimated that as many as five hundred thousand to a million voters harbored Republican views in their "hearts." Eisenhower's candidacy presented Republicans an opportunity not merely to crack the Solid South as they had in 1928, but to perhaps shatter it. The groundswell for Eisenhower captured precincts and counties with surprising ease, but the Old Guard ejected the upstarts at the Mineral Wells state convention and awarded Texas' delegates to Taft. The Eisenhower forces walked out and sent a competing delegation to the national convention outfitted with a pamphlet explaining their side of the events at Mineral Wells titled *The Texas Steal.* At the national convention, of course, Eisenhower prevailed.[19]

MEANWHILE, THE DEMOCRATS NOMINATED ILLINOIS GOVERNOR ADLAI Stevenson to be their standard-bearer. He had not been the clear favorite going in, nor was he the favorite of the Texas delegation, which—along with a number of other southern delegations—supported Georgia senator Richard Russell. Stevenson's views on many significant issues remained nebulous. Shivers therefore did not immediately turn on the nominee. He needed to draw Stevenson out into the open in order to gain a pretext for bolting the party. Writing the nominee in late July, Shivers praised him as a "strong and able candidate," but asked for a conference to "exchange views" on problems of interest to Texas and the national Democratic Party. Stevenson quickly assented to a "sober consideration of all the equities," although he admitted he was "woefully ignorant about the Tidelands business." Stevenson agreed to meet Shivers in Springfield, hoping that such a meeting might ease the "passion" surrounding the issue. The two governors did not get together immediately, however, as the Shivers's fourth child, Brian, was due any day.[20]

It is not an easy task to determine Shivers's precise expectations and plans for his meeting with Stevenson. Contemporaries had varied opinions about his purposes and schemes. Shivers's own comments on his activities are not very revealing. Senator Lyndon Johnson believed the governor's purpose in meeting with Stevenson was to trap him on the tidelands issue. D. B. Hardeman speculated that Shivers held out hope for "a *modus vivendi* . . . to save his face and save the state, and while he might not support Stevenson publicly, he wouldn't leave the party." Asked about the meeting seventeen years later, Shivers claimed that his "political enemies" had fueled rumors about the meeting being a "trap" for the Democratic nominee. "Stevenson's smarter than that," he insisted, claiming he had genuinely sought common ground with the Illinois governor. As usual, Shivers's own memories are only partially correct. Stevenson could not possibly have been deceived: he knew the tidelands issue would come up and that Shivers would want a commitment from him. However, as Shivers also admitted, the offshore lands amounted to nothing more than "a symbol of opposition." He went to Springfield with more than the tidelands on his mind. Prominent conservatives pushed him to bring up the oil depletion allowance and Fair Employment Practices Commission. When Shivers's office announced that the two governors would meet on August 25, it made clear that Shivers would quiz Stevenson on "foreign policy, corruption in government, taxation and spending, the federal budget, civil rights," and the tidelands.[21]

The two governors met over lunch. Shivers brought a brief outlining Texas' tidelands claims, which Stevenson agreed to examine following their meal. The meal was polite and agreeable, with Interior Secretary Oscar Chapman and historian Arthur Schlesinger Jr. joining the two governors. Stevenson listened and seemed sympathetic, although Shivers thought the other men's presence indicated pressure from the Truman administration to tow the line. After eating, Stevenson asked for a few hours to consider his response. Governor Shivers believed the outcome had already been decided, but agreed to return later that afternoon. Their late-afternoon conference confirmed his impression. Stevenson insisted that he, too, would oppose any bill vesting title in the tidelands to Texas. Shivers pressed him. Could Stevenson permit a quitclaim to become law without his signature? No. Although the press claimed otherwise, others reported that the two became angry and "their body chemistry didn't mix." With dusk approaching, Shivers emerged and announced that he could not support Stevenson for president. Both men told the waiting reporters that had they been in the other's shoes they might have done the same thing. In Washington, Lyndon Johnson reacted angrily, privately excoriating Stevenson as a "goddamned fool" for permitting Shivers to place him in such a situation.[22]

Johnson's fury stemmed from Stevenson's failure to use a "very careful" tidelands statement the senator had prepared to outflank Shivers. According to Johnson aide George Reedy, LBJ's suggested response "didn't say anything." Smoothly explaining that Stevenson intended to give Texas' claims "honest consideration," the memo tested the heights of Johnsonian evasion. It was a real "beaut," Reedy later recalled. It bears repeating that Stevenson hardly fell into a "trap" prepared by the Texas governor. The Democratic nominee knew the agenda well in advance of the meeting because Shivers had given him ample notice. Confused by the tidelands uproar, Stevenson phoned Maury Maverick for advice. Maverick told him that if he wanted to win Texas, he should agree with Shivers. On the other hand, if he wanted to tell the truth, he should insist that the tidelands belonged to all Americans.[23]

The Shivers-Stevenson confrontation represented pure theatrics on Shivers's part. Texas' Democratic governor had supported cross-filing, and orchestrated an intraparty battle to the death with liberal Texas Democrats in 1951. Moreover, after knowingly assisting Price Daniel's smothering of a tideland's compromise,

Shivers had nonetheless used the issue to bludgeon Texans' traditional Democratic loyalties by demonizing Harry Truman and his policies. Warned repeatedly, the national party leadership tried to placate Shivers, confident that Texas stood as firm as it had in 1948. Shivers had gone to Springfield intent on acting out a play that he had scripted. According to Jake Pickle, the tidelands issue was simply "an excuse." Shivers aide John Osorio recalled the governor's meeting with the Democratic nominee as a "formality." Had Stevenson hedged or hidden behind Johnson's talking points, the Texan had plenty of other issues with which to widen the gap between himself and the Democratic contender. With Texas' "true" Democratic Party in lockstep behind him and his dominion established, he could return to home and back the Republican nominee without serious repercussions. Allan Shivers had effectively repudiated the national Democratic Party for the rest of his life.[24]

The tidelands wedge proved devastatingly effective. "Most people in Texas didn't give a damn about the Tidelands," Weldon Hart later recalled. "We made them feel they were losing something." Separating the state Democratic leadership from the national party in the public's mind was "central to the 1952 campaign." The Texas Democrats' fury at Stevenson was so great that there was talk of removing him from the Democratic ballot. According to a source close to Shivers, Price Daniel and Arch Rowan proposed replacing Stevenson's name with Eisenhower's on the Democratic ballot. Other sources argue that Daniel's advisory opinion *against* such a move prevented Shivers from purging Stevenson from the ballot. Whatever the case, Shivers claimed that such a slight would be "morally wrong" and a concession to "brute force" in the heat of battle.[25]

Shivers and his allies prepared for the upcoming second state Democratic convention in Amarillo that September. The Shivercrat gathering endorsed the Eisenhower-Nixon ticket. Texas Democrats were "legally and morally" free to vote for whomever they chose, but the convention platform blasted the national party's stand on the tidelands and civil rights. The document articulated a link between the two in a section called "The Rights of the States." For the Shivercrats, federal "exploitation of minority groups through . . . hate-breeding, class legislation" inhabited the same plain as an effort to alter Senate cloture rules and the tidelands. The Amarillo platform, however, represented an agenda more moderate than some in the party had desired. Shivers managed to turn back delegates' effort to replace Stevenson with Eisenhower on the Democratic ticket. A possible separate "Texas Democratic" ticket came under legal assault from the LDT and had to be abandoned. Shivers apparently had taken neither possibility seriously given his "pledge" to Rayburn in Chicago.[26]

As in other Deep South states, Texas' Eisenhower forces found themselves divorced from the normal Republican Party machinery and therefore dependent upon existing conservative Democratic power brokers temporarily favorable to a GOP nominee. Dallas attorney Wallace Savage, chair of the SDEC, led Texans for Eisenhower at the same time his law partner, Alvin Lane, led Republican Party work for Ike. Porter and the Republicans were utterly beholden to Shivers for money, brains, and organizational support. The result was a blending of Republican economic conservatism and southern racial and states' rights worries. Shivers kept up contacts with South Carolina's James Byrnes and other pro-Eisenhower southerners, but as much for his own reasons as to help the general. He also became an important figure in the regional revolt against the national Democratic leadership. The Texas revolt mirrored, with more success, trends elsewhere in the South. While other southerners were urging Shivers to visit their states and campaign for Eisenhower, Texas' Democratic establishment brought in Byrnes to bolster the southern look of Shivers's defection.[27]

Motivating Texans to vote for Eisenhower took a special touch. Weldon Hart left the governor's staff to work full time as an adviser to the Eisenhower campaign. He coordinated Ike's symbolic appearance at the Alamo on October 14. Hart drove home that Texans voted Democratic out of habit and because of memories of the Depression. Suggesting that Ike appeal to tidelands, state pride, and avoid "stressing the GOP" in his address, Hart put together a perfect package for the Republican nominee to sell in Texas. Eisenhower's support of Texas' position on the tidelands dominated his campaign in the state, although even his fellow Republicans conceded he "oversimplified" the matter. The tidelands issue struck home emotionally and, given other Shivercrat concerns, also communicated sympathy in matters such as civil rights and the general assault on "big government." Hart suggested that the general avoid public discussion of both civil rights and the FEPC because he considered neither topic to be "necessary or desirable." Privately, however, Eisenhower and his staff knew fully the connotations Texans and other southerners derived from references to "states' rights," whether talk involved the tidelands or civil rights. Hart later acknowledged that the "national [Democratic] party's engrossment with civil rights" helped the Shivercrats and Ike.[28]

The 1952 Texas Eisenhower campaign had a seamier underside that presaged the increasingly ugly races of the future. Dallas independent oilman Clint Murchison funded a newsletter titled *The Native Texan*, sent out of Denison, Eisenhower's birthplace. First published in early October, it featured headlines designed to pique the interest of the four hundred thousand rural farm delivery patrons it targeted: "Nation Sickened By Mess," "A.D.A. Ghosts Haunt Adlai," and "Adlai's Ideas Aid Kremlin." One story related the nudist colony capers of "Washington bureaucrats" uncovered by Texas congressman Martin Dies. Such broadsheets had been a part of Texas politics since the days of Gov. James "Farmer Jim" Ferguson (1915–17). Intended to reach rural voters who had neither radio nor television, but possessed a voracious appetite for reading material, the tabloid newsletters straddled the line between half-truth and outright lies. Murchison notified Shivers of a second *Native Texan* slated for mailing just a week before the election. "The first edition is probably too mild," he wrote the governor apologetically. "The editor will try to spice up the second, to give either a savory or unsavory tint dependent upon the reader's imagination."[29]

With Shivers's machine against them, loyal Democrats faced what San Antonio organizer Kathleen Voigt called a "sad, sad situation." The Stevenson campaign set up shop in Dallas's posh Adolphus Hotel with none other than Sam Rayburn in charge. Several of the more liberal loyalists strained against Rayburn's leadership with some frequency. The sheer harshness of the campaign in Texas resulted in pressure for a more aggressive stance. Dominating radio, television, and the newspapers, the Shivercrats heaped scorn on loyalists as Texas Democratic politicos "scattered like doves in hunting season." Shivers's allies made a permanent enemy of Speaker Rayburn, calling him a "pinhead," a "peanut-brain," and a latter-day Santa Anna. The loyalists were no kinder with each other. Lyndon Johnson came in for a particularly hard bashing from both sides. One of the few established politicians in the state with the guts to campaign personally for Stevenson, he stood accused of helping "cut [the liberals'] . . . throat" at the national convention. Meanwhile, LBJ's conservative allies condemned him with equal venom. Clint Murchison warned the senator that the tidelands issue "burned so deeply that people are not going to be able to forget it for years to come." Supporting Stevenson was likely to "definitely impede" Johnson's "political future."[30]

The Shivercrat defection left the remnants of Texas' Democratic organization in alarming disarray. Creekmore Fath recalled canvassing neighborhoods in reliably Democratic Austin, where, much to his disappointment, he discovered that reliable voters intended to follow Shivers in support of Eisenhower. Remarkably, Stevenson stood a fair chance of winning Texas during the early going. In mid-August, before Shivers's trip to Springfield, Stevenson enjoyed a "lopsided" majority in Texas public opinion polls. Immediately after the Springfield meeting, the Democratic nominee lost nine points as his lead over the general shrank to 54–46 percent. An ominous 73 percent of those who liked Ike claimed to be Democrats. Stevenson's public support continued to spiral downward as conservative sources flooded the Eisenhower campaign coffers with cash. By November 1, Dallas lawyer Robert L. Clark, brother of Supreme Court Justice Tom Clark, reported to Lyndon Johnson that Stevenson could expect to lose Dallas County by the same margin he had been expected to win three months earlier. "I have never seen so much money spent in Dallas County on anything as has been poured out the last three days," Clark wrote, "with much more to come Sunday and Monday, in hammering away these fantastic charges and claims over radio and TV, in the newspapers, over batteries of telephones and through the mails." Estimates of Eisenhower's campaign expenditures in Texas exceeded $1 million, of which nearly a quarter came from Democrats for Eisenhower. Loyalists spent less than $500,000.[31]

Both Shivers and the state's Eisenhower forces benefited from visits by South Carolina governor James Byrnes and John Roosevelt, FDR's son, who came to Texas to campaign for the Republican nominee. The only real publicity scare for the Eisenhower forces came in October, when they learned former president Herbert Hoover planned to make a nationwide radio address in which he would endorse the general. Weldon Hart scrambled to prevent it from being broadcast in Texas, only to discover that a number of Hoover admirers had funded the project and the national GOP leadership could do nothing to stop it. "Surely some responsible person should listen to our recommendation that this situation not be further aggravated," he pleaded with Eisenhower's national campaign headquarters. Trying to defuse the situation, the Shivercrats produced Rocksprings state senator Claud Gilmer and South Carolina's governor Byrnes to refute the link between Hoover and Ike. Byrnes told Texans that blaming Eisenhower for the "Hoover depression" made as much sense as blaming FDR for the 1919–20 depression during Woodrow Wilson's presidency. Gilmer, after first reminding voters that Stevenson's own grandfather had served as vice president during the 1893 depression, argued that blaming Truman's "hand-picked yes man" for ills long past made no sense. Shivers, not wanting to be outdone, showered Eisenhower with the highest compliments possible in Democratic Texas while making his final speech of the campaign in Beaumont the night before the election.[32]

"Truman has done more to wreck the program Franklin D. Roosevelt started than I would have thought possible," the governor told his fellow Texans. "Like most Texas Democrats, I always supported Roosevelt. Roosevelt picked Eisenhower for the most important assignment ever given an American—that of leading allied forces to victory in our greatest war. I firmly believe that if FDR were alive, he would pick Dwight D. Eisenhower for the most important job in the world today—that of cleaning house in Washington and supplying leadership for world peace."

The next day, Eisenhower defeated Stevenson in Texas and the nation. Arguably, the GOP nominee might have carried Texas without Governor Shivers's active intervention. The Democrats lacked an attractive candidate and Stevenson ultimately was unable to inspire voters. The polls suggest, however, that the crucial moment in the Texas race came at the end of August, when Shivers announced that he was endorsing Ike. From that point on, Stevenson's poll numbers slipped downward. Praise for Shivers came in from across the nation and Texas. "No one can thank you adequately," Eisenhower aide Sherman Adams wrote

Shivers, crediting him for breaking new ground for the GOP in Texas and the South. In Florida, the *Orlando Morning Sentinel* featured Shivers's story, along with the observation that "the recent election indicated that most people are sick of both Trumanism and its blind adherent, the Trumancrat."[33]

Eisenhower tallied 1,102,878 votes in Texas to Stevenson's 969,228. The general's victory depended upon a strong urban vote, with 46.3 percent of his total vote coming from Texas' ten most populous counties. By contrast, less than 40 percent of Stevenson's support came from these counties. Harris, Dallas, and Bexar contributed 27 percent of the total vote in the presidential race, and Ike ran significantly better in those counties than he did statewide. Stevenson managed to win in McLennan, Jefferson, and Nueces Counties. McLennan (Waco) had a strong yellow-dog tradition; Jefferson (Beaumont–Port Arthur) rejected Shivers's lead with its heavily unionized electorate; and Nueces (Corpus Christi) went for Stevenson, who attracted a strong Hispanic turnout. Statewide, Stevenson won 114 of 254 counties, doing significantly better than Yarborough had against Shivers that summer.[34]

Political analyst Samuel Lubbell saw in Eisenhower's political ascendancy a "triumph of moderation" indicating the "balance of political power rests with those moderate voting elements who are in restless revolt against both parties." Nationally, voters appeared to move away from party identification and instead focused on economic determinants. Lubbell, however, did not apply this argument too broadly to the South. "Eisenhower's 1952 showing can be attributed to the skill with which Southern leaders who supported him merged . . . racial and economic grievances," he explained. In Texas, however, the results amounted to a "rehearsal for two-party politics." Finding evidence of some urban voting being "dominated almost entirely by economics," Lubbell implicitly suggested that the Texas vote mirrored national trends more than regional concerns.[35]

With respect to the South, Lubbell tempered his optimism about moderation—and should have done the same in his analysis of events in Texas. Shivers's leadership facilitated Eisenhower's Texas victory, and the governor's purposes and tone were hardly moderate. The 1952 presidential race in Texas was the culmination of an effort by Texas Democracy's most conservative elements that dated back to 1936. Their goal had been to hijack the state Democratic Party and use the state's electoral strength to help reverse objectionable Roosevelt-Truman reforms. It thus does not necessarily follow that Texas' vote for Eisenhower indicated any emulation of national trends. Only 40 percent of the state's electorate turned out in November, 1952, so a proper understanding of the voters' mood cannot be inferred. Shivers's general election vote in the Democratic column exceeded Eisenhower's presidential vote by 273,000, indicating that many Democrats accepted Shivers as governor, but opposed his choice for president.[36]

The 1952 race helped popularize presidential Republicanism in Texas and the South, but calling it a "rehearsal" for a two-party system might be too generous an assessment. Few Republicans ran down-ballot races in Texas that year, owing to cross-filing and traditional Democratic allegiances. Lubbell's emphasis on national issues such as communism, corruption, and Korea, obscured how southern Democrats supporting Eisenhower in 1952 worked to attract Democrats to the Republican presidential ticket. In Texas, the 1952 campaign's rhetoric and issues seemed more typical of the southern one-party system described by V. O. Key than a move toward a campaign oriented toward truly national issues.

The Tidelands Controversy dominated the presidential campaign in Texas. Shivercrats also harped on federal power, states' rights, civil rights, and the internal communist threat in a manner that reflected both southern political habit and the general trepidation many regional leaders felt toward developments of the previous two decades. Moreover, television, the crucial mass-communication tool for a truly national politics, was still in its infancy. Politics remained very much a local affair, particularly in the South. Television's potential influence upon Texas politics did not become manifest until 1954. The 1952 election demonstrated the determination of many southern conservatives to dominate state Democratic organizations while leveraging greater national influence by playing the two parties against one another in presidential years.

In 1949, V. O. Key predicted the development of two-party politics would occur in Texas ahead of the rest of the region. However, he also envisioned a prolonged struggle by Democratic factions for control of the state party. The "haves" would defect to the new Republican Party afterward and, by implication, try to squelch the new class-based politics Key expected to emerge. Their weapons of choice would remain diversionary issues that distracted voters from the more practical concerns of pocketbook and government services. The modern South's Republican Party derives much of its strength today from similar appeals. Texas and Allan Shivers took a significant step in the direction of this sort of two-party South in 1952.[37]

CHAPTER SEVEN

Self-Perpetuation and a Third Term
1953–54

EISENHOWER'S 1952 TEXAS VICTORY REPRESENTED THE HIGH POINT OF Allan Shivers's political career. Struggles with an increasingly determined opposition dimmed hopes for later successes. In order to hold on to power, Governor Shivers needed a beneficial relationship with the new Eisenhower administration. The forty-five-year-old politician also made tentative efforts to mend fences with the national Democratic Party. Considering a race for an unprecedented third term, he needed to create new issues. Shivers's political philosophy left him with one foot planted squarely in the past while the toes of his other foot tested the future. Such politicians, according to historian Numan Bartley, were decidedly conservative "advocates of modernization" but also "defenders of tradition." By embracing Eisenhower, Shivers had advanced Texas' evolution toward two-party politics. He was, however, determined to maintain one-party rule organized around him. Shivers explained his position to an irate liberal activist this way: "The fact is, young lady, I hold this state in the palm of my hand."[1]

The governor's 1952 defection might have harmed him without favorable federal action on the tidelands. Before leaving office, Harry Truman transferred control of offshore oil from the Interior Department to the Navy Department hoping to dramatize the national security ramifications of the tidelands debate. Shivers asked the incoming administration to reverse the transfer. Eisenhower's chief of staff, Sherman Adams, explained that this was not possible because such a move might bring criticism of the president. Instead, Adams insisted that Congress have the final word on the tidelands. After legislative advisers convinced Eisenhower to avoid any direct involvement in pushing a quitclaim bill, the president made no mention of offshore oil rights in his first State of the Union

President Dwight Eisenhower and Shivers, October, 1953. Eisenhower disappointed Texas Republicans by favoring Shivers's control over state politics rather than working to build a strong Republican organization in Texas. Under Eisenhower, Shivers had influence over federal patronage in Texas and easy access to the White House. Shivers supported Eisenhower in 1956 and helped deliver Texas to the Republican even as his own personal power ebbed.

message. These developments signaled divisions within the administration and caused Shivers some worries.[2]

Attorney General Herbert Brownell then shocked Texans by suggesting that quitclaim legislation was not needed in congressional testimony. He claimed the administration preferred simpler legislation granting states administrative and developmental rights. Meanwhile, Interior Secretary Douglas McKay, addressing the same committee, said he supported state ownership within "historical boundaries." Brownell quickly backed away from the apparent contradiction and the quitclaim bill sailed through the House of Representatives. However, when the bill reached the Senate, federal ownership advocates filibustered. Majority Leader Robert Taft and Minority Leader Lyndon Johnson both supported the bill but were unable to summon the votes needed to end debate. Only then did Eisenhower finally endorse the quitclaim bill. The Senate passed the Submerged Lands Act on May 5 and the president signed it on May 23.[3]

Shivers enjoyed significant influence within the administration. Two Texans, both from Houston, received cabinet posts. Attorney Robert B. Anderson became secretary of the navy on Shivers's recommendation. Oveta Culp Hobby, whose nominally Democratic *Houston Post* had supported Eisenhower, became secretary of health, education, and welfare. Shivers later claimed he declined a cabinet offer. Working through Jack Porter, the governor influenced patronage appointments from the postmaster level to federal judgeships. Although this eventually irritated Texas Republicans, Porter included, in 1953 many thought it was just a matter of time before Shivers would switch parties.[4]

H. R. Cullen told Ike's staff the Shivercrats represented the ideal next wave of Republican adherents in Texas. A growing Republican Party in the South depended upon "patriotic citizens" like Shivers and Price Daniel, who Cullen said should be consulted about important matters concerning the region. Meanwhile, Texas Republicans hoping for masses of converts found themselves disappointed. Some party activists complained that the state party had changed little from the Creager-Zweifel system under its new chair, Jack Porter. By late 1953, important Republicans close to the White House realized that Shivers had "sought not to convert" Texas to the GOP.[5]

Although Governor Shivers shied away from Republican gatherings while working to rebuild his standing as a Democrat, he sought a close relationship with Eisenhower. The president apparently liked Shivers and wanted to appoint him to the Commission on Intergovernmental Relations. Ike also offered criticism of the younger man's golf game. Eisenhower had considerable liking and empathy for southerners, so there was little surprise in 1953, when it was rumored that Eisenhower might not run again, that some suggested the Texas governor would be an appropriate replacement. Those who hoped Shivers would join the Republicans—both those who admired and those who hated him—were disappointed. Allan Shivers controlled Texas through the Democratic Party. Texas Republicans, on the other hand, saw Shivers as a force upon whom they greatly depended, but also one they hoped to either convert or replace.[6]

Although the governor still considered himself a Democrat, he desired some face-saving reconciliation with the national party. He had prevailed in 1952, but troubling signs remained. While Yarborough had won only a handful of counties in the gubernatorial primary, his showing came before Shivers endorsed Eisenhower. The much stronger vote for Stevenson in November indicated potential trouble for the governor. Loyal Democrats, intent upon retaking the state party, formed the Texas Democratic Organizing Committee in early 1953. Their literature stressed that only 634, 559 Democrats had voted for Eisenhower compared to 970,128 for Stevenson. These true Democrats needed leadership, and the committee hoped to drive Shivers from power.[7]

Governor Shivers, working to mend relations with the national party, sought restored ties to Johnson and Rayburn. Johnson, meanwhile, hoped to neutralize future opponents, including the governor. Although the senator never sought Shivers's political destruction, he did see him as a force to be reckoned with and managed. When Shivers visited Washington in mid-February, 1953, he attended a luncheon with the state's congressional delegation organized by Johnson's office. Expecting the affair for Texas' congressional delegation to be off the record, he was surprised to see Texas members of the Washington press corps there as well. In the midst of a luncheon meeting arranged for the governor, Lyndon Johnson took center stage when House Majority Leader Sam Rayburn presented his protégé a plaque and heaped lavish praise upon him. Shivers rose next and bested Rayburn in lauding Johnson. The senator gratefully embraced his guest, shutters snapped, and the story went to press. Some of Shivers's conservative allies grumbled that he had allowed himself "to get boxed in in Lyndon's own backyard."[8]

With tidelands legislation still pending, however, Shivers needed both men. He believed that better relations would help strengthen his weakened left flank in the state party as well. Johnson was willing, but Rayburn's hatred toward the governor burned hot. Shivers needed only marginally better relations with the rest of the national party to keep his Democratic credentials. The national party, more liberal than that in Texas, still offered a good target for criticism. Governor Shivers warred with the new party leadership installed by Stevenson, particularly Democratic National Committee chair Stephen Mitchell. Mitchell traveled throughout the nation during the spring of 1953 conducting a postmortem of the 1952 campaign. He interpreted much of Eisenhower's support as a rejection of Truman. Nonetheless, Mitchell discovered, "the acrimonious and vengeful attitude toward Truman so noticeable before is not so apparent generally except in the South." Shivercrats were suspicious when Mitchell came to Texas and, acting on Hart's advice, Shivers avoided direct contact with the DNC chair.[9]

Texas Democratic National Committeewoman Hilda Weinert of Seguin was the top Shivercrat to meet with Mitchell. Weinert had voted for Stevenson in 1952 by design. Her personal loyalties lay with the governor, but her vote allowed her—and, by extension, Shivers—to maintain ties to the national party. She assured the DNC chairman that most Texas Democrats who had bolted the previous year had no intention of becoming Republicans. Weinert and Mitchell got on well, and he urged her to continue to keep "one foot in each camp."[10]

Meanwhile, as Shivers worked to restore his credibility as a Democrat, his intraparty opponents feuded over how best to organize his downfall. Mitchell's visit did not cheer those in the ranks of the anti-Shivers forces, who felt constrained by the national party. More liberal loyalists grew impatient to fight Shivers, among them Maury Maverick Sr. and Creekmore Fath. "The idea of being held back by Mitchell is a bunch of crap," Maverick huffed. The Texas Democratic Organizing Committee (TDOC), which emerged in the absence of a national party effort to retake the state, met at Lake Buchanan in May, 1953. The assembled loyalists decried leaders who had "betrayed" the Democratic Party in 1952 and vowed to unseat them in 1954. The group acquired its own alternative political newspaper, the *Texas Observer*, that year and began offering amnesty to rank-and-file Democrats led astray by Shivers. Nevertheless, mistrust remained strong among Texas Democrats for decades after the 1952 election.[11]

ALLAN SHIVERS CONTROLLED THE STATE DEMOCRATIC PARTY, MOST OF THE party's campaign cash, and most of the major media outlets. However, the Shivercrat machine had been deprived of its most compelling issue with the resolution of the Tidelands Controversy. Southern one-party politics had revolved around personalities and sham issues that had little to do with the real needs of constituents. Shivers's successful use of the tidelands brouhaha is a compelling example of his talent in this regard. During 1953–54, the governor did everything he could to obstruct legislative progress on education, finance, and infrastructure. At the same time, he went on a convenient crusade against political corruption, picked a fight with a powerful federal agency, raged against communism, and positioned himself for a third-term bid in 1954.

Shivers liked to portray himself as an earnest, moral force in politics. In 1953, the governor went to war with South Texas *patrón* George Parr, the "Duke of Duval." Before 1950, Shivers had received Parr's blessing. After demolishing Boyce House in Duval County in 1946 by an astounding 4,017–17 margin, Shivers, as lieutenant governor in 1948, helped prevent a legislative investigation of Parr's role in Lyndon Johnson's eighty-seven-vote U.S. Senate victory over former governor Coke Stevenson. Later, as governor, Shivers clashed with Parr over judicial appointments. Although he appointed several pro-Parr judges, they were not the ones the *patrón* had wanted. When the "Duchy of Duval" rejected Shivers in the 1950 and 1952 primaries, the governor began gathering information on George Parr and his empire.[12]

Budget abnormalities in the Benavides Independent School District (ISD) spurred further probes. The district had paid the legal expenses of a Parr-controlled deputy sheriff who had been accused of murder. Other school moneys went into a slush fund, and the district actively promoted gambling on high school football. Informants turned in Benavides ISD records to the Internal Revenue Service, which was in the hands of a Republican administration favorable to Shivers. Working with Attorney General John Ben Shepperd and Department of Public Safety (DPS) director Homer Garrison, the governor's office arranged a press exposé of conditions in Parr's fiefdom. In August, 1953, Shivers and Shepperd went public with their attacks on the *patrón,* initiating efforts to remove pro-Parr Seventy-ninth District Court Judge Woodrow Laughlin. Laughlin's eventual ouster allowed Shivers to appoint a jurist not beholden to Parr: A. S. Broadfoot of far-off Bonham. Broadfoot's appointment came only after Shivers checked with friendly Valley bosses eager to profit at Parr's expense: Manuel Raymond of Willacy County, the Guerras of Starr County, and the Kazens of Webb County.[13]

Shivers tried without success to interest the Federal Bureau of Investigation in Parr's crimes. During a visit to San Antonio, he "offered the services of his office at any time" to M. P. Chiles, the special agent in charge there. Chiles in turn relayed the governor's worries about events in South Texas to FBI director J. Edgar Hoover. Shivers, Chiles wrote, believed that "several murders had been committed which were directly attributable to the local political situation." He even went so far as to threaten to declare martial law. Although there is no indication Hoover took any action against Parr, the governor's attack on the Duke of Duval worried another observer in Washington: Sen. Lyndon Johnson. Johnson's advisers saw Shivers's interest in Duval County as an indication the governor might be planning to run against LBJ in 1954. The unpleasant revelations about Parr helped weaken Johnson's public-approval rating in Texas in early 1954, but Shivers had no intention of challenging him. A single phone call to the senator allayed LBJ's worries.[14]

Yet, if Shivers was not preparing to challenge Johnson, why did he attack Parr? It was not part of a general effort against South Texas political corruption. Shivers's friends among the bosses of Webb, Zapata, Starr, Hidalgo, Willacy, and Cameron Counties faced no such scrutiny. Instead, he went after Parr as a matter of political survival. Shivers expected a hard-fought campaign in his bid for a third term. In a close election, Parr might prove deadly to his chances. He remembered that crossing Parr over judicial appointments had provoked conflict between the Duke and Coke Stevenson. He also knew from Stevenson's unhappy experience that close elections offered the best opportunity for theft. A federal-state investigation of goings-on in the Duchy of Duval would allow Shivers to justify using Texas Rangers to monitor the county government and elections in Parr's territory.

Governor Shivers's vigilance against overreaching federal power also led to an ill-advised clash with FBI director J. Edgar Hoover in 1953. Despite the governor's reform efforts in the 1950 special session, conditions in the state's eleemosynary institutions remained grim. Hoover used the Civil Rights Act of 1866 to justify an examination of disciplinary practices at the Gainesville State School for Girls. Without thinking of possible consequences, the governor, while in Lufkin for a gathering of Texas law enforcement officers in August, 1953, criticized the FBI for "snooping." Hoover, Shivers told the press, had conducted "hundreds" of similar probes, adding, "when they get into state affairs maybe we should ask for an investigation of them."[15]

Shivers's precipitous attack angered the FBI director and worried some of the governor's own important backers. Dallas oilman Clint Murchison told him it was "imperative that the two of you, who are among the strongest in our chain of defense against this communistic invasion of our ideals . . . present a solid front." Meanwhile, Hoover wrote to the governor and pointed out that Shivers had exaggerated the number of investigations. The FBI had received 428 complaints from Texas from 1950–53, but investigated only ninety-two. Of those, only sixteen involved state agencies. Hoover also went to the press, claiming the governor's office had known of the Gainesville inquest in advance and had even asked that the FBI not publicize it until after the July, 1952, primaries. Shivers bitterly denied the claim as mail critical of his stance poured in from around the state.[16]

Hoover also involved his titular boss, U.S. Attorney General Herbert Brownell, explaining himself in a long memo in which he claimed that Shivers had "stirred animosity" toward the director and the FBI. In September, 1953, the governor and one of his aides, former FBI agent Maurice Acers, were placed on the Bureau's "List of Persons Not To Be Contacted Without Prior Bureau Authority." The controversy eventually subsided.

The Shivers-Hoover feud highlighted two elements of the governor's personality and political style. First, he sometimes freely spouted accusations and innuendo he knew to be false. In this case, he clearly underestimated Hoover, who called his bluff. Second, Shivers also had a temper he did not always restrain. The FBI controversy also demonstrated an anxiety about the intentions of the federal government he shared with many conservative southerners. In the end, it appears that his primary purpose in attacking Hoover was to boost his own public image.[17]

AFTER HIS EMBARRASSING SKIRMISH WITH J. EDGAR HOOVER, SHIVERS MADE anticommunism an integral part of his appeal to voters. In October, he presented Wisconsin senator Joseph McCarthy a brand-new Cadillac and honorary Texas citizenship in recognition of his crusade against communism. More dramatic and controversial measures came later. Red scare hysteria had played an important role in Texas politics since the 1930s, reaching its peak in the 1950s—particularly in big cities like Dallas, Houston, and San Antonio. No evidence exists that Allan Shivers possessed any genuine fears of communism beyond the anxiety felt by many Americans during the period. He did, however, recognize the issue's potential political value. Shivers thus joined the throng of politicians of both parties who ought to have known better. Moreover, he continued the red-baiting long after it became unfashionable.[18]

Southern conservatives had long associated organized labor with communist subversion. Conservative Democrats in the region resented the national party's prolabor stance and cooperated with Republicans in restraining labor by passing the Taft-Hartley Act in 1947. Texas experienced two strong tides of antiunion sentiment in the legislature: in 1940–41 and again in 1947. Shivers opposed the first for political reasons, but embraced the second for ideological as well as political reasons. As a result, his old labor constituencies became less and less friendly. The governor knew from long experience that Texas unions were not communist fronts, but when the opportunity arose to simultaneously strike at labor and fix public attention on communism, he took it.[19]

Port Arthur retail workers began a walkout in November, 1953. Fewer than five hundred workers picketed local businesses demanding higher wages and recognition of the Distributive Processing and Office Workers Union of America (DPOWA), a CIO affiliate. Union organizers saw a pool of potential recruits in an already heavily unionized locality. The CIO had once banned the DPOWA because some of its organizers' were communist sympathizers, but readmitted the union after it purged its ranks of those with communist connections—including a few assigned to Port Arthur. City business leaders panicked and claimed the strike was communist inspired. Nonetheless, it was a very American desire for higher wages that led most workers to the DPOWA. Kitchen workers downtown averaged $14 a week in wages; store clerks and hotel maids worked six-day weeks for an average of $25 and $19.50, respectively.[20]

During this period, Shivers created an industrial commission to study communism in Texas workplaces. The governor's guidance to the five-member commission, which included a single representative from organized labor, was clear: "There can be no place in Texas organized labor for Communists. There can be no place in Texas for Communists, period." It took the commission less than two weeks to determine that there was no indication "that any member of a Texas labor union was a communist," but the stacked panel insisted there was a "clear and present danger" of communist infiltration. "The Commission finds that the present laws of Texas are inadequate to deal with this menace," they reported.[21]

PARR, THE FBI, AND PORT ARTHUR'S IMMINENT FALL TO THE COMMUNISTS ALL helped dim the memory of the inauspicious 1953 legislative session. The governor had prevented a teacher pay raise of $600 per year along with graduated, experience-based raises. Shivers favored a $240 yearly raise, although his legislative allies eventually suggested a $360 increase. The state senate passed the full $600 sought by the teachers, but the house delayed consideration until all available money had been spent. The lower chamber then passed the bill, allowing members to cast a vote for education knowing all the while that the state comptroller would negate the measure as incompatible with a balanced budget. When the teachers got nothing, Shivers blamed the "arrogant, unyielding attitude" of the Texas State Teachers Association. House Speaker Reuben Senterfitt had colluded with Shivers in the proposal's demise, demonstrating the new power the governor exercised over the legislative process. Both Senterfitt and Lt. Gov. Ben Ramsey, who owed most of his political success to Shivers, tended to defer to the governor.[22]

Speaker Senterfitt changed his chamber's rules to weaken Shivers's opponents by slowing the process of re-referring bills to more favorable committees. On an appropriations bill rider, the governor received the power to compel any state agency to submit quarterly or semiannual budgets for his approval. Bills the governor favored passed quickly with Senterfitt and Ramsey's eager cooperation. In addition, Shivers hinted that he would run for reelection in 1954 if his program did not pass in the 1953 session. Since both the speaker and lieutenant governor planned races if Shivers stepped aside, they hastened to give him what he wanted. The governor, however, had no intention of leaving his job; he was simply using guile to augment his own lawmaking power.[23]

Shivers, who had already decided to run for governor regardless of diversionary rumors, turned his back on an opportunity to run against a weakened Lyndon Johnson for U.S. Senate. Organized opposition further stiffened his resolve to stay in the governor's mansion. "I decided I'd rather get beat than let them say they ran me off," he later recalled. A strong challenger appeared assured going into 1954. Moreover, the governor appeared to have "lost his stroke" in some areas of East Texas, according to Jake Pickle, who toured the state for Johnson in early 1954. Governor Shivers, seeking a third term, could expect the toughest race of his career. Hoping to grab the spotlight and boost his political stock, the governor called a special legislative session in the spring.[24]

As he had in 1950, the governor summoned business leaders and told them the state had to spend more on education and other services. Some accounts suggest he threatened them with the prospect of Ralph Yarborough being elected governor. With their indulgence, Shivers obtained a $402 yearly pay raise for Texas teachers, thereby restoring some goodwill. Taking full advantage of the Port Arthur strike and public worries over communism, he pressed for stronger measures against subversion. Shivers proposed making Communist Party membership a capital offense, but legislators showed unusual self-restraint by rejecting his proposal. Instead, party members could be fined $20,000 and sentenced to up to twenty years' imprisonment. Other measures in the 1954 Loyalty and Subversion Acts weakened search-and-seizure protections. The senate passed the red-baiting measures unanimously; only seven legislators, including Edgar Berlin and Maury Maverick Jr., cast negative votes in the house. Eight anticommunist laws already existed in the Texas code. Perhaps no number could ever reassure citizens, but the governor did not want them reassured. He needed them to be worried for the coming campaign.[25]

In April, Ralph Yarborough announced his candidacy for governor before a statewide television audience. He attacked Shivers's likely third-term bid as an effort to perpetuate a "power-mad political machine." The challenger pledged better roads, schools, pensions, and public health measures. Directly attacking the governor and his friends in Washington, Yarborough promised an aggressive effort to obtain disaster relief for Texas farmers battered by drought. Shivers announced his decision to run for a third term shortly thereafter. The governor claimed he represented all of Texas in his race against the "CIO, PAC, ADA, NAACP, and PARR." Although he enjoyed the support of most of Texas' daily newspapers, Shivers's campaign juggernaut would spend millions of dollars compared to his opponent's $500,000. The 1954 race represented an early example of the one-party system's adaptation to television and that medium's devastating ability to communicate wedge issues. Ultimately, money allowed the governor to seize control over the tone and issues of the race.[26]

From the outset, Yarborough's chances were better in 1954 than they had been in 1952. Beyond the third-term taboo, party loyalty, and issue differences, Yarborough capitalized on two scandals that tainted the governor's public reputation. The one that most directly implicated the governor was a 1946 transaction involving Rio Grande Valley real estate. Mission developer and Shivers ally Lloyd M. Bentsen Sr. had sold Shivers an option on thirteen thousand acres for $25,000—an option Bentsen had purchased for just $10,000. For six months, the two shared the proceeds from mineral rights. As the option period drew to a close, Texan Development Company tried to purchase it from Bentsen, who insisted that Shivers controlled the option. The day after the option expired, Texan purchased it from Shivers for $450,000, but left both Bentsen and Shivers holding the mineral rights. Texan later developed the property as Texas Garden, selling thirty-two parcels to buyers from Texas, Oklahoma, Iowa, and Colorado. In 1952, when these proud owners of Valley land discovered they held no title to the groundwater, they initiated a class-action lawsuit.[27]

Yarborough's campaign seized upon the governor's weakness. Several elements of the deal smelled. First, Texan Development Company had purchased Shivers's option after it expired, but in time for him to take advantage of long-term capital gains on his 1946 income tax return. This resulted in an after-tax profit of $300,000 on an investment of $25,000. A second problem involved the legal personhood of Texan Development. On the surface, it appeared that a firm outside the Bentsen-Shivers relationship had offered the politician the sweetheart deal. In reality, Bentsen and his brother Elmer owned Texan. The third complication hurt Shivers the most. In 1949, as the state entered what proved to be a catastrophic drought, the Texas Water Board issued use permits for Rio Grande water to the Bentsens. Such permits had not been issued for the trickling river in twenty years.[28]

The governor's defenders called the controversy "pure politics." Critics argued that the governor's efforts "to minimize this transaction" represented "an insult to the public intelligence." Yarborough cited the deal as being exemplary of corrupt government and favoritism. For his part, Shivers accused Yarborough of not being able to understand or appreciate "free enterprise." The attack over the land deal angered Shivers, and may well have influenced the harshness of his response to his challenger. He sought sympathy from other Texas farmers, citing his crop losses due to freeze, drought, and bollworm. The stench of the water permit was easily explained away. Beauford Jester had appointed all of the water board members; Shivers just happened to be governor when they approved the Bentsens's permit.[29]

Another scandal involving insurance also emerged early in the primary campaign. Texas had "the worst insurance laws in the nation" in 1954. An entrepreneur with $10,000 could create a company and begin writing policies. The state's Board of Insurance Commissioners, charged with industry oversight, was ineffectual, dominated by the very industry it regulated. When Shivers became governor in 1949, Jester had just finished stocking the board with commissioners who served six-year terms. Two of the three commissioners became seriously ill and eventually died. Their lengthy illnesses insured that the commission did even less to monitor the insurance business. Shivers later claimed that the commission's weakness had worried him then, but he never proposed any meaningful reform. When the insurance mess finally broke, some cynics suggested he hide behind the dead commissioners. To his credit, Shivers "quickly and emphatically" refused to do so. However, the insurance controversies that surfaced in 1954 were only a foreshadowing of what was to come.[30]

Attorney General Shepperd sued Houston's Lloyd's of North America in late spring, 1954. Lloyd's owner, Ralph Hammonds, had created the company with a $20,000 loan and a few dollars of his own. State auditors examining the company discovered a $427,000 deficit, systematic use of premiums to pay Hammonds's personal loans, and that Hammonds had insured a piece of his own property for eight times its value. Hammonds's problems soon became Shivers's. Lloyd's had long paid a $1,000 retainer to Shivers campaign staffer John VanCronkhite for his assistance in fostering "cordial relations" with regulators. The governor himself had known the company was insolvent in 1953, but had done nothing. Early in

1954, VanCronkhite and Hammonds had a falling out and state examiners soon arrived to investigate Lloyd's.[31]

Despite warnings that VanCronkhite was a "damned crook," Shivers failed to distance himself from his aide. Attorney General Shepperd asked that Shivers be subpoenaed so he might clear himself. The state's top lawyer also subpoenaed Ralph Yarborough. Yarborough explained that he had been contacted to represent Lloyd's, but had wisely refused. Shivers testified that Hammonds had threatened him with political embarrassment unless he halted Shepperd's investigation. Their phone conversation ended when the governor explained he lacked the authority to halt the probe of Lloyd's. Although Yarborough sought to use the insurance scandal against Shivers, the issue had not yet reached maturity.[32]

The potential for ugliness in the 1954 race existed from the outset, but events outside Texas helped fuel the rancor. On May 11, just as the primary campaign began, the U.S. Supreme Court overturned segregation in public schools. Compared to other southern politicians, Governor Shivers's response reflected moderation. He certainly disapproved of the decision, but he did not resort to hysterics. He promised that Texas schools would remain open and insisted that integration would prove to be a long-term problem. The governor also specifically condemned the use of violence in response to the decision. Shivers's public warnings against violence demonstrated his skill at racial politics. The specter of possible unrest contrasted with Shivers's own paternalistic racism, but the mention of violence also sent a message to black Texans to conform. Finally, he proposed a summit of southern leaders to discuss ways of protecting the region's unique "way of life." In the early going, Shivers tried to downplay the *Brown* decision and its implications. Later, however, with Yarborough gaining ground, he turned to race as his political salvation.[33]

Brown v. Board of Education of Topeka presented a dilemma for Yarborough's campaign. The staunchest support for an anti-Shivers candidacy came from East Texas, which was the most ardently segregationist region in the state. While the governor's party regularity worried many in the east, any uncertainty on segregation would doom Yarborough. Privately, he believed the decision should be respected as the law of the land. Creekmore Fath, a liberal adviser, suggested he embrace the *Brown* decision to both attract minority votes and set a moral tone. His more conservative backers suggested he hedge on, or even ignore, the issue. The campaign adopted the latter strategy, which ultimately gave Shivers an advantage. Yarborough, however, managed to draw first blood on race.[34]

In late May, the *Austin American* disclosed that Shivers's oldest son, John, attended an integrated private school: St. Edwards in Austin. The governor was certain his opponents had leaked the information to the press. Yarborough forces featured the article in an advertisement sent to fifty-two thousand addresses.

Although involving Shivers's family in the race was risky, Yarborough managed to gain ground on the governor. The challenger's campaign literature faulted Shivers for eating with black soldiers during a visit to Korea, for his "closed meetings with Negro politicians" in Texas' big cities, and declared him the "first southern state head to openly quit the fight against public school integration."[35]

Knocked off balance by Yarborough's attacks, Shivers responded in mid-June with a strongly segregationist message in Lufkin: "All of my instincts, my political philosophy, my experiences, and my common sense revolt against this Supreme Court decision. It is an unwarranted invasion of the constitutional rights of the states, and one that could be disastrous to the children and teachers of both races." Shivers operatives also stepped up direct racial attacks on Yarborough. One group of East Texas Shivercrats sent a black man tooling through the Piney Woods in a sparkling new Cadillac sporting Yarborough bumper stickers. He stopped at service stations, behaved rudely toward white attendants, and boasted about his work for "Mr. Yarborough." Shivers grew more bellicose on the subject of segregation as the race heated up, frequently stressing the possibility of racial violence as an outcome of integration. In San Antonio, he decried integrationists' plans to "force innocent boys and girls, white and black alike to endure the emotional tension and strain of being mixed in the classrooms of our schools." In Galveston, he said that "parents who are convinced about the *dangers* of mixing white and Negro children . . . know [Yarborough's] promises to the NAACP . . . [and] will outweigh the feeble lip service he pays to Texas traditions." In Henderson, the governor pointedly told crowds that "thinking people of both races" knew the truth about integration: "The race that will *suffer most* if separate public schools are abolished is the Negro race."[36]

Yarborough's utterances and literature, no matter how mundane, drew deconstructionist critiques from Shivers's staff. A Yarborough pamphlet that introduced the candidate's family had "The Yarboroughs" printed on a background of five overlapping ovals colored white, gray, black, and gray. A Shivers worker scribbled across the pamphlet: "note — mixing of colors could well mean mixing of the races or social equality." Other Shivers supporters operated independently of the "official" campaign, as had Yarborough's segregationist allies. Some suggested funding an all-black Yarborough organization in East Texas. An advertisement featuring a doctored photo of Yarborough with black features was approved by the Shivers campaign. Although many newspaper editors refused to print the advertisement, it was circulated throughout the state.[37]

Shivers also turned toward African-American voters he had courted in 1946, but rejected in 1952. Some black leaders, including Shivers family friend Mack Hannah Jr., carried the governor's message to black Texans. Hannah thought other blacks were ignorant of the "grave issues involved" in segregation's end. The governor's operatives distributed pamphlets entitled *The Big Lie* and *Allan Shivers Speaks Against Mob Rule* in the black community. *The Big Lie* accused Yarborough of hedging on segregation in order to deceive black voters. Both publications stressed Shivers's commitment to equalizing segregation and opposition to the Ku Klux Klan. Hannah stressed the governor's "levelheaded and cool" response to *Brown* when campaigning. Shivers's black supporters also concentrated on recruiting black school principals and undertakers, two social elites endangered by integration.[38]

Both camps actively sought Tejano votes. His 1952 support of Eisenhower hurt the governor's appeal among Hispanic voters. Activists like Hector and Gus Garcia had grown disenchanted with him over his weakening of the Good Neighbor Commission. Among Tejanos, Shivers was widely known as "Gobernador Chivo"—Governor Goat—after his 1950 speech, but the word *chivo* had unflattering connotations. Yarborough's staff publicized Shivers's opposition to civil rights and its implications for Tejanos. The incumbent's allies fretted that a poor showing among Hispanic voters might defeat him in a close race. "[W]e have a real job to do with the Latins," Lloyd Bentsen, Sr. warned. "They have been handed a lot of poison over the radio . . . through the Spanish language." An orchestrated letter-writing campaign featured testimonials by one of Sharyland's longest-serving hands, Olivaro Garza. Garza claimed that Shivers was the best *patrón* he had known. Yarborough's union supporters contrasted Garza's story with the realities of Sharyland's wages and working conditions in a tract called *What Price Wetbacks?*[39]

Nasty campaigning did not involve race only. Yarborough hammered away at Governor Shivers's personal honesty and morality. Speaking in Lindale, he titillated the pious with tales of Shivers's yachting in the Gulf with a "notorious gambler," thus rattling the governor's old Sam Maceo skeleton. Shivercrats responded that by equating yachting and gambling, the challenger was pitting "class against class." Across the state, Yarborough forces spread rumors of Shivers's drinking and gambling. One concerned voter wrote Shivers's pastor, Dr. Carlyle Marney of the First Baptist Church in Austin, asking if these things could be true. Marney found himself trapped: Shivers and Yarborough were both members of his congregation. Pastor Marney averred that the governor was a born-again, dedicated Baptist. To blunt these attacks, Shivers later gave a "Little Red Arrow" speech, as Jake Pickle had suggested four years earlier.[40]

In the first primary, the two men faced an Austin builder, J. J. Holmes, and Arlon "Cyclone" Davis Jr., the son of a former congressman. The minor candidates appeared likely to force a runoff. As the July 24 election drew closer, Yarborough made much of the Eisenhower administration's earlier reluctance to recognize Texas' historical boundaries in the tidelands. When he accused the president of "welching" on state ownership, Ike invited Sen. Price Daniel to the White House to dispel any doubts there might be in Texas. However, less than a week before the primary, an assistant to Attorney General Brownell again questioned Texas' claims. Two days before the vote, Eisenhower came to the rescue by publicly restating his commitment to historic boundaries. Shivers came out of the primary with a twenty-three-thousand-vote lead over Yarborough, but the two minor candidates had drawn thirty-six thousand, forcing a runoff. The slender lead indicated a precipitous decline in Shivers's public support. His challenger had momentum.[41]

Yarborough's strong showing shocked Shivers and his staff. The campaign had to devise some method of halting the challenger's rise. Defending segregation had helped the governor, but his advisers warned him "that old dog will not hunt again" since a "standoff" now existed on the race issue. Yarborough responded by issuing a more definitive statement that condemned the "forced commingling" of the races. Segregationist rhetoric would remain part of Shivers's repertoire, but other explosive issues became melded together with race. The brutality of the first primary campaign paled next to that of the runoff. Even after he left public life, Shivers did everything in his power to ruin Yarborough's political career. Twenty years later, a Yarborough observer noted, "hating Shivers is almost an obsession with Yarborough." The result was a network of hatreds and mistrust that underlay Texas politics for nearly two decades.[42]

The miracle of Yarborough's strength was that it came despite being considerably outspent. As the runoff neared, however, Shivers forces found their own finances straitened. The governor's financial backers were able to plan for lavish spending in strongholds like Dallas County, but ran into trouble raising cash elsewhere. Eventually, Shivers aides Maurice Acers and John Osorio managed to raise $750,000 in two days, most of it by telephone. The best weapon to scare conservative backers into donating was the image of Yarborough in the governor's mansion. Osorio later recalled that money turned the tide in the runoff. The money bought mass media and mailings that spread Shivers's message.[43]

Weldon Hart drafted the roadmap to victory the Shivers team used for the runoff. Segregation would recede from statewide view and instead appear prominently in regional appeals by the "truth squad and [in] truth sheets." The governor himself gave some of his most fiery segregationist speeches in East Texas during this phase of the race. Statewide, most of the emphasis and campaign spending would center upon the "labor issue":

> I submit for your consideration a doublepronged program to bring the labor issue closer to home by:
>
> 1. Using the Port Arthur Story as a threat to businessmen everywhere.

> 2. Using the farm labor unionization threat, especially in West Texas.
>
> Both approaches have their hazards. It will be hard to develop the Port Arthur Story fully without flatly being *against* the unionization of the class of workers organized by the DWOPA. So far, you have been against the union because it was Red-controlled. This plan would involve being against the union period.

Shivers, his back against a wall, did not hesitate. He attacked the unions using communism as his cudgel.[44]

Anticommunism in the South fused together far more anxieties than did worry about the future of the free enterprise system. It touched upon racial, class, and gender concerns. Communism's atheistic worldview appeared amoral and insidious in the deeply religious region. Television was in its infancy as a political tool in 1954, but the state's roughly thirty stations reached more than three-quarters of Texas homes. The Shivers campaign used its financial advantage to orchestrate a television offensive against Yarborough. Based around a short black-and-white film called *The Port Arthur Story*, the attacks used communism and the penumbra of fears that surrounded it to reach voters. With contrived images and direct verbal and indirect visual communication, the governor's pitchmen used the medium with devastating effect.[45]

The public relations firm of Syers, Pickle, and Winn provided the struggling Shivers campaign its greatest boost with *The Port Arthur Story*. The film depicted the city as devastated and deserted as a result of the ongoing retail workers' strike. As the camera panned across empty streets and smokeless smokestacks, the narrator explained that the CIO was "supervising the death of a city." The film portrayed the picketing workers as overwhelmingly black, and their loafing took on a menacing look when juxtaposed with white citizens' complaints about the strike. All of Texas, the film asserted, could suffer Port Arthur's fate—and only Allan Shivers could stop the outside agitators. The most damning scenes depicted in the advertisement had been faked. Crews filmed downtown Port Arthur at dawn to avoid being run down by traffic. After a long, frustrating wait, cameramen were finally able to get shots of lone factory smokestack not belching smoke. The film crew also hired many of the people portrayed as "pickets." Governor Shivers previewed the piece but was not told about the faked scenes. He undoubtedly knew about the real Port Arthur, but his staff judged the film effective. Yarborough later came to believe it cost him the election.[46]

Along with *The Port Arthur Story*, pamphlets centering on the strike hit mailboxes across the state. Traveling businessmen from the stricken city toured the state speaking to chambers of commerce and civic clubs. They spoke of the "economic devastation" wrought by the strike. Pamphlets pictured a white woman and black man picketing together over the caption: "Segregation? These are a couple of Port Arthur's bitterest foes of Allan Shivers." Another Shivers leaflet contained "a personal and unsolicited letter" from a Port Arthur businessman addressed "to the Christian People of Texas." These often-faked photos subtly pressed race, class, and gender buttons.[47]

A "Duval Story" tour and pamphlets also appeared, mainly for use in East and Central Texas. Literature offered "proof" of a Yarborough-Parr "deal" to steal the election. Yarborough's defeat, the advertisement explained, would "Keep Freedom's Flag Flying Over Duval County." Although the governor's opponents fought back, meager finances limited their effectiveness. Yarborough literature spoke of the border as "open to arch criminals" because of Shivers's cozy relations with Valley bosses. Another claimed that Shivers intended to use his power "to protect his ten-cent labor supply." The irony of both 1954 primaries was that Yarborough won the counties of the Parr duchy even with Texas Rangers guarding the polls. Any South Texas votes stolen as insurance came from border counties dominated by pro-Shivers bosses.[48]

SHIVERS WON THE RUNOFF WITH 778,088 VOTES TO YARBOROUGH'S 683,132. The turnout was greater, and both men received more votes than in the first primary. In the runoff, however, Yarborough actually lost ground in areas where he had done well in July. North and Central Texas, regions with good television reception, showed reduced totals for the challenger. Shivers held his lead in the critical urban centers, adding nearly 20,000 votes to his advantage in Dallas County. The governor picked up an additional 3,000 votes in Harris County, while Bexar County Shivercrats matched Yarborough's gains in the runoff. Studies of urban voting patterns revealed division along class and racial lines. Neighborhoods in Houston with home valuations greater than $8,000 favored the governor; those with lesser valuations tended to support Yarborough. Precincts in Dallas, Tarrant, and Jefferson Counties revealed that black and labor voters preferred Yarborough. Defeated, Yarborough credited his loss to "big money, the big smear, and the big lie." His failure to articulate a clearly segregationist position early in the campaign opened him to easy attack, but the well-financed viciousness of the runoff election finished him.[49]

The governor's mansion and the state party still belonged to Allan Shivers. At the fall state party convention in Mineral Wells, armed DPS officers strolled the floor. Liberal delegations, finding themselves without seats, were shut out because standing on the convention floor violated the rules. They also found themselves without hotel rooms because state party officials had neglected to make reservations for them. The Texas Democratic Party condemned efforts at "thought control" by the national party and promised to fight for the "true" party of Jefferson, Jackson, and Wilson. Convention speakers heaped insults upon Shivers's enemies, calling them communists. Liberals seeking recognition by the chair were ignored or shouted down. Mounted police broke up a liberal caucus in a city park. The governor had survived a strong challenge and left his opponents wondering if they could ever beat him. It appeared Texas would always be nestled in his palm.[50]

CHAPTER EIGHT

Scandals and Decline

1955

ALLAN SHIVERS'S AUTHORIZED BIOGRAPHERS TITLED THEIR CHAPTER about the 1954 campaign "The Mean One." Bitter and taxing, the 1954 race had brought out the very worst in him. By the campaign's end, the election was not about whether he or Ralph Yarborough would most improve life for Texans. Instead, he explained to an Austin audience as the runoff race drew to a close, "opposition to Allan Shivers for re-election . . . is part of a nationwide conspiracy to infiltrate, then adulterate, and finally to take over and change our Democratic Party and our system of government as we know it today."

The year 1955 witnessed a marked decline in Shivers's political fortunes. Scandals within the insurance industry and state government harmed him. He also struggled to find a place in the Democratic Party, thus disappointing his Republican admirers. Ironically, he attracted more national attention than ever and already appeared to be an important actor in the coming 1956 presidential contest. As his popularity receded, Shivers chose to stake his political future on the defense of segregation. As the year closed, he pondered his chances for a fourth term as governor of Texas.[1]

Insurance company failures had complicated his bid for a third term, but those incidents represented only the beginning. The trend accelerated through 1955. By 1957, five hundred thousand customers had lost millions of dollars to Texas insurance companies. The *Saturday Evening Post* skewered the state government's handling of the crisis. Bad publicity led Shivers to hunker down and complain about the magazine's failure to properly examine the information he had provided its reporters. Shivers's papers preserved in Texas's state archives do little to illuminate the situation. The governor accused the *Saturday Evening Post* of acting against him at the behest of national Democratic leaders.

Insurance executive A. B. Shoemake suggested a national television appearance with reporter Drew Pearson to calm fears about the state's insurance industry. Shoemake's own firm had hired Pearson to do commercials, so he figured the reporter's show would be a good venue for defending the state and its insurers. Shivers aide Jack Dillard, on the other hand, advised against such an appearance, reminding the governor that it had been Pearson who had revealed his office's ties to Lloyd's of North America.[2]

Shoemake's own U.S. Trust and Guarantee failed in December, 1955. One reporter described the company as "a hybrid bank-like firm." Investors purchased policies and, when these matured, were paid the principal plus interest. Premiums taken in by the company were reinvested in four subsidiaries owned by Shoemake, whose ownership remained legally obscured. The subsidiaries then invested those funds elsewhere. When it failed, U.S. Trust had $800,000 in cash, a mortgage on a Waco residence overvalued at $100,000, and $6 million in bonds issued by U.S. Automobile Service, a subsidiary. The insurance company's 128,000 investors had $5 million invested and suffered significant losses. U.S. Trust had bloated its accounts by overappraising insured properties. For example, a farm worth $400,000 and property worth $180,000 were both insured for $1 million. Shoemake shot himself in the head, but survived. The bullet, however, passed through his brain, rendering him incapable of testifying to U.S. Trust's activities.[3]

Subsequent legislative investigations revealed that state regulators had been watching U.S. Trust for more than a year and had known of its insolvency six months before the firm's collapse. Governor Shivers could no longer duck responsibility, as he had succeeded in doing with the 1953–54 insurance company failures. He had appointed two members of the state insurance board, including its chair, Garland Smith. Smith had served in the state senate, as Shivers's 1946 campaign manager, and on the governor's personal staff. However, he had no insurance experience. The governor had relied upon insurance industry insiders to tutor the new chief regulator. A grand jury indicted Byron Saunders, Shivers's other appointee, for accepting a position with a crooked insurance company while on the insurance board. Shivers defended his appointees far longer than politically wise, then later complained that getting the best men for government positions had proved difficult because of the low pay.[4]

SCANDAL IN THE STATE AGENCY CHARGED WITH MAKING CHEAP LAND available to veterans proved even more troublesome. Shortly after Shivers defeated token Republican opposition in the November, 1954, general election, news of suspicious activities involving the three-member Veterans' Land Board (VLB) came from the town of Cuero, ninety miles southeast of Austin. The VLB was established when the legislature approved Land Commissioner Bascom Giles's proposal to set aside $100 million for assisting veterans with land purchases. Giles proposed the program at the end of World War II, shortly before the 1946 primaries. The VLB served not only returning servicemen, but also to protect Giles's political future. The board—made up of Giles, the governor, and the attorney general—bought land and then resold it to qualified veterans on easy terms: 5 percent down, with the remainder financed at 3 percent interest on a forty-year note.[5]

The system had been functioning for seven years when *Cuero Record* editor Kenneth Towery noticed unusual fraternization between the town's leading whites and black and Tejano veterans. These former servicemen found themselves invited to private all-white drinking establishments, where they signed agreements with their hosts under the impression that the state had promised them free land or cash bonuses. The papers were actually VLB loan applications. Typically, the white speculators bought tracts at market price, subdivided them, and then obtained veterans' signatures on the loan applications. This created the appearance of high demand and drove up land prices. Giles's office then appraised the properties at even higher values, after which the white speculators sold their property to the state. The minority veterans got nothing, while Bascom Giles was showered with bribes to arrange board approval for the purchases.[6]

Towery broke the story and won the Pulitzer Prize. Giles announced he would not serve his ninth term, which he won in the 1954 primaries. He then pleaded guilty to bribery charges. Three other land office staffers resigned and were eventually convicted of bribery and conspiracy. The public began to question Governor Shivers's and Attorney General John Ben Shepperd's roles in the developing scandal. As board members, they were required to give their consent for state land purchases. Both men rarely attended meetings and usually dispatched assistants. There is no evidence indicating the governor ever participated in the swindle. It is clear, however, that Maurice Acers, Shivers's usual representative at VLB meetings, recognized problems in the board's rules as early as March, 1954, but did not delve deeply into the matter.[7]

Public outrage stirred the legislature into action. A House committee investigated the VLB throughout the 1955 regular session. The snooping made people in the governor's mansion and the attorney general's office nervous. Neither official had broken the law, but both wished to limit the damage caused by the scandal. Shepperd fretted that some of Shivers's allies on the investigating committee "were not helping him on the situation." He believed he might be sacrificed to save the governor. Although he protested his loyalty to Shivers and claimed the liberals were out to get them both, Shepperd's complaints may have contained a veiled threat to tell all. Maurice Acers's position was particularly sensitive, and attorneys coached him before he gave his testimony.[8]

Two matters preoccupied the investigators and the investigated. First, the board's minutes became a focal point of the investigation. "[T]he girl who kept the minutes," Acers explained to Shivers, "wrote up pretty well whatever she thought the minutes should be." Then, after the meeting, Giles would add improper transactions to the record as though they had been lawfully approved. Second, the legislators probed the governor's and the attorney general's record of attendance at board meetings. Although this proved embarrassing to both officeholders, it was also exculpatory. Taken together, the minutes and their absences indicated that neither Shivers nor Shepperd even bothered to read the minutes before approving them, thus causing them to miss the chance to discover the fraud.[9]

The trick was to get the exculpatory information out, while at the same time not drawing attention to what had made it exculpatory. Shivers, Shepperd, and their staffs swore out affidavits, distancing themselves from Giles and their own responsibilities. That way, Acers explained to the governor, the committee "could make the proper finding, draw the proper conclusion, and make the proper statement to the press." What worried Acers—and perhaps Shivers—the most, however, was John Ben Shepperd's "handsprings" as he sought public disclosure of the affidavits. Shepperd nursed ambitions for higher office and felt threatened by the more aggressive committee members. The attorney general called the investigation "an inquisition" and grumbled about the "purely personal" nature of the questioning. Attorney General Shepperd wanted to be publicly exonerated, which gave Shivers opponents on the committee some hope of tracing the matter to the governor's mansion.[10]

The news eventually came out and no one saved face, regardless of the precautions they had taken. Legislative investigators ruled that the scandal stopped with Giles, his staff, and the land developers involved. However, the committee also criticized Shivers and Shepperd for their lax attention to duty. The mild rebuke was, as historian George Green has pointed out, administered by an "Establishment legislature." The investigation had been carefully managed from its outset because few legislators had any genuine interest in disturbing business as usual in Austin.[11]

This was not enough for some. Senator Kilmer Corbin of Lubbock demanded a broader investigation of the governor. Corbin raised three questions that the conservative investigating committee had failed to explore. First, there had been no examination of VLB transactions in Liberty, Polk, and Hidalgo Counties. Shivers had interests in each. Second, the Lubbock senator accused the governor's office of diverting state printing contracts to the Times Publishing Company of Mission, which was owned by the John Shary estate. Lastly, the senator complained that Maurice Acers, a state employee, routinely worked on Shivers's business deals on state time. The governor bitterly denied all Corbin's claims. He claimed that

Corbin and those "who fall in the same category" wanted to overturn the previous election by tying him to scandal. Despite Shivers's denials, his papers support Corbin's accusations about Acers. In the end, a resolution calling for an investigation failed in the more conservative state senate, where Shivers's allies, led by Ottis Lock of Lufkin, went so far as to have it expunged from the record.[12]

After Bascom Giles's resigned, Shivers appointed Earl Rudder to serve his term as land commissioner. In concert with the governor and Attorney General Shepperd, the new commissioner worked to pin the whole scandal on his predecessor. This proved difficult because the public had a hard time accepting that neither Shivers nor Shepperd could not have known about the illegal activity going on around them. Years later, after retiring from politics, Shivers argued that some voters unfairly blamed him because they believed he had appointed Giles. He claimed that this demonstrated the public's ignorance of state government. Although his statement was self-serving, Shivers knew the Texas electorate. Voters might well have not understood the complicated insurance crisis, but they did know that someone had defrauded veterans. In 1957, the Travis County grand jury reopened its investigation of the VLB scandal. Fred Schmidt of the Texas CIO joined other jury members in a prison field trip to question Bascom Giles. The former land commissioner told them nothing other than to offer an analogy of the scandal. Giles described driving down a highway at eighty miles per hour with everyone in the flow of traffic driving as fast or faster and he alone being pulled over. He later left prison as he had entered it: a wealthy man.[13]

The two scandals called into question Shivers's personal honesty and judgment. They also heightened his sensitivity to criticism. What the governor knew and when he knew it concerning the Veterans' Land Board fraud remains illusive. He rarely participated in board meetings, and his representative, Acers, never detected any fraud. His handling of the insurance fiasco also seems devoid of criminal intent. Statutory and constitutional limitations prevented his taking vigorous action. On the other hand, although he had worried about lax insurance laws as early as 1953, he never proposed stronger legislation or offered leadership on the issue. Insurance commission appointments, Shivers's best opportunity to influence the industry, always went to political cronies whose primary qualifications seem to have been personal loyalty to him. Political allies always urged appointments "sympathetic" to "mortgage loan and insurance business[es]." Shivers willingly complied, for his sympathies consistently lay with Texas corporations.[14]

Shivers cannot be accused of incompetence in the insurance mess. He did little to rein in insurers because it went against his view of government and business. Business success and amassing wealth tended to impress him even more than political skill. His personal fastidiousness with money was well known. It was not unusual for the governor to carefully examine a restaurant check item by item before paying. In business, he routinely required daily financial statements from his enterprises. John Osorio recalled a business deal Shivers made after leaving office in which the former governor purchased a large block of stock. He counted each share personally to make sure all were there. Did such care for his own money mean that he was honest in all things? It certainly demonstrated a vigilance he might have directed toward business interests as governor had he been so inclined.[15]

Other accusations made against Allan Shivers stick. He plainly used state employees for his private business concerns. As governor, he violated numerous campaign finance laws—almost as a matter of course. His staff kept two different lists of political contributions and contributors: one from which to draft "thank you" notes, another for the official report to the secretary of state's office. Discrepancies exist between actual donation amounts and those that were reported. At the height of the 1954 race, Lloyd Bentsen Sr. sent the governor two $1,000 checks, one for himself and one for his brother. Bentsen's note explained, "for your confidential information Elmer and my contribution, as shown on the statement of $2,000, does not represent what we did or will do." Bentsen had already paid out $1,700 to political bosses to assist in getting out the vote and assumed the Hidalgo County Shivers campaign's debt of $1,600. More than once, advertising and public relations firms forgave campaign debts in exchange for partial payment. Shivers hardly stands out among Texas politicians of the era in such transgressions. Rather, his refusal to go through the motions of hiding such venal sins is what sets him apart.[16]

AFTER THE HARD CAMPAIGN OF 1954 AND DURING THE SCANDALS OF 1955, Shivers spent time outside the state. He had become an important national figure, and the positive publicity he often received on his trips contrasted with the difficulties he faced back home. In late 1954, Shivers attracted the attention of Hollywood. Photogenic in his late forties, he made a cameo appearance in *Lucy Gallant*, a film set in Texas starring Jane Wyman and Charlton Heston. Wyman played a clothing-store owner in a fictional oil town, with Heston cast as her determined suitor. The picture culminated in a fashion show scene in which Shivers, playing the governor of Texas, introduced the runway show. Before his show business debut, the governor joined the Screen Actors Guild, ironically becoming the first Texas governor ever to join a union. After paying his dues, Tinseltown's newest talent donated his $87 paycheck to a union charity.[17]

Lucy Gallant did not make Shivers a hot Hollywood commodity. Released in the fall of 1954, the film took a beating from reviewers. Bosley Crowther of the *New York Times* saw right through the earthy atmosphere of the Texas boomtown setting. *Lucy Gallant*, he told readers, was "essentially a woman's film." The roles were well acted by both Wyman and Heston, but the story and script proved unworthy of their talents. Crowther concluded by saying the "boy-meets-girl, boy-loses-girl routines through which they have to go are too much for the talents or the patience of the longest suffering actors in the world."[18]

Shivers returned to California in the spring of 1955, this time as the commencement speaker at the University of Southern California. The USC student senate passed a resolution critical of university administrators for tendering the invitation. The students complained that commencement addresses should "inspire" recognition of virtues like "tolerance, integrity and intelligence," but Texas' governor "consistently demonstrated lack of these ideals." A large number of faculty members joined the students in criticizing Shivers's defense of segregation and spoke out against the university's plans to confer on honorary doctorate on him. The administration refused to rescind their invitation to "one of the most outstanding young public figures on the American scene." The student boycott effort "fizzled" when fourteen thousand turned out to watch the seniors receive their diplomas.[19]

Governor Shivers reassured the crowd "the South has passed far beyond the era of bigotry and prejudice and provincialism which persists in portrayals offered by commercial fiction." He turned the tables on his critics, calling for tolerance of alternative viewpoints on the day's great issues. A cadre of 150 student pickets walked the streets across from the Beverly Hills Hotel, carrying signs that read, "Shivers, you give me the chills." The public response to his speech was generally favorable. Supportive mail streamed in from the West Coast and elsewhere around the country. Robert Patterson, secretary of the Mississippi Citizens' Council praised Shivers for taking on "Communists and Left-wingers in California" and "bring[ing] truth to their mongrel state." "You can judge a man by his enemies," wrote Patterson. "We have long been admirers of yours here in Mississippi."[20]

Shivers also journeyed to New York that summer, where he offered a speech titled "A Middle of the Road Policy" at the Sales Executive Club's "Texas Day" meeting. Most of his talk justified his decision to support Eisenhower in 1952, but he also spoke to states' rights matters, trying to place them in a context that would resonate with his northern audience. Transplanted Texans present wrote glowing letters praising his remarks, but many not from Texas also seemed to have understood his points. William Peterson of New Jersey described the Texan as a "beacon" other governors should follow in the struggle against "centralism and socialism."[21]

THE TEXAS GOVERNOR'S HEIGHTENED NATIONAL IMPORTANCE CAME EVEN as he struggled to find his place within the two-party system. Nationally, he worked to keep good relations with Eisenhower's Republican administration. At the state level, however, he sought to keep power within a one-party Democratic political landscape. He did not intend to change parties, but he did intend to use both political parties to serve his own political ends. As a result, Shivers increasingly became a man without a party during the years 1955–56.

Shivers's relationship with Eisenhower remained strong, despite the governor's difficulties with scandal. The administration had bailed him out during the 1954 primaries when Ralph Yarborough questioned the wisdom of trusting Eisenhower with the tidelands. As 1954 drew to a close, the president's chief of staff, Sherman Adams, suggested the formation of a "Constitutional Party" for the 1956 elections. The president fancied himself above ordinary party politics and sometimes toyed with a departure from the two-party system. Coming under more intense Democratic criticism and never completely comfortable with congressional Republicans, Eisenhower thought Adams's suggestion was "wonderful." Shivers and Ike had originally hatched the idea over golf, and they discussed it periodically from 1954–57. Governor Shivers secretly met with like-minded media, political, and business figures to create support. Eisenhower eventually dropped the project, but the furtive third party plot illustrates Shivers's pet-Democrat status with the president.[22]

Eisenhower's distaste for politics led him to permit speculation about Vice Pres. Richard Nixon's future in late 1955. Nixon's credentials as a "professional politician" disturbed the president. When Eisenhower suffered a heart attack that year, Nixon behaved well under the pressure, but many observers voiced concerns about his suitability as a successor for the popular president. The president cruelly allowed Nixon's future to dangle into 1956, directly suggesting he might gain better "administrative experience" in the cabinet. The press seized upon the story and the "Dump Nixon" trend quickly caught fire. Nixon's enemies, Sherman Adams among them, believed his reputation as an ideologue might hurt the ticket. Allan Shivers was among those mentioned as a possible replacement. Those most involved in plotting against the vice president appear never to have seriously considered the governor. Eisenhower sought to put a stop to the speculation in April, 1956, by announcing his intention to keep Nixon as his running mate. However, rumors about Nixon's demise were still circulating when Attorney General Brownell met with Shivers that same month.[23]

Though close to Eisenhower, Shivers was a tremendous disappointment to Texas Republicans. National committeeman H. Jack Porter strengthened his hold on the Texas party from 1954–56. Although dissatisfied Republicans claimed otherwise, Porter was determined to make Texas a two-party state. Porter, meanwhile, grew increasingly frustrated with Governor Shivers. A significant Republican crossover vote had helped defeat Ralph Yarborough, but Shivers repaid this favor with efforts to curb Republican growth. When Shivers rebuffed overtures from Dallas County Republicans, they fielded a congressional candidate against his longtime ally, Shivercrat Wallace Savage. The Republican, a right-wing activist named Bruce Alger, defeated the equally conservative Savage and went to Washington as Texas's first Republican congressman in nearly thirty years.[24]

Porter bluntly informed the president that Governor Shivers's power was on the wane. As he saw Texas politics, Republicans represented the balance of power between conservative and liberal Democrats. He was convinced that a revived Texas GOP might attract more-conservative Democrats to its 1956 primary, thereby bringing a Democratic gubernatorial nominee loyal to the national party. Porter, who thought Shivers's political retirement was likely in 1956, had no intention of sharing power with the leaderless Shivercrats. He hoped to attract a hundred thousand votes in the 1956 GOP primary and run candidates for all statewide offices. However, this strategy still depended heavily upon Eisenhower. "[A]ll of our plans are predicated on your running for a second term," Porter told Ike. In Texas, "a campaign for anyone else would be futile." It was time, he concluded, to think about Texas after Shivers. "[A]s much as we might like Allan Shivers personally," the Houston oilman wrote, "he has gone to the well once too often in trying to re-establish himself in the Democrat Party."[25]

As his political strength ebbed, Shivers made pained efforts to rebuild his ties to the national Democratic Party. The DNC's new chair, Paul Butler, came to Texas in June, 1955, to examine the party's condition. Governor Shivers invited Butler to lunch, but the DNC leader declined. Responding to the slight, the governor claimed that Butler had come to plot against him with Sam Rayburn and other loyalists. He then suggested that he might moderate his stance toward the national party if it agreed to accept a Texas delegation representative of a majority of the state's Democrats at the 1956 national convention. Butler insisted he had no interest in interfering with the selection of Texas's delegation. The Butler-Shivers exchange moved the chief Shivercrat's relations with the DNC from cold to cool. Texas liberals, however, smelled a sellout. Ralph Yarborough complained, "those who are trying to appease Allan Shivers will find that the only way to appease the bunch back of him is to surrender to them." Austin lawyer John Coffer grumbled that a rapprochement between Butler and Shivers would only serve as an encouragement to the governor and his allies.[26]

Outgoing national party chief Stephen Mitchell drew nothing but scorn from the governor. In a November, 1955, television appearance, Mitchell harshly criticized Shivers. His words drew a quick, intemperate reaction from the governor's mansion. Texas liberals might have agreed with Mitchell's view of Shivers, but some complained of his poor timing. Gas House Gang alumnus George Nokes thought Mitchell's comments added fuel to Shivers's dying flame. Rayburn and Johnson, according to Nokes, had finally begun to neutralize the governor's power, but Mitchell's attacks only allowed Shivers to stand as a "super-Texan fighting the Northern Liberals." Others were not so sure. Maury Maverick Jr. delighted in the former DNC chair's baiting of Shivers. He suggested a continued drumbeat against the governor, concentrating on the scandals that bedeviled him. Maverick did not see Rayburn and Johnson as a solution to Shivers. He worried that a 1956 favorite-son candidacy for LBJ might bring a new role for the weakened politician. "[T]hree weeks ago," Maverick wrote Mitchell, "Allan Shivers was a dead duck. Less than that. Now he either has come back or is well on the way."[27]

Governor Shivers had spoken to Johnson about the senator's running for the presidency as early as November, 1954, when they met at the Southern Governors' Conference in Boca Raton, Florida. There, Shivers discussed Johnson's plans with South Carolina governor James Byrnes. Byrnes claimed he did not know Johnson well, but added that he did not like the things he did know. A journalist overhearing the conversation portrayed Byrnes as hostile to Johnson in the next day's papers. According to press accounts, Byrnes called the Texas senator a "young upstart." The governor quickly tried to repair any damage to his relationship with LBJ. Johnson brushed off the news and absolved Shivers. "I proceed on the basis which I have told you about a mighty long time that as long as we are living the break is going to come from you," Johnson reassured the governor. "As far as I am concerned I don't care what stories they put out or what conversations they overhear or what eye-witness accounts come to me. I am always going to know that whatever you do or say is not in anyway calculated to do anything but help me." Was Johnson really that placid about the incident? For what it is worth, LBJ, in the same conversation, also denied having any ambition for the presidency in 1956.[28]

Whatever Byrnes said about Johnson, he plainly told Shivers that if Adlai Stevenson received the 1956 Democratic nomination, "I'll vote for Ike and so will you." Texas loyalists knew that Shivers wanted the credibility conferred upon the leader of the state's national convention delegation, and he would need the senator's help to obtain that honor. Shivers, hoping to ingratiate himself with LBJ, worked to forward a favorite-son candidacy. He framed Johnson as an alternative to the direction of the national party. According to the governor, "radical" and "extremist" elements had ruined the Democratic Party and Johnson could correct the party's course. Democratic loyalist Byron Skelton observed: "I don't believe that Lyndon Johnson will appreciate this 'kiss of death' that Shivers has put upon him." Eight months later, Johnson suffered a massive heart attack. Although it failed to kill the senator, it effectively killed a strong presidential bid by him in 1956. However, he did not completely forgo his favorite-son chances, and the senate majority leader angled for the vice-presidential nomination. National party observers believed Johnson's "deadly serious" ambitions threatened stronger candidacies and could serve to resurrect Shivers. The governor's struggle for relevance and his deliberate appeal to Johnson's vanity and ambition thus served one another.[29]

THROUGHOUT 1955, ALLAN SHIVERS MADE OTHER SUBSTANTIVE MOVES TO bind his rift with loyal Texas Democrats. He signed legislation authored by San Antonio state representative Maury Maverick Jr. that ended cross-filing in Texas elections. He also hammered out an agreement with Johnson and Rayburn that would allow Wright Morrow's removal as a Democratic national committeeman. Morrow, who had helped lead the state's Dixiecrat movement, had long been close to Shivers. In 1953, however, the governor began to put some distance between himself and the Dixiecrats. Two years later, after failing to press Eisenhower to nominate Morrow to serve as ambassador to Mexico, the governor unceremoniously dumped him from his national committeeman's slot during a State Democratic Executive Committee meeting in Mineral Wells and appointed Lt. Gov. Ben Ramsey, a reliable Shivers ally, to fill it. An angry conservative described the meeting as "Munich Wells," while liberal Texas Democrats looked skeptically on during the proceedings. "[I]n deserting Morrow, [Shivers] has clearly abandoned every principle that he ever stood for, if any," Temple attorney Byron Skelton observed. The governor's game was self-preservation and, though he sometimes moderated his stance, he would veer sharply rightward whenever he thought it politically profitable.[30]

Governor Shivers sought political salvation in defending segregation. The U.S. Supreme Court issued its *Brown II* ruling in the spring of 1955, turning the how and when of integration over to the federal district courts. "Full implementation of these constitutional principles may require solution of varied school problems," the court held, its decision reading like something southern politicians might have written. "In fashioning and effectuating the decrees, the courts will be guided by equitable principles. Traditionally, equity has been characterized by a practical flexibility in shaping its remedies and by a facility for adjusting and reconciling public and private needs." Southern schools must, the court concluded, integrate "with all deliberate speed." Southern political leaders found solace in the opinion's language, which seemingly opened the door to endless appeals by beleaguered segregationists. Southern speed proved deliberate indeed. Allan Shivers was determined to use the situation to keep alive his hopes for yet another term as governor.[31]

The Texas NAACP had aggressively sought favorable court decisions in civil rights matters since its earliest challenges to the white primary in the 1920s. The association saw southern fringe states as a proving ground for its legal strategies and its first school integration cases began showing up on Texas federal district court dockets in late 1955.

Whites, concerned by these developments, began to organize. That summer, the Citizens' Council movement reached Texas. Kilgore citizens were the first to form a chapter in the state. The Citizens' Councils represented an elite and middle-class response to the integration threat. Council literature sought to inculcate whites of all ages with segregationist doctrine. The councils organized boycotts of integrated and "liberal" businesses and also led protests when decisions calling for desegregation were announced. Citizens' Council strength grew quickly in East Texas and some of the larger cities, but the organization never achieved statewide influence. By November, twelve chapters fused into the Associated Citizens' Councils of Texas. Governor Shivers and Attorney General Shepperd sympathized with the councils—Shepperd so much so that he created his own states' rights organization, the Committees on Correspondence.[32]

Other Texas conservatives—including Wright Morrow, J. Evetts Haley, and Coke Stevenson—became prominent leaders in Mississippi senator James O. Eastland's Federation for Constitutional Government. In early 1956, segregationist organizations collected over 150,000 signatures to force three referenda on the July primary ballot. Shivers gladly complied. One referendum sounded out voters on "interposition" to prevent "illegal federal encroachment." A second asked if voters preferred stronger laws against mixed-race marriages. Still another sought voters' opinions on exempting students from mandatory attendance at integrated schools. Governor Shivers, not content with merely allowing angry whites to delude themselves about halting integration, actively encouraged resistance and exhorted the segregationist faithful.[33]

Shivers created a special committee to study segregation in Texas public schools in the midsummer of 1955. He charged the organization, the Texas Advisory Committee on Segregation (TACS), with objectively examining ways to meet the challenge of integration, then stacked the committee with staunch segregationists. Charles Howell, a committee member from Beaumont, received his appointment because he "would hardly give an inch on this subject." Although segregationist in mind-set, Shivers wanted TACS to work "with dignity and without bombast." Of the forty-two members, four were black. Three of the four were college presidents and the other a mortician—professions economically cushioned under segregation. Shivers appointed thirty-four of the committee's members, with Lieutenant Governor Ramsey and Speaker Reuben Senterfitt naming the other eight. Only four of the appointees resided west of modern-day Interstate 35, a geographic bias that was intentional. Some eighty school districts in western Texas had already moved to end segregation voluntarily. Victoria teacher and "Womanpower for Eisenhower" leader Nan Procter typified the alarm with which those in the east viewed these developments. If integration came, Procter wrote Shivers, standards would decline and "our white children will be the losers."[34]

Rather than propose ways to comply with constitutional requirements, the committee planned a systematic defense of segregation by all legal means. African Americans on the committee simply served to legitimize the process. Each had been carefully chosen, but some segregationists were not pleased with even a token black presence. Bishop College president M. K. Curry Jr.'s appointment drew fire from the owner of his hometown newspaper, the *Marshall News Messenger.* Millard Cope protested Curry's appointment because the college president had failed to join Marshall's chapter of the Federation for Constitutional Government. Shivers aides quieted the controversy by assuring Cope that the all-white Legal and Legislative Affairs Subcommittee was "carrying the ball and will continue to do so" in drafting TACS's recommendations. The governor's office wanted to avoid tampering with the committee's black membership since it might cause a "major stir" and things already were "under control."[35]

The committee was part of a regionwide effort to draft formal state policies in defense of segregation and to suggest legislative methods of reinforcing the institution. Throughout 1955, the news media, politicians, and other opinion-shaping forces focused on the doctrine of interposition as the proper rebuttal to demands for integration. Interposition, according to historian Numan Bartley, became "the theory and battle cry of massive resistance." Interposition dated from the Virginia and Kentucky Resolutions, and stipulated that states might interpose their authority to protect their citizens from unconstitutional federal action. Authored by Thomas Jefferson and James Madison, the resolutions represented reactions to the Alien and Sedition Acts in the 1790s. Later embellished and distorted by John C. Calhoun, among others, interposition remained part of the southern political gospel even after the Civil War. Yet, however good its intellectual pedigree, interposition had no basis in law. It instead represented a rallying construct that elevated arguments against integration from the shameful muck of sectional racism by allowing good people who favored segregation to deny their own racism and cast the debate in terms of conservatism versus liberalism, modernization versus the "Southern Way of Life."[36]

The central problem with interposition, apart from its illegality, was that the concept proved damnably hard to explain to the masses. Under the Constitution, the argument ran, states surrendered only the enumerated powers given to Congress. All others, including the power over education, remained with the states through the rarely litigated Tenth Amendment. The Fourteenth Amendment, passed during Reconstruction, failed to alter the basic makeup of the federal Union and did not explicitly prohibit segregation. Following interposition's logic, the *Brown* decision represented a constitutional amendment by judicial fiat. Resistance therefore became the duty of all loyal white southerners. At Shivers's urging, TACS built its official position on integration upon interposition.[37]

Texas courts rejected interposition outright a few months later. Big Spring's Citizens' Council sued to prevent voluntary school integration for grades one through six. The angry parents contended that the school district's compliance with *Brown* violated both the Texas state constitution and the Gilmer-Aikin education law. The plaintiffs sought a declaratory judgment affirming segregation and an injunction against the Big Spring school district to prevent integration. The Citizens' Council legal staff lost every hearing, right up to the Texas Supreme Court. The state's high court unanimously rejected the parents' efforts to use state laws to prevent integration. Associate Justice Will Wilson recalled that he and the other justices dealt with the case with detachment, fully recognizing *Brown* as the law of the land. Rather than give strength to interposition, the court invalidated those provisions of the state constitution and Gilmer-Aikin that mandated racial separation. The ruling shocked many, but Governor Shivers assured Texans that he would continue to defend segregation. "Neither the Texas nor the United States Supreme Court has said that schools must desegregate immediately," he explained. "[N]o school district should feel compelled to take hasty or unnecessary action."[38]

While Shivers's public pronouncements lacked the fire of some southern governors, he had not hesitated to use segregation as an issue in 1954 and appeared determined to ride it into 1956. His behavior during this period does not fit with the moderation of some of his contemporaries, such as LeRoy Collins of Florida or North Carolina's Luther Hodges. On the other hand, Arkansas's Orval Faubus showed greater moderation than Shivers during the period. All three men courted modernization in their states, and all three saw racial progress at least in some measure as being key to attracting industrial development. While Allan Shivers was no enemy of industrialization, there is no evidence that he saw racial moderation as a necessary or desirable step toward modernization. Like Virginia governor Thomas Stanley, Shivers created a special committee ostensibly to study the problems of integration. Virginia's Gray Commission delivered its recommendations as the Texas committee deliberated. The Virginia panel appeared somewhat accepting of token integration, and even Governor Stanley embraced its findings in the early going. Shivers's panel was not reconciled to tokenism. Indeed, it moved to reverse the voluntary integration undertaken in western Texas. The state's government could hardly be mistaken as being moderate, let alone progressive, about integration in the 1950s.[39]

Segregation might yet have rescued Shivers, but political reality had grown much bleaker during 1955. The conservative bloc he had ridden to power began to crumble. The prospects of a Johnson presidential candidacy divided Shivercrats, as did Shivers's own tentative embrace of the senator's ambitions. Reliable Shivercrat Wallace Savage reported that meetings held across the state "to get conservatives together" seemed torn between loyalty to the governor and uncertainty about his political future. Although Savage confessed to being "baffled and a little vexed" as he looked toward 1956, the Dallas attorney was convinced segregation was "the best single issue to weld together conservative forces." Allan Shivers no doubt realized that as well. Yet, his popularity had slipped markedly during the year—from 64 percent in January to 52 percent in May, to 22 percent by September. Weldon Hart, seeking to put a better face on the news, observed that the numbers did not reflect peoples' personal feelings for their governor but rather the public's disgust with government in general after a year of scandal.[40]

Things had not gone as smoothly in Texas as they had on the set of *Lucy Gallant* or before the New York Sales Executive Club. Deterioration of the political situation showed in Shivers's own behavior and personal concerns. In late 1955, the governor howled that "wild-eyed pinks" had conspired to keep him from attending the coming Democratic national convention. Maury Maverick Jr. saw such comments as evidence "Allan must be getting pretty desperate. . . . It's not like him to make silly statements like that." The ruthless 1954 race had brought into question his personal honesty and business practices, and developments in 1955 had resulted in heightened scrutiny. Governor Shivers responded by lashing out against opponents with increasing frequency—and with much less discretion than in better days.[41]

The hectic pace and mounting criticism apparently led Shivers to worry about his health. He collected articles, including one entitled "Way to Heart Attack," which warned against work habits much like his own. Two notable cardiac arrests in 1955—Lyndon Johnson's and Dwight Eisenhower's—likely intensified his anxiety. Johnson's illness must have been particularly troubling. Both men were the same age, and both possessed the same liking (in intensity if not in volume) for harmful habits: overwork, heavy southern food, cigarettes, and alcohol. Still, as he looked toward another election year, Allan Shivers studied his prospects for a fourth term and began organizing people and issues for the race. Hoping to continue to draw attention on the national stage, he prepared himself to influence both Democratic and Republican presidential strategies.[42]

CHAPTER NINE

Last Fights and Departure 1956–57

GOVERNOR SHIVERS'S POLITICAL FORTUNES HAD SUFFERED tremendously in 1955. Public approval of his leadership diminished to its lowest level ever. Still, Shivers left the press, political insiders, and public guessing as to his plans for 1956. Although he decided against seeking a fourth term as governor, he worked to leave political life while still on top. Allan Shivers, determined to dominate Texas politics until his departure from office, defended segregation in the hope of engineering a political resurgence. Riding white fear of racial equality, he hoped to keep control over the state Democratic Party. By doing so, he would be in position to command national attention in a presidential election year. Moreover, he might lay the groundwork for a possible future return to public life. Instead, he failed to achieve these goals, but remained a powerful behind-the-scenes force in state politics. The last months of 1956 saw him influence national events while his conduct in office devolved into pettiness.

Sometime in early 1956, Shivers decided not to seek a fourth term. The governor and his staff began devising an exit strategy in February. Weldon Hart advised against an early retirement announcement. He suggested the governor allow suspense to build by making a statewide television and radio appearance featuring a canned question-and-answer session. "If we announced in advance that you were going to 'announce,'" Hart explained, a larger audience would tune in. The governor's office intended to keep attention focused upon Shivers. The contrived suspense was to draw attention away from U.S. senator Price Daniel, a likely gubernatorial candidate in the summer primary. Hart noted that all suspense would disappear "if you don't do it [make an announcement about his political future] before Price announces." Rumors that Shivers would not seek reelection had reached Daniel, who desperately wanted to be governor.

The senator was simply awaiting Shivers's own word on retirement before announcing.[1]

Using the canned press conference to rattle Daniel, Governor Shivers explained that he was "seriously considering" a fourth term and planned to clarify his intentions within two weeks. Mail poured into the governor's office from across the state, commenting upon prospects for a fourth term. The majority of the letters that have been preserved favored his continuing in politics. Correspondents cheered his "near announcement," many of them praising Shivers as the only man capable of leading Texas through the challenges of the coming years. Most of those favoring a fourth term downplayed the significance of the previous year's scandals. The minority who advised retirement tended to so from a position of sympathy for the governor. One praised him as being presidential material and urged him not to "get sucked into" another state race. Another letter writer bluntly told Shivers that a fourth-term effort would divide conservatives and land Ralph Yarborough in the governor's mansion.[2]

On March 1, the day after Dwight Eisenhower told Americans he would seek a second term as president, the *Dallas Morning News* announced Shivers would make a broadcast that evening. The governor told Texans he would not run, but would instead finish his term in a crusade for local self-government against "socialistic, do-nothing boys who want to federalize, to centralize all parts of the government." To further this crusade, he urged voters to support the interposition and segregation referenda that would be on the ballot in July. He reassured Texans that they could trust their insurance companies and blamed Bascom Giles for the Veterans' Land Board scandal. He also declared his intention to lead the state Democratic Party in the coming primary and convention season. Although he was leaving politics, Shivers insisted he would fight the national party and bring it back to its roots. The governor intended to carry the struggle to the national convention at the head of Texas' delegation.[3]

Others, however, had similar designs. As early as September, 1955, Sam Rayburn and Lyndon Johnson had begun plotting to seize the Texas delegation as a part of Johnson's efforts to get on the national ticket. In November, Johnson went on record saying that the state's delegation should be pledged in advance to the national party nominee. That same fall, Governor Shivers began searching for an acceptable presidential nominee, suggesting Ohio governor Frank Lausche in a southern-midwestern-western alliance against party liberals. He reiterated this vision in a March, 1956, appearance on NBC's *Meet the Press*. Shivers also refused to pledge himself to the party nominee in advance. Later that spring he initiated a network of precinct and county convention "schools" to prepare Shivercrats for the coming convention battles. At Rayburn's instigation, loyal and liberal Democrats responded in kind.[4]

Johnson wanted a favorite-son nomination, which Rayburn hoped would land the senator the second slot on the national ticket. Mister Sam also wanted to drive Shivers out of the state party and force Johnson to defend party loyalty more actively. At home in Bonham, Rayburn announced a "little squib" for the hometown paper. He endorsed Johnson for favorite son and for state delegation leader. The senate majority leader, the Speaker explained, could put Texas Democrats' "house in order" and "prevent a repetition" of 1952. Rayburn acted without Johnson's consent, and he also left LBJ with no place to hide. On March 25, Shivers had claimed that he would not seek the delegation chairmanship and four days later promised not to deny Johnson the honor. However, the governor left open the chance that "issues" and "principles" might yet bring him into the race.[5]

Senator Johnson worked feverishly to avoid a conflict with Shivers. He negotiated with the governor throughout late March and early April. At one point they appeared agreed that Johnson and railroad commissioner Ernest O. Thompson would cochair the delegation. Shivers, however, was simply playing for time. He hoped to delay a possible alliance between Johnson and Rayburn and party liberals. If he could keep Johnson talking until May, the governor would be able to take control of the county conventions. He then could negotiate from a position of strength. Johnson, meanwhile, grew impatient with the governor's delays. Determined to destroy Shivers's power in the party, Rayburn, with Johnson's blessing, cooperated with Texas liberals in a coup against the Shivercrats. Liberals were not thrilled at the prospect. They preferred a "weekend romance with Lyndon" to marriage. Still, the desire to defeat Allan Shivers trumped all such reservations. By the end of April, the Speaker succeeded in "driv[ing] a sharp wedge between Lyndon and Shivers," according to his aide, D. B. Hardeman, thus forcing Johnson to "join up and fight or suffer a terrible loss of face."[6]

JOHNSON AND SHIVERS HAD HOPED TO AVOID A CONFLICT. THEY FIRST MET when Shivers came to the state senate and Johnson was managing the National Youth Administration in Texas. They attended the same parties and often relied upon the same contacts to advance their careers. Both were tall, dark-haired, hard-driving children of obscure backgrounds. When Johnson went to Congress, they kept in contact. The congressman had helped arrange an early return from war for Major Shivers—in time for the 1945 legislative session. Johnson subsequently helped Shivers with his 1946 race for statewide office. Both shared the friendship and services of Jake Pickle. From time to time, the governor asked Senator Johnson for help with the Internal Revenue Service or to influence legislation in which he had a financial stake.[7]

However, Johnson's career focused on national power and issues. He had stayed with the national party in 1952. He found the tidelands furor silly and

With two rivals, Shivers speaks at the 1952 Tyler Rose Festival. On the far right, Senator Lyndon Johnson cooperated with Shivers on matters important to Texas, but the two clashed in a bid for control over the state Democratic party in 1956. On the far left is Attorney General, later U.S. Senator, Price Daniel. Their rivalry was less ideological and largely personal with each man working to frustrate the designs of the other. Courtesy LBJ Library.

"troublesome." A certain tension existed between the two, as if they were always sizing each other up. "Johnson always figured . . . that the two of them had a rendezvous," mutual friend Horace Busby recalled. "He figured Shivers would be the principal challenger in his life." Johnson must have felt relief when the governor decided not to challenge him in 1954. It seems he liked Shivers, though he hoped to control him and prevent his making mischief. Each man a had formidable personality and ego, along with great talent for political calculation and planning.[8]

Rayburn greatly influenced the senator. Johnson's father had served with Rayburn in the Texas legislature. The Speaker enjoyed a familial closeness with LBJ, his wife, and their children. The old man hated Shivers. Throughout 1952–55, Johnson tried to keep communications open between the two men. Rayburn, however, remained determined to "collect [his] rent off Mr. Shivers," and would not allow a thaw in their chilly relationship. The Speaker pressed Johnson out onto a ledge in 1956. "But I don't want to see Allan kicked around," LBJ protested. "I'll kick him around every chance I get," Rayburn replied. Forced to choose between Rayburn and Shivers, Johnson unhesitatingly chose the former.[9]

The governor knew Rayburn and Johnson needed the support of party liberals to succeed against him. His best hope of influencing Johnson came from this situation. By the time he sent Weldon Hart to meet with the senator in early April to hammer out a compromise, LBJ was tired of waiting. There would be no negotiation. Johnson explained that he could not afford the appearance of a "secret deal" with Shivers. The liberals, he pointed out, had always mistrusted the governor and were looking for any sign of betrayal. Besides, he already had commitments from 199 of Texas' 254 counties. The Shivercrats could either play ball or lose. Shivers's intransigence seemed to pain Johnson, who wanted to know just what Shivers hoped to get from him. The senator pressed Hart for answers. After all, had he not consistently helped the governor in every way during the previous twenty years of their association?[10]

An exasperated LBJ said that with no race of his own to run, Shivers should fall in behind him. A role remained for the governor provided he dropped his rhetoric and reconciled with the party. Hart later wrote in a memo to Shivers describing the meeting: "I rather fear he has listened to his own conversation so long that he is convinced of his own propaganda . . . i.e., that he has sold himself rather completely on the idea of the Big Play now—possibly feeling that the admitted risks are worth the taking, for if he wins he will wind up as an Olympian figure in Texas politics—far, far above Rayburn, Shivers, the gubernatorial candidates and all other small fry . . . a prospect that is entrancing to a man whose Parr used to be 87." Johnson closed the meeting bluntly: "I am running for delegation leader." No quarter was sought or given by either side during the clash.[11]

With the May county conventions just over a month away, Hart told Shivers of a "growing feeling of pessimism" among the faithful. The candidates exchanged harsh words throughout April. Shivers repeatedly demanded to know where Johnson stood on interposition. His staff suggested he accuse Johnson forces of "raising the smokescreen of race to obscure the real principle: whether or not the federal government is to absorb local government." He also hit hard at Sam Rayburn, comparing the House Speaker to Mexican dictator Santa Anna. In addition, Shivers lashed out at Ralph Yarborough, who was in a large field of gubernatorial candidates, calling him a man who "seems determined to set a new record for running in second place." Then, taking a different tack, the governor suggested that he would be willing to support Johnson if the senator professed faith in interposition.[12]

Shivers's shrill attacks on Rayburn and Johnson, both clearly mainstream politicians, demonstrated the desperate energy of his attempt to rally his followers.

Normally loyal Shivercrats showed signs of flagging support as Johnson and Shivers both tapped the same sources for campaign funds. Rancher G. T. McLaughlin's response to Shivers's plea for financial help typified the ambivalence of some of the governor's allies. The cattleman argued that the senator represented Texas' "best hope," adding, "it must be apparent to all that we cannot serve our best purpose withdrawn from both parties." Shivers, McLaughlin continued, had put "many trusted friends on the spot" by challenging Johnson for the delegation chairmanship. Other Shivercrats agreed with Gibb Gilchrist, who wanted "to rise or fall with Allan Shivers" in the fight against Johnson. The numbers of such ardent friends proved too few, however. When the May county conventions concluded, Johnson had won apparent control of the state party, although more fireworks lay ahead. The senator claimed his victory represented popular repudiation of "the demagogue." The governor had lost his last political race.[13]

The summer Democratic primary did not lack excitement, even without Shivers on the ballot. The State Democratic Executive Committee, with Shivers's backing, had placed segregationist referenda on the ballot. Voters were asked to endorse interposition, a stricter ban on interracial marriage, and exemptions from compulsory attendance for students attending integrated schools. Although nonbinding, the referenda promised to attract conservatives to the polls. Running as a conservative with support from the same interests that had supported Shivers, Sen. Price Daniel sought the gubernatorial nomination. Texas House Speaker Reuben Senterfitt also campaigned on the respectable right, but he lacked Daniel's resources. On Daniel's extreme right, West Texas rancher and author J. Evetts Haley and former governor W. Lee O'Daniel ran using segregation and communism as their key issues. Haley sputtered about the red menace, while O'Daniel warned that there would be "blood in the streets" if the federal government tried to integrate Texas schools. Some worried that the four candidates might dilute conservative voting strength, which would benefit Ralph Yarborough, the liberal alternative.[14]

Yarborough promised to "clean up the mess in Austin" and delighted in calling Daniel a "political buddy of Allan Shivers." Though hardly credible, the accusation demonstrated Yarborough's awareness of Shivers's declining stature. The three-time candidate for governor loved the stump and drew enthusiastic crowds. Daniel, on the other hand, had never been a strong campaigner. Even in the midst of a stifling Texas summer, the senator worked the crowds in a coat and tie, looking quite uncomfortable. Both candidates took the high road during the first primary campaign, allowing Haley and O'Daniel to inhabit the gutter. Senator Daniel stressed his commitment to "states' rights," but avoided excess. To prevent any misunderstanding, Yarborough reiterated his opposition to integration, but did not dwell on the issue. Generally, he attacked corruption and elitism while championing the little man. In the July primary, Daniel received 628,817 votes to Yarborough's 463,396. However, the three other conservatives together drew 474,315, forcing the Daniel into a runoff.[15]

Based on these results, Daniel had every reason to expect victory in August. If the conservative voters who had supported his opponents flocked to him, he could expect to gain hundreds of thousands of votes. Matters quickly grew more complicated, however. O'Daniel endorsed Yarborough, boosting him with rural and elderly voters. As in 1954, it appeared the liberal candidate had gained momentum coming out of the first primary. Daniel thus felt compelled to resort to tougher antilabor and prosegregation rhetoric. He also accused his opponent of engaging in a "smear" campaign. Meanwhile, the senator had picked up some needed endorsements of his own. Fellow senator Lyndon Johnson spoke out for Daniel, but so did Allan Shivers. The outgoing governor put aside his disdain for Daniel and attacked his old enemy for dealing in "personalities and wild, unsubstantiated charges." Yarborough responded by calling Daniel the "hand-picked heir to the Shivers throne." The liberal candidate, somewhat unfairly, tied Daniel to the Veteran's Land Board scandal and, somewhat hypocritically, to South Texas' Parr machine.[16]

The bitter runoff favored Daniel by 3,171 votes. With 50.1 percent of the vote, the senator won Texas' major urban areas, whereas Yarborough had an advantage in rural areas and small urban centers. Charges of fraud flew back and forth between the rival camps. Sources close to Daniel described him as "quite upset" by the narrowness of his victory. Yarborough forces cited irregularities in counties all over the state. Ballots went missing or were burned under mysterious circumstances. Liberals and other Yarborough supporters were deeply disappointed. Luckily for them, however, they had helped Johnson and Rayburn take control of the state Democratic Party away from Allan Shivers. The liberals, expecting their reward when the party held its September state convention, were stunned when Johnson, Rayburn, Daniel, and Shivers froze them out of power. Denied seats on the SDEC and prevented from having a seat on Texas' national committee, the liberals cursed Johnson and Rayburn for their duplicity. Shivers was gone, but the Establishment remained in control.[17]

SHORTLY AFTER YARBOROUGH'S DEFEAT, THE TEXAS ADVISORY COMMITTEE on Segregation issued its preliminary report. Weldon Hart reviewed the document for the Governor Shivers and came away appalled. A "lengthy section on constitutional theory" needed a complete revision. The committee's suggestions for state action were "blatantly 'loaded'," Hart told his boss. "If that is what you want, a good job has been done," Shivers's longtime adviser remarked. "I question, however, if leaving ourselves too obviously open to charges of evasion and extremism will accomplish the desired purpose." Committee members suggested legislation that would punish school districts for integrating voluntarily or pursuant to a court order. Hart noted the irony of an administration devoted to local self-government taking such a stand:

> I hope no one will be offended by my somewhat facetious comments. Frankly, this whole approach is contrary to my personal views and sentiments . . . but, then as you know, I am somewhat a reformed liberal and should not be taken too seriously in these matters.
>
> While I am making myself generally obnoxious, I will go one step further and make myself unbearable: I don't think it is a completely satisfactory argument against integration to say that the people of Texas don't like it.

After all, Hart explained, Texans had not liked Prohibition, nor did they like income taxes. At Hart's suggestion, Shivers convinced the committee to drop some of its wilder proposals before it submitted its final report. The advisory panel did excise its recommendation for a state nullification statute to blunt federal laws, but changed little else in the otherwise extremist document.[18]

The TACS presented its final report in September, 1956. The panel's legislative subcommittee proposed that the "white" and "Negro" designations assigned to schools remain. It further recommended legislation that would force integrated districts to resegregate or face losing state funds. Students who felt discriminated against might apply for transfer within a school district, thereby complying, in the committee's view, with *Brown*. Such transfers must take into account matters pertaining to student "welfare," including "compatibility with the children" of the new school, the "welfare" of students at the new school, a comparison of the "academic standards" at the new and old schools, and "any and all [other] reasonable factors." Those ruling on transfer requests would be forbidden to take "race or color" into consideration. Children not wishing to attend integrated schools could be exempted from doing so. The subcommittee members further suggested that state funds be made available for pupils unwilling to attend integrated public schools so that they might receive a nonsectarian private education. The state attorney general's office should be tasked with providing legal advice to those creating such private schools. Moreover, inadequate physical facilities for such nonsectarian private schools should not be a bar to state accreditation.[19]

Even as the state strengthened its commitment to segregation, black communities became more assertive against separation. Segregated school districts often allowed African Americans to serve as subtrustees and represent black students' interests before the white, elected trustees. In early 1955, the black subtrustees of

Mansfield, a small farm town outside Fort Worth, sought improvements for the existing African-American school. They requested a lunch program, better teaching materials, and a bus to transport local black students to Fort Worth's I. W. Terrell High School. Like many smaller districts, Mansfield did not have a black high school, so the district paid transportation and tuition to send its black students to Terrell. When the white trustees failed to act, the subtrustees and local NAACP petitioned for "immediate steps to end segregation" in the district. The trustees belatedly offered to purchase a bus to continue exporting students to Fort Worth. This proved to be too little, too late. In October, L. Clifford Davis, a Fort Worth–based NAACP attorney, filed suit on behalf of three of twelve black high school students seeking integration.[20]

United States District Judge Joseph E. Estes heard the suit in Fort Worth in early November, 1955. Estes was an Eisenhower appointee and new to the federal bench. The school district's lawyers claimed the district needed more time to plan compliance with *Brown*. Public sentiment in the town ran against integration, and the trustees desired to move slowly because of the possibility of violence. Davis, in laying out the plaintiffs' case, simply summarized the U.S. Supreme Court holdings in *Brown* and *Brown II*. He pointed out that the Texas high court had invalidated segregated schools just a few weeks earlier in *McKinney v. Blankenship*. To demonstrate the Mansfield trustees' delaying tactics, he pressed them to explain their proposed timetable for integration. The white trustees had none. Estes stunned the plaintiffs by ruling for the school district and criticizing the lawsuit as "precipitate and without equitable justification." Although school trustees had done nothing to comply with the law, the judge praised their "good faith effort" to "start" in that direction. Having lost the first round, the black students appealed to the Fifth Circuit Court of Appeals in New Orleans.[21]

The Fifth Circuit showed little patience with the trustees' evasions. That spring, it ordered the district to integrate during the coming school year. The appellate justices said Estes's decision for the district violated "plainest principles governing cases of this kind." Moreover, the court held that district officials had "not given any serious consideration to its paramount duty not to delay but to proceed with integration." The case was remanded to Judge Estes's supervision. Tensions rose throughout the summer in anticipation of the new school year. In the August Democratic primary, Mansfield's polling places reported a 95 percent favorable vote in favor of Shivers's segregation referenda.[22]

Meanwhile, a campaign of intimidation against Mansfield's African American community began on August 22. Threatening phone calls awakened community leaders and crosses burned on two consecutive nights in the black section of town. When Judge Estes issued his final integration order on Saturday, August 25, school officials prevailed upon him to delay publicizing his edict until Monday. He complied, but citizens driving through town on Tuesday morning were shocked to see the figure of a black man hanging in effigy over U.S. Highway 287, Mansfield's main street. "This Negro tried to go to a White School," read an attached sign, "wouldn't this be a horrible way to die." On Wednesday, August 29, the white trustees sought a yearlong stay from Estes, but he refused. The Fifth Circuit had specifically rejected public animosity or disorder as justification for delaying integration.[23]

When Thursday dawned, some five hundred whites ringed the high school, determined to obstruct the registration of black students. Mansfield's mayor, police chief, and many other members of the local "power structure" left town. Fanatics from the local Citizens' Council seized power. The crowd outside the school roughed up newsmen from Dallas and Fort Worth. Some in the mob carried firearms. A Tarrant County district attorney narrowly avoided injury after issuing a warning against lawlessness. Sheriff's deputies hustled him away and then left themselves. The mob beat an Episcopal minister who had shown up to urge restraint. Bands of local whites manning roadblocks sought to prevent "outside agitators" from entering town. On Friday, August 31, the pattern repeated itself. Clifford Davis, representing the black students, sent a telegram to Governor Shivers urging him to intervene.[24]

Shivers dispatched two Texas Rangers to Mansfield with orders to arrest anyone who disturbed public order. He then encouraged school officials to expel "any scholastics, white or colored, whose attendance . . . would reasonably be calculated to incite violence." The governor plainly intended to inhibit integration. He assured the town's citizens that legal channels remained to fight desegregation orders. Suggesting an appeal to the U.S. Supreme Court, Shivers argued that such a hearing would offer the justices "an opportunity to view the effect of [*Brown*] on a typical law-abiding Texas community." The governor viewed the public disorder in Mansfield as sufficient justification for his intervention to stop desegregation. If the federal courts wanted to cite local officials for contempt for failing to integrate, Shivers declared, "the charge should be laid against the Governor" instead. "It is not my intention to permit the use of state officers or troops to shoot down or intimidate Texas citizens who are now making orderly protest against a situation instigated and agitated by the National Association for the Advancement of Colored People," Shivers wrote. "At the same time we will protect persons of all races who are not themselves contributing to the breach of the peace. If this course is not satisfactory under the circumstances to the federal government, I respectfully suggest further that the Supreme Court, which is responsible for the order, be given the task of enforcing it."

Shivers had taken the next step down the road to Little Rock, Ole Miss, and Selma. Fortunately, no one died at Mansfield. Black students, however, were still barred from entering the town's schools. A man who had nothing to gain or lose politically had deliberately obstructed a cause of great moral importance. An African-American preacher wrote Shivers from Mansfield a short time later: "[T]he negro cleans house [for whites] cook for [them] nurse thair babyes and keep them clean and go to the navy and army and help fight and die to save this country after all he is accounted less than a dog. . . . [T]he way you did them in Mansfield . . . such as that just prove to the negro who you is."[25]

Mansfield placed the Eisenhower administration in a tricky position. That same week—in Clinton, Tennessee, and Sturgis, Kentucky—two other governors had squelched mob violence and complied with integration orders. In Clinton, the Justice Department had cooperated in prosecuting segregationist mob leaders for contempt of court. The president, however, did not want himself associated with the fight against segregation. Eisenhower thus was loath to act against his ally in Texas. Attorney General Herbert Brownell weakly argued that the administration had been "powerless to intervene." Brownell advised Eisenhower that, absent a contempt citation from Judge Estes, the Justice Department could do nothing in Texas. The attorney general took this line even though his own assistants supported action in Mansfield.[26]

Eisenhower's responses to press questions about Mansfield appeared painfully improvised. On September 5, Ike went to his regularly scheduled press conference well briefed on events in Tennessee, but not those in Texas. Moreover, the president's handlers expected most reporters to be focused on the developing Suez crisis. Asked about the national government's commitment to enforce integration orders, the president seemed unprepared to answer.

> Well in each case I think the local governments have moved very promptly to stop the violence. And let us remember this: under the law, the Federal government cannot—on the ordinary normal case of keeping law and order and preventing rioting—cannot move into a State until the State is not able to handle the matter.
>
> Now in the Texas case there was—the attorney for the students did report this violence and ask help, which apparently was the result of unreadiness to obey a Federal court order. Then before anyone could move, the Texas authorities had moved and order was restored. So the question became unimportant.

When *El Paso Times* reporter Sarah McClendon told the president of Shivers's personal defiance, Eisenhower denied any knowledge of the governor's statements. However, the questions kept coming. Did the president merely accept or did he wholeheartedly endorse the *Brown* decision? "I think it makes no difference whether or not I endorse it," he replied.[27]

The next presidential press conference, conducted on September 11, found Eisenhower better prepared to answer questions about integration in Texas. By that time, not only had Shivers obstructed desegregation in Mansfield, the Texas governor had also intervened at Texarkana Junior College. The president told reporters that since the federal court system had ordered integration in Texas, it was up to those courts to determine what action, if any, should be taken in light of Shivers's defiance. He added that the Justice Department would not intervene unless a federal court issued a contempt citation. Eisenhower then attempted to divert attention from events in Texas by pointing to the successful integration of Louisville, Kentucky's school system. The journalists refused to take the bait and instead probed him all the more about violent encounters in the Lone Star State. "Now," Eisenhower replied, "no one could deplore violence in this thing more than I do. I think that violence sets us back—well, I—years. I think the youngsters that are indulging in violence are not being counseled properly at home."[28]

Eisenhower's mishandling of the Mansfield affair stemmed from more than mere bumbling. The administration clearly had no intention of intervening on the side of integration in 1956. White House press secretary James C. Hagerty described the president as "perfectly well aware" of the euphemistic value of states' rights rhetoric in dealing with white southerners. Eisenhower's press conference performances are more an indication of his determination to mine southern votes than of any deep intellectual crisis over federal power. Ike coupled his nonintervention at Mansfield with equally intentional silence on the virtues of desegregation at Clinton and Sturgis. He viewed civil rights with ambivalence, believing that African Americans had "a place" of their own. White House staffer Frederic Morrow found Ike's position "vexing." Although he had advised the president to make "some kind of gesture" toward the black community in the wake of these incidents, Eisenhower refused to meet with African-American leaders.[29]

Other white southerners also noticed Eisenhower's response to Mansfield. The next summer, when Little Rock, Arkansas, school officials received a federal integration order, Gov. Orval Faubus, an embattled politician who "had no strong feeling about the Negroes," fought against integration despite the local school board's acceptance of it. Faubus had been goaded to take such action in part by a series of full-page advertisements appearing in the *Arkansas Democrat*: "If Governor Shivers of Texas can stop integration, why can't you?" Arkansas's interference with integration drew a strong response from Eisenhower. Years later, Faubus admitted that the president's nonreaction to Mansfield had emboldened him because "Eisenhower did not say a word" in response to Shivers's defiant stand.[30]

JUST OVER A MONTH AFTER THE MANSFIELD DEBACLE, SHIVERS HIT THE campaign trail in support of Eisenhower. He appeared with James F. Byrnes in campaign advertisements televised in Florida, Georgia, North Carolina, South Carolina, Kentucky, Tennessee, Louisiana, and Mississippi. The Texan spoke in person to crowds in Memphis, Nashville, Jacksonville, and Orlando. Weldon Hart advised him to keep to a two-speech schedule, one each in Tennessee and Florida. In Memphis, former Texas Dixiecrat Lamar Fleming Jr., who had connections with that city's Citizens for Eisenhower organization, made the arrangements for Shivers's appearance. Shortly before his trip began, Tennessee governor Frank Clement offered Shivers a bed and a meal at the governor's mansion in Nashville. The Texan begged off the invitation, coming as it did from the man who had integrated Clinton.[31]

The Texas governor used the same basic speech at each appearance. Eisenhower, Shivers explained, "has reversed the trend toward centralization of government and demonstrated a respect for states' rights that his opponent does not hold." He slammed Adlai Stevenson's link with the feared CIO. Southerners, he told crowds, should mistrust a candidate who said one thing about segregation in New Orleans and something else in Harlem. The governor told audiences that his struggles at home were simply part of a larger effort by southerners against agents of the national Democratic Party. "Lyndon Johnson and Sam Rayburn are doing their best to convince the people of Texas that this is a race between them and Allan Shivers," he said. He railed against the Americans for Democratic Action and an organization on which he bestowed the acronym WAACP: the "Washington association for the advancement of certain politicians."[32]

Eisenhower again won nationally. Moreover, despite the efforts of Governor-elect Daniel, House Speaker Rayburn, and Senator Johnson, he carried Texas as well. Both the numbers and percentage of the president's Texas vote increased over 1952. The Republicans, however, remained dependent upon urban and suburban voters. Had urban voters not turned out strongly for the president, he might have lost Texas. This constituency had consistently backed Allan Shivers from his first statewide race to 1954. By 1956, Dallas and Harris Counties together contributed roughly 20 percent of the total state vote for president. Eisenhower increased his percentages in all but one of Texas' five largest counties. On the other hand, rural support for the Republican nominee diminished somewhat, owing to feelings that the administration had failed to deal adequately with farmers' problems. Significantly, these areas had demonstrated strong support for Yarborough since 1954, indicating a relationship between rural voters' views of Shivers and their view of the president.[33]

From early November until January, Governor Shivers waited out his lame-duck period as Daniel's inauguration drew near. In an interview with *U.S. News and World Report*, the outgoing governor pronounced Texas' potential for growth "unlimited." Texas' low taxes and probusiness climate would insure his prediction,

Shivers explained. Shivers fibbed a bit about Texas' low taxes, implying that consumers bore relatively little of the state's tax burden. He insisted that natural resource extraction bore the highest tax burden of all state industries. Somewhat presciently, he predicted that Texas might one day suffer a check on its growth due to water supply issues. He allowed with equal foresight that the day might arrive when Texas would have to look beyond oil for revenue. The tidelands settlement had postponed such a reckoning far into the future, Shivers promised.[34]

For unclear reasons, Shivers labored to make Price Daniel's transition as difficult as possible. The departing politician's behavior toward his successor dripped with pettiness. Early in 1957, with Daniel's inauguration only days away, Shivers appointed a slate of regents for the University of Texas and Texas A&M College. Ordinarily, an incoming governor might expect to nominate his own friends regents. Daniel was furious. He struggled to have the appointments withdrawn in the senate, but Shivers's friends frustrated that effort. Governor Daniel eventually accepted a compromise whereby the nominations would be withdrawn and he would then reappoint the same people. Throughout his service as governor, Daniel faced determined opposition from Shivercrats in the legislature.[35]

Shivers and Daniel engaged in a bitter dispute over how the latter would be replaced in the U.S. Senate. Daniel's victory over Yarborough in the summer Democratic runoff left little doubt about his election as governor. Just over a month later, Daniel announced his conditional resignation as senator effective January 15, 1957. This allowed him to remain in the Senate until inaugurated governor. He then could fulfill his constitutional responsibility to name a successor and set a special election for the unexpired term. Questions arose about whether Daniel's conditional resignation allowed Governor Shivers to call a special election. Shivers refused to do so on the basis of a conditional resignation and flatly accused Daniel of trying to "control both offices." There can be little doubt this was the governor-elect's intention. However, there can be equally little doubt that Shivers wished to control the situation himself.[36]

On December 12, Shivers demanded that Daniel resign his Senate seat. Governor-elect Daniel accused Shivers of wanting to appoint a Republican in his place. Nationally, Eisenhower's coattails had endangered Lyndon Johnson's position as Senate majority leader. The GOP would gain control of the body if Shivers selected a Republican replacement for Daniel. The situation offered a delicious opportunity for revenge against LBJ. However, looking ahead, a misstep might end any hope Shivers had of a return to politics. At this point, President Eisenhower called Shivers to sound out the departing governor about the possibility of a Republican senator from Texas. He told the president he could not appoint a Republican. Ike magnanimously agreed, saying simply, "you can't afford to do it." Years later, Shivers recalled that he had never seriously considered appointing a Republican to succeed Daniel. Instead, barely two hours before Daniel's inauguration, he nominated Dallas millionaire William "Dollar Bill" Blakely, a conservative Democrat. Blakely had ingratiated himself with Shivers during the spring struggle with Johnson over the delegation chairmanship. The senator-designate had returned the more than $13,000 the governor paid for radio and television ads during the failed campaign.[37]

Although the outgoing governor had appointed Blakely, as governor, Price Daniel was able to set the date for the special election: April 2, 1957. Twenty-two hopefuls eventually signed up for the race, including Republican Thad Hutcheson, Rep. Martin Dies, and Ralph Yarborough. From the outset, it appeared likely that conservative voters would be divided among many candidates. This gave Yarborough a good shot at being elected because Texas election law required only a plurality to win. With Johnson and Rayburn's approval, a bill was introduced in the state house in January, 1957, requiring a majority and mandating a runoff should a candidate not obtain one. The bill's sponsor, Rep. Joe Pool of Dallas, had been an important Shivercrat. Because Yarborough's regular host of foes appeared to be in collusion, opponents called the proposal a "gut Yarborough" bill.[38]

However, the dynamics behind Pool's legislation proved much more complex than simply a desire to "gut Yarborough." Rayburn and LBJ genuinely feared a Republican victory under the old rules, which would reduce Johnson to Senate minority leader. Pool, meanwhile, had his eyes on Martin Dies's at-large congressional seat, which would open if Dies won the special election. Even though he was out of office, it appeared to some observers that Shivers and his allies might have a chance to defeat Yarborough yet again. To their surprise, the former governor sought to influence his friends to vote against the proposal. Weldon Hart lobbied legislators against any change. State senator R. A. Weinert of Seguin, one of the former governor's major supporters, deserves most of the credit for defeating the "gut Yarborough" measure. In the end, it may have been Shivers's intention to frustrate Daniel, Rayburn, and Johnson that overrode his distaste for Yarborough. There would be later opportunities for Allan Shivers to act against his liberal nemesis.[39]

ON THE DAY OF PRICE DANIEL'S INAUGURATION, BEFORE LEAVING THE governor's office for the last time, Allan Shivers followed a tradition dating to 1925. That year, Gov. Pat Neff left an open Bible on his desk with a passage marked for his successor, Miriam A. "Ma" Ferguson. Each departing governor since then had chosen a new verse for the entering leader. Daniel, who had always been rankled by Shivers's clean-cut, straight arrow image, thought the outgoing governor's piety was largely for public consumption. The new governor also exhibited less ease with power and had a more fretful personality than his retiring rival. Shivers marked Philippians 4:6 for the new governor: "Be careful for nothing; but in everything by prayer and supplication with thanksgiving let your requests be made known to God."[40]

With that last reverent act, Shivers left public life, although he remained influential in state politics, business, and higher education for nearly thirty years afterward. He had demonstrated remarkable political longevity and instinct. He reached for and grasped greater power than most governors before and since. Allan Shivers made an indelible mark upon the politics of his state and region, but he remains a very elusive figure. His extant public papers reveal little about his personality, and even his allies testify to his aloofness. One of those who puzzled over Shivers was Lyndon Johnson, himself a complex political operator.

Sometime after the 1956 precinct and county battles, Johnson received a call from his defeated opponent. They had not spoken since the bitter fight, but Shivers invited his rival over for drinks. It was midafternoon and they drank, talked, and argued until midnight—at times growing angry. Senator Johnson described the two of them "throwing lances at each other, dodging, jumping like stuck pigs when we was hit." When they parted, all was forgiven—at least for the time being. "I think both of us considered it just another political campaign," Shivers later recalled. "It did get pretty rough at times. We referred to each other in uncomplimentary terms."[41]

Johnson told the story at a dinner party in 1958, according to Johnson aide Billy Brammer, who recalled the following exchange afterward:

"Too bad about Shivers," somebody said.

"Yes," Johnson replied. "He had everything almost. He had the head and he had the heels, and he knew how to use them, but he didn't have a heart. No emotion. Didn't love the people."

"He used to love the people," someone interrupted.

"Yes," Johnson said, but not any longer. The senator gestured broadly around the room, noting its decor and furnishings.

"Here's how you forget," he explained. "You sit here at a big dining table before a cracking fire and carpets three inches thick. Now tell me. Are you very much worried about the suffering in the world at this moment? That's what you have to watch out for."[42]

EPILOGUE

ALLAN SHIVERS'S INFLUENCE ON TEXAS POLITICS GRADUALLY FADED after 1957. He did, however, remain active in state Democratic circles as late as the 1980s. He participated in every conservative attempt to drive Sen. Ralph Yarborough from office. The record indicates the former governor's implacable hatred fed much of his continued interest in state affairs. The feeling was mutual; hating Shivers was an "obsession" with the liberal senator. In 1958, Shivers promoted William Blakely's candidacy for the Democratic U.S. Senate nomination after considering running against Yarborough himself. That effort failed, but six years later, allied with Gov. John Connally and Fort Worth oilman Sid Richardson, Shivers helped raise $500,000 to back right-wing Valley congressman Joe Kilgore. Only determined intervention by Pres. Lyndon B. Johnson, hardly on the best terms with Yarborough himself, saved the liberal senator's seat. When Kilgore dropped out of the running, the former governor attached himself to the Republican candidate, a transplanted Connecticut oilman named George Herbert Walker Bush. Finally, in 1970, Shivers helped recruit and promote the successful challenge of former South Texas congressman Lloyd M. Bentsen Jr.[1]

Shivers's endorsement mattered in state politics long after he left office. He backed his sometime enemy Lyndon Johnson's 1960 bid for the Democratic presidential nomination, but then sided with Richard Nixon against John Kennedy. When Johnson faced ultraconservative Arizona senator Barry Goldwater in 1964, Shivers shocked friend and foe alike by supporting the Democratic incumbent. A Johnson presidency, the former governor argued, was best for Texas and the nation. Shivers rejected both Hubert Humphrey and George McGovern, coming out publicly for Richard Nixon in 1968 and 1972. His last major endorsement of a presidential candidate came in 1984. That year he helped form "Texans for Reagan," a nonpartisan-sounding citizens group intended to attract Democratic voters to the Republican president. He attacked the Democratic ticket, referring to the candidates as "Mondale and the lady." Seventy-six years old, his gray hair still bearing coal-black streaks, Shivers attacked Geraldine Ferraro's critique of Ronald Reagan's religious rhetoric. Reagan was "a good Christian," according to the retired governor, and "the lady" had erred "by getting religion and politics mixed up."[2]

Although he never again sought public office, Allan Shivers served in two important semipolitical capacities in retirement. With Johnson's backing, he became president of the National Chambers of Commerce in 1967. As the nation's leading businessman, he offered mixed reviews of the War on Poverty and the Great Society. He agreed with providing job training to help the impoverished since it helped business as well, but criticized Johnson's close relationship with unions because it rewarded organized labor for "using the public as hostages to enforce its demands on an employer." Throughout the 1970s, the former University of Texas student body president served on and led the university system's board of regents. During his tenure as board chairman, he proved to be a powerful advocate of state higher education, presided over a period of rapid growth, and improved the academic stature of the system's campuses. He announced the end of the "era of destructive students" and urged legislators to see higher-education dollars as money "productively and responsibly spent."[3]

He died in his Austin office of a massive heart attack on January 15, 1985. A silent and aloof man, he unfortunately kept to himself much of what a historian needs to explain his personality and worldview. However, the record shows that he was a powerful political figure who complemented his success with business prowess. To his credit, he and his wife raised a strong family despite living in the fishbowl of politics. They suffered the tragic loss of one child and the debilitating injury of another. Despite his limited and parsimonious approach to government, Shivers and his family gave generously to charities, hospitals, and educational institutions. Memory of Allan Shivers has faded, but the impact he had on the modern politics of Texas and the South continues to be felt.

OF ALL TEXAS GOVERNORS, SHIVERS REMAINS A POLITICAL POWER SUI GENERIS. He looms as the state's most powerful governor since Reconstruction. Shivers emerged as the closest representation of a machine "boss" in modern state politics. He faced no real opposition from any other statewide officeholder, particularly after 1950. Attorney General Price Daniel dared not challenge him. The only dissident state officer, Agriculture Commissioner John White, found himself marginalized outside the Shivercrat camp. Party elements ideologically hostile to Shivers failed to undo him until 1956, and then they succeeded only with the cooperation of Senator Johnson and Speaker Rayburn.

After Shivers, other governors controlled the Democratic Party machinery, but none ever approached his level of dominance. Price Daniel, John Connally, Preston Smith, and Dolph Briscoe each faced vigorous dissent within the party organization and from statewide politicians capable of challenging their leadership. Governor Shivers also proved more adept at controlling the state legislative agenda than most governors before or since. Both Lt. Gov. Ben Ramsey and House Speaker Reuben Senterfitt displayed little independence. His years as state senator and lieutenant governor allowed him to observe other chief executives' interaction with the legislature. Shivers clearly understood the tremendous symbolic and ceremonial importance of the governor's office. Most Texans did not understand and do not yet understand their governor's relative weakness. As governor, he used this to his advantage, going directly to the people to set the public agenda. He early on used television to maximize his public exposure and the impact of his personal strengths: his looks, bearing, and rhetorical skills.

This great power and political acumen might well have been used to bring great advances to Texas. At times, Shivers demonstrated a visionary understanding of the complexities of modern Texas and how state government might best serve its people. He recognized early in his career the limitations of the Constitution of 1876. As lieutenant governor, he backed measures that dramatically improved education funding, proposed an end to the poll tax, and made lynching a state crime. After his ascent to the governor's mansion, he took a risk by proposing a tax increase to remedy scandalous conditions in state eleemosynary institutions. However, he turned his back on efforts to modernize and make the state's rickety tax structure more progressive. He also wasted later opportunities to improve education and other public services. Shivers fought against equality for black Texans and Tejanos. Too often, he fought contrived enemies in set-piece battles over meaningless issues like the tidelands, communist subversion, and petty differences with opponents. The 1950 Goat Speech presaged modern "compassionate conservatism" in Texas. Shivers's reforms served primarily to humanize a business-dominated state government bent upon licensing rapacity. Even at its best, Texas state government has done little else since. Governor Shivers influenced Texas politics long after he left office and helped insure that Texas remains, as one commentator has put it, "Mississippi with good roads."[4]

As a regional political figure, Allan Shivers helped make presidential Republicanism respectable in the Democratic South. Voting Republican for president made it ever easier to vote for the GOP down ballot. By 1994, the region's politics had come to be dominated by a conservative, predominantly white Republican Party that worked to keep state services minimal, taxes low, and business conditions favorable. Southern Republicans exercised national power in Congress and within the national party, working to make its policies ever more like its southern wing.

NOTES

Introduction

1. For the purposes of this study, the South consists of the eleven states that seceded from the Union in 1860–61 and suffered defeat in the American Civil War.

Chapter One. Portrait of the Politician As a Young Man

1. The debate over Texas' proper regional affiliation is ongoing. Few make the unqualified claim that Texas is a part of the West. Some argue that Texas politics is influenced by both western and southern cultural elements. For the purposes of this study, Walter Buenger's recent work is most informative. Buenger has asserted the prevalence of southern attitudes and folkways across the whole of the state. He has also made a compelling argument that late nineteenth-century and early twentieth-century Texans forged a very strong state identity distinct from the rest of the region, which helped move Texas toward modernity. See Walter Buenger, "Texas and the South," *Southwestern Historical Quarterly* 103 (Jan., 2000): 309–24; and *The Path to a Modern South: Northeast Texas Between Reconstruction and the Great Depression*. Patricia Limerick's *The Legacy of Conquest* includes Texas as part of the West, but scarcely mentions the state. George Green's excellent book on Texas politics from 1938–57 is premised on the notion of western and southern cultural elements shaping Texas' political history. See George Green, *The Establishment in Texas Politics: The Primitive Years, 1938–1957*, 3–10. A more recent work emphasizing Texas' southern elements is Randolph B. Campbell, *Gone to Texas: A History of the Lone Star State*.

2. Sam Kinch and Stuart Long, *Allan Shivers: The Pied Piper of Texas Politics*, 8; Frank Lawrence Owsley, *Plain Folk of the Old South*, 58–61; Lou Ella Moseley, *Pioneer Days of Tyler County*, 101, 125; *Population Schedules of the Ninth Census of the United States: 1870*, Manuscript Returns, "Texas," "Tyler County," 426; Randolph B. Campbell, *An Empire for Slavery: The Peculiar Institution in Texas, 1821–1836*, 69–73, 191–94, 209–10; Eugene D. Genovese, *Roll, Jordan, Roll: The World the Slaves Made*, 7–9, 296.

3. "Robert M. Shivers," Confederate Pension Application no. 13100, Tyler County, Texas, Texas State Archives, Texas State Library, Austin (hereafter TSA); Campbell, *Empire for Slavery*, 249; *Ninth Census*, Manuscript Returns; *Population Schedules of the Tenth Census of the United States: 1880*, Manuscript Returns, "Texas," "Tyler County," 390.

4. *Tenth Census*, Manuscript Returns; *Population Schedules of the Twelfth Census of the United States: 1900*, Manuscript Returns, "Texas," "Tyler County"; *Population Schedules of the Thirteenth Census of the United States: 1910*, Manuscript Returns, "Texas," "Tyler County"; Kinch and Long, *Allan Shivers*, 8–9; Moseley, *Pioneer Days*, 164, 194.

5. Martin Sandlin to Martin Dies, Feb. 18, 1933, box 95, Martin Dies Papers, Sam Houston Regional Library and Research Center, Liberty, Tex. (hereafter SHRLRC); George W. Barclay, "Tyler County School Superintendents and Their Administrations, 1912–1978," MS in SHRLRC; Kinch and Long, *Allan Shivers*, 8–9; Bureau of the Census, *Thirteenth Census of the United States*, vol. 3, *Population*, 846–47; ibid., vol. 7, *Agriculture*, 675, 698, 706.

6. Robert S. Maxwell, "One Man's Legacy: W. Goodrich Jones and Texas Conservation," *Southwest Historical Quarterly* 77, no. 3 (Jan., 1974): 359–60; George T. Morgan Jr., "The Gospel of Wealth Goes South: John H. Kirby and Labor's Struggle for Self-Determination, 1901–1916," *Southwest Historical Quarterly* 75, no. 2 (Oct., 1971): 187, 191–92, 194–95.

7. Morgan, "Gospel of Wealth," 188–89, 195–97; Moseley, *Pioneer Days*, 51–52.

8. Kinch and Long, *Allan Shivers*, 8–9.

9. Ibid.; Barclay, "Tyler County School Superintendents"; *Population Schedules of the Fourteenth Census of the United States: 1920*, Manuscript Returns; Lewis L. Gould, *Progressives and Prohibitionists: Texas Democrats in the Wilson Era*, 271–72, 272–73, 275–76. In later years, Allan Shivers tended to exaggerate his father's participation in the campaign, calling him Neff's "county campaign manager." Neff's correspondence relating to the 1920 campaign in Tyler County contains no mention of Robert Andrew Shivers, and there are no letters from him to Neff. The elder Shivers did approach Neff about a judicial appointment in late 1921, but did not receive the job. In his application, Shivers made no mention of having worked for Neff in such a capacity (Robert Andrew Shivers to Neff, Dec. 26, 1921, boxes 2E22 and 2E97, and Neff to Shivers, Dec. 27, 1921, box 2E77, Pat Neff Papers, Texas Collection, Baylor University, Waco, Tex.).

10. Kinch and Long, *Allan Shivers*, 9–10; Jane A. Preddy, "Port Arthur in 1923," *East Texas Historical Journal* 24, no. 1 (1986): 41–45; Keith L. Bryant, "Arthur Stilwell and the Founding of Port Arthur: A Case of Entrepreneurial Error," *Southwestern Historical Quarterly* 75, no. 1 (July, 1971): 19, 28, 29; William Ford Stewart, *Collision of Giants: The Port Arthur Story*, 41–46.

11. Kinch and Long, *Allan Shivers*, 10; Edgar Berlin, interview by author, Oct. 17, 1995, Austin.

12. Ronnie Dugger, "When the Governor Was President—The Saga of a Wheel That Kept Rolling," *Texas Ranger*, Oct., 1949, clipping in Allan Shivers Scrapbooks, Center for American History, University of Texas, Austin (hereafter CAH); *Cactus* (1931, 1932);

J. J. "Jake" Pickle, interview by author, Feb. 6, 1996; Kinch and Long, *Allan Shivers*, 11; D. B. Hardeman, "Shivers of Texas: A Tragedy in Three Acts," *Harper's*, Nov., 1956, 52.

13. Margaret Berry, *UT Austin: Traditions and Nostalgia*, 105; Pickle, interview by author; Creekmore Fath, interview by author, Feb. 20, 1996, Austin; Robert Eckhardt, interview by author, July 10, 1997, Austin.

14. Dugger, "When the Governor"; *Cactus* (1931, 1932).

15. Dugger, "When the Governor"; *Cactus* (1932, 1933); *Daily Texan*, Apr. n.d., 1932; Green, *Establishment*, 135.

16. *Cactus* (1932, 1933); Dugger, "When the Governor."

17. Kinch and Long, *Allan Shivers*, 11–12; Pickle, interview by author; Fath interview; Eckhardt interview; Dugger, "When the Governor." The *Blunderbuss* was actually a bit of a UT tradition having appeared sporadically since April 1, 1914. University administrators struggled to quash it, but it kept coming back (Berry, *UT Austin*, 107–109). Patric was expelled for the *Blunderbuss* broadside five days after his fight with Shivers. He went on to fame as a playwright and screenwriter, satirizing military government in the *Teahouse of the August Moon.*

18. Green, *Establishment*, 13; Kinch and Long, *Allan Shivers*, 12–13.

19. Bureau of the Census, *Fifteenth Census of the United States:* 1930, vol. 3, *Agriculture*, pt. 2, *The Southern States*, 1370–74, 1432–44; idem., *Sixteenth Census of the United States:* 1940, vol. 1, *Agriculture*, pt. 5, *West South Central*, 341–49, 367–71; idem., *Fifteenth Census*, vol. 4, *Occupations by States*, 1560, 1571, 1574; ibid., vol. 1, *Unemployment*, 952–53, 973–79.

20. Kinch and Long, *Allan Shivers*, 12–13; Allan Shivers, paid political advertisement (1934), box 1977/81-425, Allan Shivers Papers, TSA (hereafter Shivers Papers).

21. Shivers, paid political advertisement (1934); W. R. Cousins handbill (1934), box 1977/81-425, Shivers Papers; Kinch and Long, *Allan Shivers*, 13; William Free to Alf Roark, June 25, 1934, box 1, Alfred Roark Papers, SHRLRC (hereafter Roark Papers).

22. Kinch and Long, *Allan Shivers*, 13.

23. Ibid., 13–14. Shivers defeated Cousins, 17,365 to 14,199 (Fourth State Senate District, Election Returns, Democratic Primary, July, 1934, Elections Division, Texas Secretary of State, TSA [hereafter Elections Division]).

24. Shivers to Roark, Dec. 11, 1934, and July 8, 1935, box 1; and E. H. Thornton to Roark, Dec. 3, 1935, box 2, Roark Papers.

25. Shivers to Roark, Aug. 11, Sept. 21, and Nov. 1, 1936; and Quentin Keith to Roark, Oct. 3, 1936, box 3, Roark Papers.

26. Kinch and Long, *Allan Shivers*, 25–27; Shivers to Roark, Nov. 1 and 10, 1936, box 3; and ibid., n.d. (late 1936), and Roark to Shivers, Aug. 24, 1937, box 5, Roark Papers.

27. Kinch and Long, *Allan Shivers*, 44; Berlin interview; Will Wilson, interview by author, Sept. 12, 1995, Austin; Fred Schmidt, interview by author, Oct. 10, 1995, Fredericksburg, Tex.

28. Among those who viewed Shivers as plainly conservative were Jake Pickle and John Osorio, a former aide, lawyer, and business partner (Pickle, interview by author; John Osorio, interview by author, Dec. 29, 1997, Dallas, Tex.).

29. Regarding Allred, his reputation as a liberal, and his program, see William Eugene Atkinson, "James V. Allred: A Political Biography, 1899–1935" (Ph.D. diss., Texas Christian University, 1978); Green, *Establishment*, 14–16; *Texas Food Journal* 10, no. 10 (Oct., 1935): 6–7, copy in box 1977/81-425, Shivers Papers.

30. Kinch and Long, *Allan Shivers*, 18–19, 23; W. C. Todd to James Allred, Feb. 1 and Feb. 4, 1936, box 106, James V. Allred Papers, Department of Special Collections, University of Houston, Houston (hereafter Allred Papers); *State Observer* (Austin), Jan. 24, 1938.

31. Kinch and Long, *Allan Shivers*, 18–19, 23; *State Observer* (Austin), Jan. 24, 1938.

32. Kinch and Long, *Allan Shivers*, 31; Green, *Establishment*, 22; "18th Biennial Report of the Joint Railway Legislative Board of Texas and the Texas Federation of Labor for 1937 and 1938," box 1977/81-425, Shivers Papers.

33. Kinch and Long, *Allan Shivers*, 31; Fourth State Senate District, Election Returns, Democratic Primary, July, 1938, Elections Division.

Chapter Two. Turmoil and Transition

1. V. O. Key Jr., *Southern Politics in State and Nation*, 4, 5–9, 307; Chandler Davidson, *Race and Class in Texas Politics*, 3–6.

2. Key, *Southern Politics*, 254–76 (specifics on Texas), 299–301, 307, 310–11, 510–11, 646, 669–70, 673–75; Davidson, *Race and Class*, 12–15.

3. Green, *Establishment*, 16–17.

4. Key, *Southern Politics*, 265–67; Green, *Establishment*, 22–25; radio address, Sept. 8, 1940, box 4-14/194, W. Lee O'Daniel Papers, TSA (hereafter O'Daniel Papers).

5. Green, *Establishment*, 26–27.

6. Ibid., 29, 31–32; radio address, Mar. 16, 1941, box 4-14/194, O'Daniel Papers. Letters reporting suspicious activity to O'Daniel can be found in box 4-14/242, O'Daniel Papers. One such letter reported a Nazi cell operated on John Shary's Valley citrus plantation (Ernest Mullins to O'Daniel, May 21, 1940, ibid.).

7. Green, *Establishment*, 32–38.

8. Ibid., 24–27; *Journal of the Texas Senate* (hereafter *Senate Journal*), 46th Leg. reg. sess. (1939), 1845; E. N. Wadley to Shivers, Apr. n.d., 1939, box 4-14/194, O'Daniel Papers.

9. Green, *Establishment*, 26; *Senate Journal*, 46th Leg. reg. sess. (1939), 1154; ibid., 47th Leg. reg. sess. (1941), 682.

10. Green, *Establishment*, 31–32; "46th Legislature Report Card, Nineteenth Biennial Report of the Joint Railway Legislative Board of Texas and the Texas Federation of Labor," "47th Legislative Report Card, Twentieth Biennial Report of the Joint Railway Legislative Board of Texas and the Texas Federation of Labor," and W. R. Cousins handbill (1942), all in box 1977/81-425, Shivers Papers.

11. Green, *Establishment*, 32–39; list of guests at Port Arthur dinner honoring Lyndon B. Johnson, Nov. 11, 1941, box 146, Allred Papers; Joe Betsy Allred to John Shary, May 30, 1942, box 1977/81-425, Shivers Papers.

12. Kinch and Long, *Allan Shivers*, 33.

13. On wider southern dissatisfaction with Roosevelt and the New Deal, see Kari Frederickson, *The Dixiecrat Revolt and the End of the Solid South, 1932–1968*, 16–27.

14. Robert Dalleck, *Lone Star Rising: Lyndon Johnson and His Times, 1907–1960*, 192–96; Richard Henderson, *Maury Maverick: A Political Biography*, 203–205; David M. Kennedy, *Freedom from Fear: The American People in Depression and War, 1929–1945*, 456–57; D. B. Hardeman and Donald C. Bacon, *Rayburn: A Biography*, 232–33, 235–39; Green, *Establishment*, 29–30.

15. Green, *Establishment*, 29–30; Bacon and Hardeman, *Rayburn*, 232–33, 235, 239; Henderson, *Maury Maverick*, 203–208; Dalleck, *Lone Star Rising*, 192–96.

16. *Congressional Record*, 75th Cong., 2d sess., Nov. 16 and 17, 1937; Carl White to Shivers, Feb. 20, 1937; Wendell Willkie, "We the People, a foundation for a platform for recovery"; idem., "The Faith That Is America"; E. B. Germany, "Pioneers of the Future," to the Young Democrats of Texas, Apr. 1, 1939; and Frank Gannett at Indiana State Fair, Sept., 1939, in *Congressional Record*, 76th Cong., 1st sess., Oct. 25, 1939, clipping, all in box 1977/81-424; and Shivers to Tom Connally, Dec. 21, 1937, box 1977/81-423, Shivers Papers.

17. "Friend Jasper," by Harvey Briggs, n.d., ca. 1939–40, box 1977/81-424, Shivers Papers; Jimmy Banks, *Money, Marbles, and Chalk: The Wondrous World of Texas Politics*, 120.

18. Green, *Establishment*, 12–13, 72–73, 83–86; Schmidt interview.

19. Green, *Establishment*, 84–89.

20. William McGill to Shivers, July 31 and Aug. 2, 1937, box 1977/81-423; and Lennox Lee Moak, "Manager Government in Port Arthur, Texas"; A. W. Walker Jr. to Shivers, Mar. 1, 1943; and Shivers to Walker, Mar. 8 and Apr. 9, 1943, all in box 1977/81-424, Shivers Papers.

21. Green, *Establishment*, 43–47; Key, *Southern Politics*, 256.

22. Green, *Establishment*, 49–52; Key, *Southern Politics*, 256.

23. Green, *Establishment*, 49–50, 143, 146; Kinch and Long, *Allan Shivers*, 17–18, 39, 111–12; Davidson, *Race and Class*, 75–76.

24. Robert A. Calvert and Arnoldo DeLeón, *The History of Texas*, 325–28, 336; Numan V. Bartley, *The New South, 1945–1980: The Story of the South's Modernization*, 8–11; Bureau of the Census, *Sixteenth Census of the United States: 1940*, pt. 6, *Pennsylvania–Texas*, 1, 10; idem., *1950 Census of Population*, vol. 2, *Characteristics of Population*, pt. 43, *Texas*, 13, 55.

25. Calvert and DeLeón, *History of Texas*, 333–36; Bartley, *New South*, 110–11.

26. Frederickson, *Dixiecrat Revolt*, 30–32, 39–40; Bartley, *New South*, 7–9, 12–15; Calvert and DeLen, *History of Texas*, 329.

27. Lorry A. Jacobs to Stevenson, Sept. 28, 1942, box 4-14/164; J. L. Block to Stevenson, Apr. 26, 1943; John C. Thompson, June 18, 1943; and E. K. Anderson to Stevenson, July 1, 1943, all in box 4-14/136; Stevenson to Leonard Brinn, June 7, 1944; Malcolm Ross to Stevenson, June 11, 1944; and W. Don Ellinger to Stevenson, July 11, 1944, all in box 4-14/170; and L. H. Kassel to Stevenson, Sept. 13, 1945, box 4-14/145, Coke Stevenson Papers, TSA (hereafter Stevenson Papers).

28. Green, *Establishment*, 79–80.

29. Ibid., 80–81. Regarding the relationship between Anglos and Hispanics in Texas, see Arnoldo DeLeón, *They Called Them Greasers: Anglo Attitudes Toward Mexicans in*

Texas, 1821–1900; David Montejano, *Anglos and Mexicans in the Making of Texas, 1836–1986*; and Stevenson to Eziquiel Padilla, July 12, 1943, box 4-14/155, Stevenson Papers.

30. Green, *Establishment*, 80–81; *Senate Journal*, 49th Leg., reg. sess. (1945), 300, 617, 643–44, 803, 869–70.

31. Green, *Establishment*, 81; B. E. Howell and G. F. Porter to Stevenson, Aug. 3, 1943, and Elosa Galn to Stevenson, Sept. 15, 1943, box 4-14/136; and Malcolm Ross to Stevenson, June 11, 1944, box 4-14/170, Stevenson Papers.

32. Calvert and DeLeón, *History of Texas*, 343–46; Bartley, *New South*, 29; Green, *Establishment*, 98. Polls indicated that 44 percent of Texans favored the *Smith* decision with a crucial difference in opinion evident from one region of the state to another. Only 38 percent of East Texas residents favored an end to the white primary, compared to 55 percent in West Texas (Allan Scott, "Twenty-five Years of Opinion on Integration in Texas," *Southwestern Social Science Quarterly* 48 [Sept., 1967]: 156).

33. *Beaumont Journal*, May 31, 1945; Kinch and Long, *Allan Shivers*, 3–5, 37.

Chapter Three. "That All Depends upon God and Allan Shivers"

1. *Beaumont Journal*, May 31, 1945; Herman Brown to Shivers, Apr. 6, 1945, and Maynard Robinson to Shivers, Oct. 25, 1945, box 1977/81-423, Shivers Papers.

2. Bartley, *New South*, 26–27, 40–41.

3. SR-46 draft, Mar. n.d., 1945; Bob Blanton to Shivers, Mar. 20, 1945; L. Welch to Shivers, Mar. 30, 1945; O'Daniel to Shivers, Mar. 30, 1945; Emile Zoller to Shivers, July 12, 1945; Joe Steadham to Shivers, July 16, 1945, Charles Richker et al. to Shivers, Oct. 8, 1945; and Shivers to Richker, Oct. 10, 1945, all in box 1977/81-325, Shivers Papers; *Senate Journal*, 49th Leg., reg. sess. (1945), 379, 577, 1053–54.

4. Kinch and Long, *Allan Shivers*, 39–40; *Beaumont Journal*, Jan. 30, 1946; *Beaumont Enterprise*, Feb. 17, 1946; *Port Arthur News*, Feb. 17 and Mar. 10 and 11, 1946.

5. Green, *Establishment*, 103–104; Bartley, *New South*, 39–42, 44–49, 76–77; Coke Stevenson to Louis Bailey, Mar. 20, 1946, and *Sweatt v. Painter*, typescript of opinion from 126th District Court, Travis County, Tex., June 17, 1946, box 4-14/147, Stevenson Papers. Additional coverage of the tensions during that year can be found in Frederickson, *Dixiecrat Revolt.*

6. Green, *Establishment*, 90–96; Hazel Avery to Shivers, May 8, 1946, and Bessie Pierce to Shivers, June 4, 1946, box 1977/81-375, Shivers Papers. Emphasis in the original. Kinch and Long portray the lieutenant governor's race as a gentlemanly contest, but this understanding was based upon twenty years of reflection and runs quite contrary to the written record (*Allan Shivers*, 40–41).

7. Kinch and Long, *Allan Shivers*, 40–41.

8. "Boyce House's Rival Welcomes CIO-PAC Support for 12 Years," broadside, box 1977/81-424, Shivers Papers; *Houston Post*, Aug. 22, 1946.

9. *Houston Post*, July 25, 1946; J. Evetts Haley to Shivers, July 26, 1946, and H. L. Mills to Shivers, Aug. 21, 1946, box 1977/81-375, Shivers Papers.

10. *San Antonio Express*, Aug. 17, 1946; *Fort Worth Star-Telegram*, Aug. 18, 1946.

11. *Port Arthur News*, July 31 and Aug. 2, 1946; *Beaumont Enterprise*, Aug. 3, 1946.

12. Affidavit granting proxy of Richard Young to Allan Shivers for Jefferson County Democratic Convention, Aug. 3, 1946, box 1977/81-423, Shivers Papers; *Beaumont Enterprise*, Aug. 4, 1946.

13. *Texas Almanac: 1947–1948*, 404, 417–19. The Pearson correlation of Rainey voters to Shivers voters is .958; .878 between Rainey and House voters; .924 between Jester and House voters, and .934 between Jester and Shivers.

14. Bartley, *New South*, 38–43; Shivers to Richker, Oct. 10, 1945; *Port Arthur News*, July 31 and Aug. 2, 1946; *Beaumont Enterprise*, Aug. 3, 1946.

15. *Dallas Morning News*, June 28, 1946; Shivers radio address, July 27, 1946, and *Gonzales Enquirer*, Aug. 22, 1946, clipping, box 1977/81-422, Shivers Papers; *Houston Post*, July 16, 1946. See Williamson, *The Crucible of Race*, 22–23, 82–83, 292–95 on various styles of southern white racism.

16. Mack H. Hannah to Shivers, Sept. 28, 1946, and Shivers to Hannah, Oct. 10, 1946, box 1977/81-431, Shivers Papers.

17. C. W. Hansen to Shivers, Aug. 25, 1946; *Texas CIO Notes*, Sept. 3, 1946; and Leon Brown to Shivers, Aug. 26, 1946, all in box 1977/81-375, Shivers Papers.

18. Calvert and DeLeón, *History of Texas*, 146–51. A good overview of the executive branch is in Eugene Jones, Joe Ericson, Lyle Brown, and Robert Trotter Jr., *Practicing Texas Politics*, 200–310.

19. Jones et. al., *Practicing Texas Politics*, 306–307; Kinch and Long, *Allan Shivers*, 46–47.

20. Kinch and Long, *Allan Shivers*, 49; Berlin interview.

21. *Austin American*, Jan. 28, 1949; *Corpus Christi Caller-Times*, Jan. 30, 1949; *Houston Post*, Jan. 31, 1947.

22. Shivers repeatedly favored similar legislation while a senator, although it never passed (Allan Shivers paid political advertisement [1934], box 1977/81-425; *Port Arthur News*, Oct. 12, 1942, clipping, box 1977/81-424; and Irene Lohman Davis to 50th Leg., Mar. 12, 1947, box 1977/81-417, Shivers Papers). In 1948, Davis became an active member and financial backer of the Texas Dixiecrats (*Senate Journal*, 50th Leg., reg. sess. [1947], 66, 542, 1347, 1349).

23. Green, *Establishment*, 80–81, 139–40; GNC minutes, Oct. 2, 1945, box 1989/59–1, Good Neighbor Commission Papers, TSA (hereafter GNC Papers); Arnoldo DeLeón, "Our Gringo Amigos: Anglo Americans and the Tejano Experience," *East Texas Historical Journal* 32 (1993): 74; Montejano, *Anglos and Mexicans*, 270–71.

24. Green, *Establishment*, 81, 139–40; Pauline Kibbe, *Latin Americans in Texas*; GNC minutes, Mar. 24, 1947, box 1989/59–1; and Kibbe, report to GNC on Lower Rio Grande Valley Trip, Apr. 17–27, 1947, box 1990/16–1, GNC Papers; M. B. Morgan to Beauford Jester, Nov. 21, 1947, box 4-14/62, Beauford Jester Papers, TSA (hereafter Jester Papers).

25. Green, *Establishment*, 139–40; R. E. Smith to William McGill, May 22, 1947; Pauline Kibbe to McGill, July 30, 1947; R. E. Smith to Jester, Nov. 18 and Aug. 6, 1947; and Oscar C. Dancy to Jester, July 9, 1947, all in box 4-14/122, Jester Papers; Eckhardt interview. Eckhardt worked as a lawyer for the GNC and resigned when Kibbe did in 1947. Smith

believed Eckhardt's presence on the GNC was proof that CIO sympathizers dominated the agency (*Austin Statesman*, Sept. 4, 1947; *Dallas Morning News*, Sept. 5, 1947). The whole Kibbe affair seemed to tax the patience of the male power structure. Jester and Smith agreed not only to "cull out political misfits" in choosing a new director for the GNC, but also that the new director not be a woman. Whether the male leaders feared having to pull their punches with a woman agency director or whether they feared a woman might be too soft was not indicated.

26. Green, *Establishment*, 104–105; *Dallas Morning News*, Apr. 3 and 8, 1947.

27. Harvard Sitkoff, "Harry Truman and the Election of 1948: The Coming of Age of Civil Rights in American Politics," *Journal of Southern History* 37, no. 4 (Nov., 1971): 615.

28. Ibid., 597; David McCullough, *Truman*, 570, 586–88, 589–90, 593; Green, *Establishment*, 108–11; *Fort Worth Star-Telegram*, Feb. 4, 1948; *Dallas Morning News*, Feb. 4, 1948.

29. Paul Brown and Allen Duckworth, telephone transcript, Feb. 19, 1948; Paul Brown to Jester, telegram, Mar. 4, 1948; and John Lee Smith to Jester, Apr. 27, 1948, all in box 4-14/93, Jester Papers; Green, *Establishment*, 109–10; *Beaumont Enterprise* and *Port Arthur News*, May 26, 1948.

30. Shivers to W. M. Townsend and Shivers to Lillie Garrett, Mar. 1, 1948, box 1977/81-418, Shivers Papers.

31. Shivers to E. N. Holmgreen, May 3, 1948, box 1977/81-418, Shivers Papers; *Austin American*, Apr. 14, 1948; Kinch and Long, *Allan Shivers*, 50. Shivers's lack of determined opposition was not reflected in other statewide races. Jester drew seven opponents and avoided a run-off with 52 percent of the vote.

32. Wilson interview; Shivers to W. M. Townsend, Feb. 24, 1948, box 1977/81-418, Shivers Papers; McCullough, *Truman*, 674–79; Green, *Establishment*, 112. Prior to LBJ's entry into the 1948 U.S. Senate race, Shivers's favored candidate had been George Peddy, a Houston lawyer connected to the Dixiecrats (Shivers to Holmgreen, May 3, 1948). Regarding Peddy's ideology, see Dale Baum and James L. Haley, "Lyndon Johnson's Victory in the 1948 Texas Senate Race: A Reappraisal," *Political Science Quarterly* 109, no. 4 (fall, 1994): 595–602.

33. John C. Calhoun to Jester, Dec. 21, 1948; Weldon Hart to Melvin Hildreth, Dec. 28, 1948; and Jester to Wright Morrow, Jan. 11, 1949, all in box 4-14/82, Jester Papers; Johnson to Shivers, Feb. 7, 1949, box 1977/81-477, Shivers Papers; McCullough, *Truman*, 733.

34. Green, *Establishment*, 117; *Senate Journal*, 51st Leg., reg. sess. (1949), 26, 163, 623–30, 769, 1361, 1393, 1413; *Journal of the Texas House of Representatives* (hereafter *House Journal*), 51st Leg., reg. sess., (1949), 2:1686, 2:1696, 2:1954–56; Kinch and Long, *Allan Shivers*, 57; Berlin interview.

35. Jester radio address, May 21, 1948; Jester to S. J. Isaacks, Jan. 11, 1949; William McGill to Jester, memo, May 30, 1949; and Jester to Hill Hudson, June 19, 1949, all in box 4-14/106, Jester Papers; *Senate Journal*, 51st Leg., reg. sess. (1949), 344, 348, 416, 1045, 1294, 1667.

36. Green, *Establishment*, 117–19; Report of the Gilmer-Aikin Committee, n.d., 1948, and Jester, memo to Gilmer-Aikin Committee, n.d., 1948, box 4-14/103, Jester Papers.

37. Gilmer-Aikin Committee Report; Jester, memo to Gilmer-Aikin Committee; *Senate Journal*, 51st Leg., reg. sess. (1949), 143.

38. L. O. Ireson to Jester, Mar. 6, 1948, and Robert Johnson to Jester, Mar. 7, 1948, box 4-14/69; and William McGill to Jester, memo, Feb. 13, 1949, box 4-14/110, Jester Papers; *Senate Journal*, 51st Leg., reg. sess. (1949), 143, 191, 1114; *Austin Statesman*, Feb. 17, 1949; Green, *Establishment*, 115.

39. *Austin Statesman*, Feb. 17, 1949; *Senate Journal*, 51st Leg., reg. sess. (1949), 143, 191, 1114.

40. Bartley, *New South*, 149–51; Green, *Establishment*, 117–19; Gilmer-Aikin Technical Memo no. 2, Feb. 15, 1948, box 4-14/69, Jester Papers; Gilmer-Aikin Committee Report. The foundation funding system ended up in the U.S. Supreme Court in 1973 (*San Antonio Independent School District v. Rodriguez*, 411 U.S. 1). In 1989, the Texas Supreme Court unanimously overturned the state's school finance system, touching off a series of legislative and legal battles that have yet to be fully resolved.

41. Green, *Establishment*, 119; Kinch and Long, *Allan Shivers*, 47–48; "Factors Related to House Bill 52, Creating Lamar State College of Technology," memo, n.d. (1949), box 4-14/46, Jester Papers.

42. Kinch and Long, *Allan Shivers*, 56–57; Green, *Establishment*, 147.

43. Joe Pool to Shivers, Dec. 5, 1946, box 1977/81-375; and David Read to Shivers, July 25, 1947, and Doyle Willis to Shivers, Aug. n.d., 1947, box 1977/81-418, Shivers Papers; *Port Arthur News*, July 27, 1947; *Beaumont Enterprise* and *Port Arthur News*, May 26, 1948; *Austin American* and *Dallas Morning News*, June 10, 1949. Regarding Culberson as a conservative rival, see Green, *Establishment*, 137–38.

44. *San Antonio Light*, Apr. 24, 1949; Daniel to Tom P. Cooper, Mar. 7, 1949; Cooper to Shivers, Mar. 25, 1949; and Price and Shivers to Cooper, Mar. 31, 1949, all in box 1977/81-477; and Bernard Ladon to Shivers, May 4, 1949, and Ken Harper to Shivers, May 10, 1949, box 1977/81-472, Shivers Papers; *Beaumont Journal*, May 20, 1949; *Fort Worth Star-Telegram*, May 25, 1949; *Beaumont Enterprise*, May 25, 1949.

45. *Austin Statesman*, July 11, 1949; *Houston Post*, July 12, 1949.

46. Kinch and Long, *Allan Shivers*, 59–63.

Chapter Four. Ascent and Election in His Own Right

1. Banks, *Money, Marbles, and Chalk*, 143.

2. Green, *Establishment*, 137–38; Jake Pickle to Shivers, memo, "General Political Picture," n.d. (1950), box 1977/81-283, Shivers Papers.

3. Banks, *Money, Marbles, and Chalk*, 119; Richard Morehead, *Fifty Years in Texas Politics*, 91; George Christian, interview by author, July 27, 1997, Austin; Osorio interview; Berlin interview.

4. Green, *Establishment*, 137–38; Pickle to Shivers, memo, "General Political Picture"; Pickle's "Field Notes," Oct. 1–15, 1949, and Feb. 13–18, 1950, box 1977/81-283, Shivers Papers. Pickle's "Little Red Arrow" suggestion refers to former Texas attorney general Gerald Mann. Mann earned the nickname for both his running ability and his piety

while playing football at Southern Methodist University (Schmidt interview; J. J. "Jake" Pickle, interview by Joe Frantz, Mar. 1, 1971, AC81-76, Oral History Collection [OHC], Lyndon Baines Johnson Library, Austin [hereafter LBJL]).

5. Green, *Establishment*, 137; Hart to Shivers, Oct. 12, 1949, box 1977/81-239, and Dec. 30, 1949, box 1977/81-372, Shivers Papers; Banks, *Money, Marbles, and Chalk*, 143–46; Osorio interview.

6. Frank Rawlings to Shivers, Jan. 26, 1950, box 1977/81-125; Hart to Shivers, Jan. 2, 1950, box 1977/81-239; Fred Korth to Shivers, Jan. 24, 1950, box 1977/81-282; and Arch Rowan to Shivers, Jan. 21 and Feb. 6, 1950, and Shivers to Rowan, Feb. 3, 1950, box 1977/81-143, Shivers Papers.

7. Green, *Establishment*, 137–38; Morehead, *Fifty Years*, 93; Osorio interview; Christian interview.

8. Green, *Establishment*, 137–38; Kinch and Long, *Allan Shivers*, 70–75; Osorio interview; Christian interview; Bill Youngblood to William McGill, Jan. 23, 1950, box 1977/81-125, Shivers Papers.

9. McGill to Shivers, n.d. (Nov. or Dec., 1949), and Dec. 30, 1949, box 1977/81-126; and Jan. 13, 22, and 24, 1950, box 1977/81-134, Shivers Papers.

10. McGill to Shivers, Jan. 13, 22, and 24, 1950.

11. *Senate Journal*, 51st Leg., 1st called sess., 145, 148, 158, 175, 228–30, 242; *House Journal*, 51st Leg., 2d called sess., 265, 404–407; *Austin Statesman*, Feb. 28, 1950; *Beal v. Holcombe*, 103 F.Supp. 218 (D.C.S.D.C.Tx); *Beal v. Holcombe*, 193 F. 2d. 384; *Beal v. Holcombe*, cert. denied, 347 U.S. 974.

12. Green, *Establishment*, 81, 140.

13. Ibid., 140; Robert Dalleck, *Lone Star Rising*, 369; Hector Garcia to Lyndon Johnson, Jan. 10, 1949; John B. Connally to Johnson, memo, Jan. 14, 1949; Johnson to Three Rivers Chamber of Commerce, telegram, Jan. 17, 1949; R. E. Smith to Gus Garcia, Jan. 17, 1949; and Shag Floore to Lt. Col. Stanley Partridge, Jan. 21, 1949, all in box 2; and Gus Garcia to Johnson, Mar. 16 and 25, 1949, box 3, Pre-Presidential Confidential Files, Lyndon B. Johnson Papers, LBJL; Tom Sutherland to William McGill, memo, Mar. 5, 1949; McGill to Sutherland, memo, Mar. 7, 1949; and telephone transcript R. E. Smith and McGill, Feb. 3, 1949, all in box 4-14/69, Jester Papers; *House Journal*, 51st Leg., reg. sess., Feb. 17, 1949.

14. Green, *Establishment*, 140–41; Neville Penrose, "Log of the Good Neighbor Commission, Sept., 1949–Feb., 1950, and Penrose to John C. Gregg, Dec. 19, 1949, box 1977/81-259; and Hector Garcia to McGill, May 9, 1950, and Marlin Sandlin to Shivers, May 8, 1950, box 1977/81-131, Shivers Papers; Shivers press memo, May 4, 1950, box 1989/59–19, GNC Papers.

15. McGill to Shivers, Aug. 2, 1949, box 1977/81-232; and American G.I. Forum Resolution, Sept. 26, 1949, and McGill to J. W. Edgar, Mar. 21, 1950, box 1977/81-127, Shivers Papers; Montejano, *Anglos and Mexicans*, 260–61.

16. McGill to Sutherland, Oct. 15, 1949; Sutherland to McGill, memo, Nov. 2, 1949; and Garcia to Sutherland, Dec. 2, 1949, all in box 1977/81-132; and Garcia to Shivers, telegram, Feb. 20, 1950, and *La Verdad* (Corpus Christi), Feb. 24, 1950, clipping, box 1977/81-139, Shivers Papers.

17. Clifton Carter to Weldon Hart, Jan. 28, 1950, and Creekmore Fath notation on H. M. Morgan et al. to Shivers, Mar. 3, 1950, 1977/81-372; McGill to O. E. Cannon, Mar. 1, 1950, and McGill to Shivers, Mar. 2 and 8, 1950, box 1977-81/139; and John VanCronkhite to Shivers, June 6, 1950, box 1977/81-195, Shivers Papers; Green, *Establishment*, 186.

18. *Houston Informer*, Apr. 25, 1950; *Dallas Morning News*, May 28, 1950; *Houston Chronicle*, June 3, 1950. Ironically, Texas' Young Democrats voted the same day to integrate chapters on a local-option basis.

19. *Dallas Morning News*, June 6, 1950; *San Antonio Express*, June 16, 1950; *Sweatt v. Painter*, 339 U.S. 629 (1950). Two other important civil rights cases were also decided that day. *Henderson v. United States*, 339 U.S. 816 (1950), integrated railroad dining cars, while *McLaurin v. Oklahoma*, 339 U.S. 637 (1950), in a vein similar to *Sweatt*, integrated Oklahoma University's graduate school. *Sweatt* and *McLaurin* argued that professional, graduate, and undergraduate schools all provided a specialized variety of education that could not be made "separate, but equal" because the connections, opportunities, experiences, and relationships they engendered could not be duplicated. In other words, the slapdash "law school" Texas provided Heman Sweatt would never be equal to that of the University of Texas.

20. D. K. Woodward to Beauford Jester, May 18, 1949, and Jester to Shivers and Jester to Durwood Manford, May 25, 1949, all in box 4-14/52, Jester Papers; *Dallas Morning News*, June 6, 1950.

21. Lindsy Pack, "The Political Aspects of the Texas Tidelands Controversy" (Ph.D. diss., Texas A&M University, 1979), 1, 10–21; *Pollard v. Hogan*, 3 How. 212 (1845); Alvin J. Wirtz to Lyndon Johnson, Mar. 11, 1949, box 48, Tom C. Clark Papers, Harry S. Truman Library (hereafter HSTL), Independence, Mo. (hereafter Clark Papers). For the purposes of this study, the term *tidelands* refers to the offshore lands claimed by Texas, as well as similar lands in other states.

22. Pack, "Political Aspects," 22–29.

23. Ibid., 31–37; Harold Ickes to Truman, July 17, 1945, box 336, Official File (hereafter OF), Harry S. Truman Papers, HSTL (hereafter Truman Papers).

24. *United States v. California*, 332 U.S. 19 (1947); Pack, "Political Aspects," 39, 44–45; *Austin Statesman*, June 24, 1947; *Dallas Times Herald*, Aug. 8, 1947; Tom Clark to William Burrow, Dec. 15, 1947, box 76, Clark Papers.

25. Pack, "Political Aspects," 40–42, 54–56, 60–61; press memo, Sept. 22, 1947, box 4-14/46; and William McGill to Jester, memo, Dec. 17, 1947, box 4-14/110, Jester Papers. Emphasis added. The comment on the limitations of drilling technology is based on the author's interview with Dr. Don Carleton, Sept. 5, 1995, Austin.

26. Pack, "Political Aspects," 57–61; Myron Blaylock to J. Howard McGrath, Mar. 6, 1948, box 22, Clark Papers; *Austin American*, Dec. 27, 1949; Green, *Establishment*, 111; McCullough, *Truman*, 674–78; William Batt to Clark Clifford, Sept. 14, 1948, box 35, Clark Clifford Papers, HSTL (hereafter Clifford Papers); J. B. C. Howe to John Steelman, Sept. 14, 1948, box 337, OF, HSTL.

27. Regarding Truman's views about state leasing of offshore properties, see Truman to Clark, Aug. 10, 1948; Clark to Steelman, Dec. 21, 1948; and Julius Krug to John Steelman,

Dec. 29, 1948, all in box 337, OF, HSTL; *Houston*, Feb., 1949, clipping, box 22; and Clark to George Wilson, Dec. 28, 1948, and Clark to Douglas McGregor, Feb. 28, 1949, box 77, Clark Papers.

28. Pack, "Political Aspects," 70–71, 79–82; Statement of the School Land Board, May 4, 1949, box 1977/81-235, Shivers Papers; *Houston Chronicle*, Apr. 29, 1949. Emphasis in original. The Rayburn-Johnson compromise originated with Johnson confidant Alvin J. Wirtz, an Austin lawyer. Rayburn modified it slightly into the form presented above (Wirtz to Johnson, Mar. 11, 1949, and Johnson to Tom Clark, Mar. 14, 1949, box 48, Clark Papers). For Truman's expression of interest in a revenue-sharing compromise to Clark, see Clark to Amon Carter, Apr. 22, 1949, box 77, Clark Papers; and Jester to Rayburn, May 20, 1949, box 1977/81-325, Shivers Papers. Concerning Giles, see Clark to Carter, July 15, 1949, box 77, Clark Papers.

29. Pack, "Political Aspects," 70–74, 82; Statement of the School Land Board, May 4, 1949; *Austin Statesman*, July 24, 1947; Allan Shivers, interview by Joe B. Frantz, May 29, 1970, AC74-42, OHC, LBJL.

30. Pack, "Political Aspects," 77–79, 83–86; Wilson interview; Shivers to Tom P. Cooper, May 31, 1949, box 1977/81-477, Shivers Papers; Tom Clark to Sam Rayburn, July 20, 1949, box 68, Clark Papers; Kinch and Long, *Allan Shivers*, 84–86.

31. *San Antonio Express*, Apr. 6, 1950; *Houston Chronicle*, Apr. 6, 1950; Joe Belden and Associates, "The Governor's Race in 1950. Report Number 5, June 26, 1950," box 1977/81-195, Shivers Papers; David Chrisman, "The Public Life of Caso March: Anti-Establishment Campaigns in the Democratic Party, 1946–1950" (M.A. thesis, Baylor University, 1990), 150, 151–56, 159–62, 165–66, 183–84. Shivers won in 253 counties; March won only Parr's Duval County—by a ratio of 39–1.

32. Green, *Establishment*, 141; Bartley, *New South*, 78–81.

33. *Austin American*, Sept. 12, 1950; *Dallas Morning News*, Sept. 12, 1950; Pickle, interview by Frantz.

34. Green, *Establishment*, 141; Margaret Carter to Byron Skelton, Aug. 16, 1951, box 11, Byron Skelton Papers, LBJL (hereafter Skelton Papers); *Dallas Morning News*, Sept. 11 and 12, 1950; *Austin American*, Sept. 12 and 13, 1950.

35. *Dallas Morning News*, Sept. 11 and 12, 1950; *Austin American*, Sept. 12 and 13, 1950.

36. Walter G. Hall to Byron Skelton, Oct. 4, 1950, and Skelton to Hall, Nov. 7, 1950, box 11, Skelton Papers.

37. Texas Democratic Platform, Mineral Wells Convention, Sept. 12, 1950, and *States' Righter* (Jackson, Miss.), clipping, Oct. 1, 1950, box 1977/81-258, Shivers Papers; Green, *Establishment*, 141; *Austin American*, Sept. 13, 1950. Emphasis added.

38. Maury Maverick to Harry S. Truman, Oct. 7, 1950, and Henri Warren to Truman, Aug. 17, 1950, box 61, OF, HSTL; Maury Maverick to Donald S. Dawson, Oct. 7, 1950, and Byron Skelton to Donald S. Dawson, Nov. 8, 1950, box 983, OF, HSTL.

Chapter Five. Maneuvers, Intrigues, and Party Leadership

1. Kinch and Long, *Allan Shivers*, 103–104. The draconian measures suggested by the TMA in 1950 might give a clear idea of the scope of cuts proposed by business. Lobbyists

for the TMA suggested a 10–15 percent cut in spending, including a moratorium on textbook purchases. The Fort Worth Chamber of Commerce suggested reductions that would force closing all state departments for a year and shutting down state higher education for six months (Green, *Establishment*, 137).

2. Green, *Establishment*, 135, 137; Kinch and Long, *Allan Shivers*, 93; Maurice Acers to Shivers, Oct. 15 and Dec. 12, 1951, and Apr. 15, 1952, box 1977/81-372, Shivers Papers; Christian interview; Osorio interview.

3. Kinch and Long, *Allan Shivers*, 103–104.

4. Ibid.; Green, *Establishment*, 138; Berlin interview; Maury Maverick Jr., interview by author, Nov. 28, 1995, San Antonio.

5. Kinch and Long, *Allan Shivers*, 104–106.

6. Hart to Shivers, May 23, 1951, box 1977/81-373, Shivers Papers; Maverick interview.

7. Kinch and Long, *Allan Shivers*, 104–107; D. B. Hardeman, interview by John Luter, Jan. 3, 1970, OH-213, Dwight D. Eisenhower Library, Abilene, Kans. (hereafter DDEL); Barefoot Sanders, interview by author, Dec. 29, 1995, Dallas; Green, *Establishment*, 138–39.

8. *House Journal*, 52d. Leg., reg. sess. (1951), 70, 1201, 2292, 2911–12, 2920, 2929; *Senate Journal*, 52d. Leg., reg. sess. (1951), 950 (Shivers's message endorsing H.B. 6), 1142, 1274; *Austin Statesman*, May 30, 1951; Seth McKay, *Texas and the Fair Deal*, 348.

9. *House Journal*, 52d. Leg., reg. sess., 86–87, 600, 732; Berlin interview; Green, *Establishment*, 143; McKay, *Texas*, 348; *Senate Journal*, 52d Leg., reg. sess., 353, 371, 422, 500, 522; Edward Dicker, OH-178, interview by John Luter, Dec. 23, 1969; H. Jack Porter, OH-228, interview by John Luter, Dec. 30, 1969; and Joe Ingraham and H. Jack Porter, OH-349, interview by Maclyn Burg, Nov. 9, 1972, DDEL.

10. *Senate Journal*, 52d. Leg., reg. sess., 1472; Byron Skelton to Shivers, June 6, 1951, box 11, Skelton Papers; Hart to Shivers, June 21, 1951, box 1977/81-372, Shivers Papers; Green, *Establishment*, 143; *Austin Statesman*, May 30, 1951; McGill to Shivers, Aug. 30, 1951, box 1977/81-373, Shivers Papers.

11. Calvert and DeLeón, *History of Texas*, 139–47, 201, 203, 207, 210. On disfranchisement and its effect upon voting and the Republican Party, see Michael Perman, *The Struggle for Mastery: Disfranchisement in the South, 1888–1908*, 270–81. The other major study of disfranchisement is J. Morgan Kousser, *The Shaping of Southern Politics: Suffrage Restriction and the Establishment of the One Party South, 1880–1910*, 203–208.

12. Alvin Lane, interview by John Luter, Dec. 22, 1969, OH-217; Joe S. Sheldon, interview by Maclyn Burg, Nov. 6, 1972, OH-329; Ingraham and Porter, OH-349, DDEL; and Green *Establishment*, 45–48. On Bentsen Sr. and Creager, see Davidson, *Race and Class*, 198.

13. W. C. Briggs to Herbert Brownell, Nov. 27, 1949, box 24, Herbert Brownell Papers, DDEL; Dillon Anderson, interview by John Luter, Dec. 30, 1969, OH-165; Dicker, OH-178; Lane, OH-217; Porter, OH-228; Sheldon, OH-329; and Herbert Brownell, interview by Thomas Soapes, Feb. 24, 1977, OH 362, DDEL.

14. Pack, "Political Aspects," 106–107; *Austin Statesman*, Dec. 27, 1949; J. J. "Jake" Pickle to Lyndon Johnson, Apr. 16, 1951, box 30, Lyndon Baines Johnson Archives (hereafter LBJA Files), LBJL.

15. Pickle to Johnson, Apr. 16 and June 4, 1951, box 30, LBJA Files, LBJL; Mrs. Cordye Hall to Shivers, May 4, 1951, and Shivers to Hall, May 9, 1951, box 1977/81-143, Shivers Papers.

16. Pickle to Johnson, June 4, 1951.

17. Green, *Establishment*, 143; Fath interview; Kathleen Voigt, interview by author, Nov. 28, 1995, San Antonio, Texas; Weldon Hart to Shivers, memo, July 19, 1951, box 1977/81-372, Shivers Papers.

18. *Dallas Morning News*, July 31, 1951; Kinch and Long, *Allan Shivers*, 112–13.

19. Kinch and Long, *Allan Shivers*, 110–11; *Dallas Morning News*, Nov. 13, 1951.

20. Kinch and Long, *Allan Shivers*, 110–11; *Dallas Morning News*, Nov. 13 and 15, 1951; and Gordon Persons to Shivers, Nov. 20, 1951, box 1977/81-146, Shivers Papers. On Truman's and Byrnes's troubled relationship, see McCullough, *Truman*, 478–80.

21. Kinch and Long, *Allan Shivers*, 110–11; *Dallas Morning News*, Nov. 12, 13, and 15, 1951; *Forth Worth Star-Telegram*, Nov. 13, 1951; *Houston Chronicle*, Nov. 13, 1951.

22. *Houston Post*, Nov. 13 and 14, 1951.

23. Green, *Establishment*, 144, 148–49; McGill to Shivers, memo, Apr. 26, 1951, box 1977/81-373, Shivers Papers.

24. J. K. Mumford to J. Edgar Hoover, memo, Jan. 21, 1952, "Robert Allan Shivers," file 94–42122, Federal Bureau of Investigation, Department of Justice, Washington, D.C. (hereafter Shivers FBI file). This file was obtained by filing a Freedom of Information Act request. The photos clearly show Shivers and the Maceo party throwing beer bottles off the back of a yacht into the Gulf. The Maceo accusations were hoary tales by 1952. Price Daniel had the Maceo photos in his possession as early as 1949 or 1950, according to Joe R. Greenhill Sr., a close Daniel associate. Daniel seemed to think they would make great ammunition against Shivers, as much for their proof that he drank as of his friendship with a gangster. Daniel chafed at Shivers's reputation as a moral straight arrow (Joe R. Greenhill Sr., interview by author, Jan. 10, 2000, Austin; David Marsh Barton, "The Governor As Party Leader: Allan Shivers in 1952" [honor's thesis, Austin College, 1968], 12).

25. Green, *Establishment*, 148; Wilson interview; Price Daniel, interview by Joe Frantz, June 5, 1970, AC78-40; and Shivers, AC74-42, OHC, LBJL; Banks, *Money, Marbles, and Chalk*, 143; Hart to Shivers, memo, Aug. 27, 1951, box 1977/81-372, Shivers Papers; Byron Skelton to Daniel, Dec. 31, 1951, box 11, Skelton Papers.

26. Hardeman, OH-213; and Allan Shivers, interview by John Luter, Dec. 23, 1969, OH-238, DDEL; Maverick interview; Berlin interview; Osorio interview. Of all those interviewed, only Joe Greenhill Sr. held that Shivers and Daniel had a good relationship and did little to undermine each other.

27. Pack, "Political Aspects," 104–106; *Fort Worth Star-Telegram*, July 14, 1950; George Kirksey to Weldon Hart, Feb. 8 and 14, 1950; June n.d., 1950; and June 30, 1950; and Kirksey to Shivers, June 30 and Oct. 15, 1950, all in box 1977/81-235, Shivers Papers. The extent of out-of-state lobbying on the Tidelands before the TPDA's formation is discussed in Curtis Morris to Beauford Jester, Mar. 26, 1949, box 4-14/46, Jester Papers.

28. Pack, "Political Aspects," 106–107; Hart to Shivers, memo, July 3, 1951, box 1977/81-372, Shivers Papers.

29. Hart to Shivers, memo, Oct. 22, 1951, box 1977/81-235, Shivers Papers.

30. Kinch and Long, *Allan Shivers*, 113; *Orlando Morning Sentinel*, Dec. 14, 1951; Hart to Shivers, memo, Jan. 18, 1952, box 1977/81-372, Shivers Papers.

31. Osorio interview; Osorio to author, Feb. 8, 1999.

32. McCullough, *Truman*, 770–71, 891–93.

33. Hart to Shivers, memo, Mar. 30, 1952, and governor's press statement, Mar. 31, 1952, box 1977/81-372, Shivers Papers.

34. Kinch and Long, *Allan Shivers*, 112–13, 120; Dalleck, *Lone Star Rising*, 417–18; Hart to Shivers, memo, Feb. 29, 1952, box 1977/81-372, Shivers Papers.

35. Hart to Shivers, memo, "The Latino Attitude," Feb. 27, 1952, box 1977/81-372, Shivers Papers; idem., memo, Feb. 29, 1952.

36. "Remarks of Governor Allan Shivers, State Democratic Executive Committee Meeting, New Braunfels, Apr. 18, 1952," enclosed with Fagan Dickson to Truman, May 2, 1952, box 983, OF, HSTL.

37. Ibid.

38. Shivers quote, ibid.

Chapter Six. Vote Texan, Vote Ike

1. Hardeman and Bacon, *Rayburn*, 363; Green, *Establishment*, 142–43; Voigt interview. On Johnson's role as intermediary, see Hart to Shivers, memo, Apr. 24, 1950, box 1977/81-372, Shivers Papers.

2. Hart to Shivers, memos, Feb. 4 and May 2, 1952, box 1977/81-372, Shivers Papers; Green, *Establishment*, 145; Kinch and Long, *Allan Shivers*, 92–93, 95–96, 116–17; Pickle, interview by author; Sanders interview.

3. Davidson, *Race and Class*, 156, 160–62.

4. Hart to Shivers, memos, Feb. 4 and May 2, 1952; Patrick Cox, *Ralph Yarborough: The People's Senator*, 101; Green, *Establishment*, 145; Kinch and Long, *Allan Shivers*, 92–93, 95–96, 116–17; Pickle, interview by author; Sanders interview.

5. Green, *Establishment*, 145; Kinch and Long, *Allan Shivers*, 117; Voigt interview. *Austin American*, May 28, 1952.

6. *San Antonio Evening News*, May 28, 1952; *Austin Statesman*, May 28, 1952; Voigt interview; Cox, *Ralph Yarborough*, 98.

7. Green, *Establishment*, 141–42; Schmidt interview; William McGill to Shivers, memo, July 29, 1951, box 1977/81-373; Maurice Acers to Shivers, memo, Apr. 28, 1952, box 1977/81-372; and J. R. Parten to Shivers, telegram, July 17, 1952, box 1977/81-256, Shivers Papers; Fath interview.

8. Ralph Yarborough to Harry S. Truman, Sept. 12, 1952, box 983, OF, HSTL; William McGill to Shivers, memo, June 13, 1952, box 1977/81-372, Shivers Papers; Green, *Establishment*, 142, 145; Kinch and Long, *Allan Shivers*, 118; "Yarborough Ideas," memo, n.d. (1952), box 1977/81-6, Shivers Papers; Fath interview.

9. Green, *Establishment*, 145; Cox, *Ralph Yarborough*, 98–103; Numan V. Bartley and Hugh Graham, *Southern Elections: County and Precinct Data, 1950–1972*, 245–50. Bartley

and Graham have Yarborough winning Callahan, Comanche, Fisher, Haskell, Howard, Mills, San Saba, Taylor, Throckmorton (West Central); Collin, Coryell, Franklin, Navarro, Wise (Central); Fannin, Hardin, Henderson, Jasper, Newton, and Van Zandt (East). Duval County does not fit any geographical pattern, but was a stronghold of political boss George Parr, who disliked Shivers and favored the loyalists. In addition, Yarborough held Shivers to less than 52 percent of the vote in Angelina, Atascosa, Bell, Bosque, Denton, Eastland, Erath, Falls, Grayson, Hamilton, Hill, Hood, Kent, Nueces, Orange, Shackelford, and Upshur Counties. All of these except Atascosa and Nueces are contiguous with counties Yarborough won. Atascosa saw an unusual turnout for a third minor candidate. Yarborough's strong showing in Nueces is likely a reflection of the Mexican-American vote in Corpus Christi.

10. Hart and VanCronkhite to Shivers, June 15, 1952, box 1977/81-372; and Shivers for Governor press release, July 17, 1952, box 1977/81-46, Shivers Papers; Loyal Democrats of Texas, *The Texas Story*, box 983, OF, HSTL.

11. Bacon and Hardeman, *Rayburn*, 363–64; Frederickson, *Dixiecrat Revolt*, 226–28; Maynard Robinson to Shivers, June 4, 1952, box 1977/81-182; and H. Roy Cullen to Shivers, two telephone messages, July 17, 1952, box 1977/81-46, Shivers Papers; Fath interview.

12. Green, *Establishment*, 145; Bacon and Hardeman, *Rayburn*, 363, 491 n 3; Voigt interview.

13. Byron G. Skelton, interview by T. H. Baker, Oct. 15, 1968, AC74-252, OHC, LBJL; Acers to Shivers, memo, Sept. 5, 1952, box 1977/81-372, Shivers Papers.

14. Maury Maverick to Truman, telegram, July 19, 1952; William D. Kimbrough to Truman, Aug. 1, 1952; and Dallas Scarborough to Truman, Aug. 12, 1952, all in box 983, OF, HSTL.

15. Frederickson, *Dixiecrat Revolt*, 228–32.

16. Clark Clifford and Wright Morrow, meeting notes, Feb. 5, 1952, and "1952" scratch paper tally sheet, box 24, Clifford Papers; Creekmore Fath to Truman, Sept. 6, 1952, and Truman to Fath, Sept. 10, 1952, box 337, OF, HSTL.

17. Parmet, *Eisenhower*, 73–76.

18. H. R. Cullen to Eisenhower, Jan. 10, 1952, box 29, Pre-Presidential Papers, DDEL; Anderson, OH-165; Ingraham and Porter, OH-349; and Brownell, OH-362, DDEL.

19. Anderson, OH-165; Dicker, OH-178; Ingraham and Porter, OH-349; and Brownell, OH-362, DDEL.

20. Shivers to Stevenson, July 30, 1952, box 1977/81-46; and Stevenson to Shivers, Aug. 3, 1952, and Shivers to Stevenson, Aug. 11, 1952, box 1977/81-334, Shivers Papers.

21. Dalleck, *Lone Star Rising*, 419; Hardeman, OH-213, and Shivers, OH-238, DDEL; Hart to Shivers, memo, Aug. 9, 1952, box 1977/81-334; and governor's press memo, Aug. 21, 1952, box 1977/81-258, Shivers Papers.

22. Kinch and Long, *Allan Shivers*, 120–21; Hardeman, OH-213, and Shivers, OH-238, DDEL; Dalleck, *Lone Star Rising*, 419; Barton, "Governor," 44, 46.

23. Dalleck, *Lone Star Rising*, 419; George Reedy, interview by Michael Gillette, May 25, 1982, AC84-40, OHC, LBJL; Reedy to author, Oct. 7, 1995; Maverick interview; Osorio interview. No text of Johnson's memo exists at the LBJL.

24. Pickle, interview by author; Osorio interview.

25. Barton, "Governor," 15, 72; Banks, *Money, Marbles, and Chalk*, 117. Democrats supporting Eisenhower in other southern states schemed to have him listed as the Democratic nominee, thinking it a more reliable way to rack up Democratic votes for the GOP candidate. For example, Leander Perez unsuccessfully struggled to have Ike listed as a Democrat on Louisiana's ballot (Frederickson, *Dixiecrat Revolt*, 228–30).

26. Maurice Acers to Shivers, memo, Sept. 5, 1952, box 1977/81-372; and State Democratic Party Platform, Amarillo Convention, Sept. 9, 1952, box 1977/81-253, Shivers Papers; Fath interview.

27. "Eisenhower Political Situations," memo, n.d. (ca. 1952), box 528, General File, Central Files, Eisenhower Papers, DDEL (hereafter Eisenhower Papers); Hart to Shivers, memo, Sept. 23, 1952, box 1977/81-372; and Lea Harris to Shivers, Oct. 20, 1952, box 1977/81-38, Shivers Papers.

28. Weldon Hart to C. D. Jackson, Oct. 5, 1952, box 1977/81-372, Shivers Papers; James C. Hagerty, interview by Ed Edwin, Feb. 6, 1968, OH-91; Anderson, OH-165; and Stephen Benedicts, interview by John T. Mason, Oct. 18, 1968, OH-210, DDEL; Barton, "Governor," 16.

29. Copy of *The Native Texan* and Clint Murchison to Shivers, Oct. 7, 1952, both in box 1977/81-523, Shivers Papers; Fath interview. On Ferguson, see Gould, *Progressives and Prohibitionists*.

30. Voigt interview; Hardeman, OH-213, DDEL; Fath interview; Bacon and Hardeman, *Rayburn*, 371–72; Maury Maverick Jr. to Johnson, Aug. 16, 1952, box 27; Clint Murchison to Johnson, Sept. 30, 1952, box 8; and Robert L. Clark to Johnson, Nov. 1, 1952, box 9, LBJA Files, LBJL; Dalleck, *Lone Star Rising*, 420–21. According to several polls cited by Dalleck, Johnson took some risk with his own fragile but rising popularity in backing Stevenson.

31. Fath interview; Joe Belden and Associates, "The Texas Poll," Aug. 31 and Sept. 14, 1952, box 8, LBJA Files, LBJL; Barton, "Governor," 70–71. Given the lassitude of campaign finance and reporting laws in the state, it is likely that far more was spent, particularly for Eisenhower.

32. Shivers to Eisenhower, Nov. 5, 1952; Weldon Hart to Ralph Cake, Oct. n.d., 1952; Claud Gilmer, radio address, Nov. 3, 1952; and Texas Democrats for Eisenhower, press release, Nov. 2, 1952, all in box 1977/81-198, Shivers Papers.

33. Texas Democrats for Eisenhower, press release, Nov. 2, 1952; Adams to Shivers, Nov. 21, 1952, box 1977/81-523, Shivers Papers; Green, *Establishment*, 147; Porter, OH-228, DDEL; *Orlando Morning Sentinel*, Nov. 20, 1952.

34. *Texas Almanac: 1954–1955*, 461–63; Bartley and Graham, *Southern Elections*, 245–50; Green, *Establishment*, 216–27; Davidson, *Race and Class*, 48.

35. Samuel Lubbell, *Revolt of the Moderates*, 6, 41–42, 51, 55, 180–85, 282–83, 282 n 1.

36. *Texas Almanac: 1954–1955*, 463. Voter participation in general elections and Democratic primaries from 1880–1988 is charted in Davidson, *Race and Class*, 24.

37. Key's theory of southern politics and its broader implications for modern two-party Texas are summarized in Davidson, *Race and Class*, 3–15.

Chapter Seven. Self-Perpetuation and a Third Term

1. Bartley, *New South*, 98–99, 101–104; Shivers speaking to Billie Carr, as quoted in Davidson, *Race and Class*, 163.

2. Pack, "Political Aspects," 172–74.

3. Ibid., 177–78, 180, 182, 185–87.

4. Jack Nossaman to Shivers, Jan. 16, 1953, and Sam D. Young to Shivers, Jan. 28, 1953, box 1977/81-6, Shivers Papers; Porter, OH-228, and Shivers, OH-238, DDEL.

5. H. R. Cullen to Robert Harris, Dec. 8, 1952; "Eisenhower Political Situations," memo, n.d. (1953?); and William Burrow to Sherman Adams, Apr. 18, 1953, all in box 528; and Dillon Anderson to Wilson B. Persons, Oct. 5, 1953, box 530, General File, Central Files, Eisenhower Papers.

6. Kinch and Long, *Allan Shivers*, 141–45.

7. Texas Democratic Organizing Committee, "Let's Talk Some Sense About the Democratic Party," n.d. (1953), box 1977/81-282, Shivers Papers. The TDOC apparently based its assertion on Eisenhower's total vote less the number of Republican votes for Shivers via cross-filing.

8. Dalleck, *Lone Star Rising*, 438.

9. Ibid.; Mitchell to Adlai Stevenson, May 28, 1953, box 37, Stephen Mitchell Papers, HSTL (hereafter Mitchell Papers); Hart to Shivers, June 17, 1953, box 1977/81-372, Shivers Papers. Pickle argued that Rayburn's hatred toward Shivers extended to those professionally associated with him as well. Despite his personal closeness to LBJ, Pickle recalled that Rayburn never had any "use" for him. Pickle's connection to Shivers caused him problems with more people that Rayburn into the 1960s (Pickle, interview by author).

10. Kinch and Long, *Allan Shivers*, 155–56; Texas Democratic Organizing Committee, "Let's Talk Some Sense"; Hilda Weinert to Allan Shivers, handwritten note on Stuart Long to "Dear Democrat," n.d. (1953), box 1977/81-525, Shivers Papers; Mitchell to Rayburn, Jan. 15, 1953, box 40, Mitchell Papers; *Dallas Morning News*, Jan. 18, 1953; Jim Sewell to Maury Maverick Sr., June 19, 1953, box 2L42, Maury Maverick Sr. Papers, CAH.

11. Kinch and Long, *Allan Shivers*, 155–56; Green, *Establishment*, 165–66; Texas Democratic Organizing Committee, "Let's Talk Some Sense"; Sewell to Maverick Sr., June 19, 1953.

12. Stuart Long, *Austin Report*, Feb. 7, 1954, box 1977/81-86, Shivers Papers; Jack R. Pope, oral history interview by Bill Brands, Feb. 13, 1986, Tarlton Law Library, University of Texas School of Law, Austin.

13. John Osorio to Shivers, Nov. 24 and Dec. 8, 1952, and James L. McDonald to Shivers, Sept. 11, 1954, all in box 1977/81-182; and *Obiter Dictum*, Mar. 17, 1954, box 1977/81-486, Shivers Papers; Kinch and Long, *Allan Shivers*, 149.

14. SAC, San Antonio (Chiles), to Director, FBI (Hoover), memo, Apr. 3, 1953, and Hoover to Shivers, Apr. 10, 1953, Shivers FBI file; Dalleck, *Lone Star Rising*, 448–49; Kinch and Long, *Allan Shivers*, 149. Sarah McClendon wrote of the Shivers-Johnson relationship at this time: "whatever one does will undoubtedly have been agreed to by the other in a well thought out pattern before it is announced" (*Austin American*, Feb. 27, 1954).

15. Kinch and Long, *Allan Shivers*, 137; *Austin Statesman*, Aug. 26, 1953; *Houston Chronicle*, Aug. 30, 1953.

16. Murchison to Shivers, Nov. 18, 1953; Shivers to Murchison, Nov. 25, 1953; and Hoover to Shivers, Sept. 1, 1953, all in box 1977/81-486, Shivers Papers. Shivers staffer and former FBI agent Maurice Acers represented the flashpoint in the FBI controversy. Acers supposedly had received bureau notification of the Gainesville probe, but he and Shivers denied it. Acers even claimed to have recorded his telephone conversations with FBI operatives, and said that these proved no notification had come from the Bureau. Acers's recordings and transcripts seem to back his story. However, these same sources indicate Shivers heard about the investigation from a third party earlier than he claimed (Kinch and Long, *Allan Shivers*, 137–38). See box 1977/81-482, Shivers Papers, for Acers recordings and transcripts.

17. SAC, San Antonio (Chiles), to Director, FBI (Hoover), telegram, Sept. 1, 1953; Hoover to Brownell, memo, Sept. 2, 1953; and M. A. Jones to Mr. Nichols, memo, Sept. 21, 1953, all in Shivers FBI file; Maurice Acers to Jack Love, Sept. 8, 1953, box 1977/81-483, Shivers Papers.

18. Green, *Establishment*, 31–32, 106–107, 121–34. Regarding anticommunism in Houston specifically, see Don Carleton, *The Red Scare: Right Wing Hysteria, Fifties Fanaticism and Their Legacies in Texas.*

19. Green, *Establishment*, 153; Frederickson, *Dixiecrat Revolt*, 21–25; Bartley, *New South*, 41–42, 46–50, 59–60.

20. Green, *Establishment*, 153, 155; Resolution of Kilgore Local 207, OWIU-CIO, Dec. n.d., 1954, box 1977/81-115, Shivers Papers; Schmidt interview; Berlin interview.

21. Governor's press memo, Nov. 27, 1953; William Harris to Shivers, Nov. 30, 1953; and "Preliminary Report of the Industrial Commission," Dec. 7, 1953, all in box 1977/81-115, Shivers Papers; Green, *Establishment*, 153–54.

22. Kinch and Long, *Allan Shivers*, 99, 128–31.

23. Ibid., 131–33.

24. Ibid., 154, 156; Dalleck, *Lone Star Rising*, 438, 448–49; J. J. "Jake" Pickle to Johnson, July 3, 1953; Pickle to Johnson, July 27, 1953; and Pickle to Johnson, Mar. 29, 1954, all in box 30, LBJA Files, LBJL.

25. Green, *Establishment*, 154–55. The new communist control laws likely violated the Fifth Amendment's protection against self-incrimination since existing laws already required communists to register with the secretary of state's office (Berlin interview; Maverick interview).

26. Yarborough press releases, Apr. 19 and June 18, 1954, box 1977/81-6, Shivers Papers; Cox, *Ralph Yarborough*, 108–109; Kinch and Long, *Allan Shivers*, 147, 156; Green, *Establishment*, 163.

27. *Brownsville Herald*, July 23, 1954; "Plaintiffs in Texas Garden Case," typed list, box 1977/81-2, Shivers Papers; Green, *Establishment*, 153.

28. Notes on cleaning receipt from Stephen F. Austin Hotel, box 1977/81-2, Shivers Papers; *Brownsville Herald*, July 23, 1954; *Texas (Austin) Observer*, July 28, 1954. The

Observer's story was based upon access to Shivers's deposition in the Texas Garden Case (Green, *Establishment*, 153).

29. Shivers press release, July 2, 1954, box 1977/81-6, Shivers Papers; *Brownsville Herald*, July 23, 1954; Cox, *Ralph Yarborough*, 110–11; *Texas (Austin) Observer*, July 28, 1954; Green, *Establishment*, 153.

30. *Time*, May 31, 1954; Kinch and Long, *Allan Shivers*, 173, 175; Banks, *Money, Marbles, and Chalk*, 120.

31. *Time*, May 31, 1954; Green, *Establishment*, 152.

32. *Time*, May 31, 1954; *Houston Press*, May 10, 1954; *Austin Statesman*, June 5, 1954; *Austin American*, June 5 and 8, 1954; Green, *Establishment*, 152.

33. Green, *Establishment*, 155–56; Francis Wilhoit, *The Politics of Massive Resistance*, 34; Numan Bartley, *The Rise of Massive Resistance*, 138; *Brown v. Board of Education of Topeka*, 347 U.S. 483 (1954).

34. Green, *Establishment*, 155–56; Fath interview.

35. Yarborough flyer, box 1977/81-6; and "Where Does Governor Shivers Stand on Segregation?" n.d. (1954), box 1977/81-363, Shivers Papers; Green, *Establishment*, 156.

36. Green, *Establishment*, 156; Cox, *Ralph Yarborough*, 112; Shivers speeches: Alamo Rally, Aug. 23, 1954; Galveston, Aug. 20, 1954; and Henderson, Aug. 26, 1954, all in box 1977/81-4, Shivers Papers. Emphasis added.

37. "The Yarboroughs," box 1977/81-6, Shivers Papers; Green, *Establishment*, 158.

38. Hobart Taylor to Mack Hannah Jr., June 3, 1954; and Hannah to Ottis Lock, June 29 and July 14, 1954, all in box 1977/81-182, Shivers Papers; Green, *Establishment*, 156.

39. R. N. Jones to Lyndon Johnson, Nov. 7, 1952, box 9, LBJ Senate Political Files, LBJL. J. Evetts Haley to Shivers, July 27, 1954; Sam Aldridge to Ottis Lock, July 30, 1954; and Olivaro Garza to Lupe Rosas, Aug. 10, 1954, all in box 1977/81-204, Shivers Papers; Schmidt interview. One Yarborough ad warned against rumors about voting rules designed to discourage turnout. Another, called *Se Vende Un Chivo* (*Goat for Sale*), described Shivers as a goat with "insatiable hunger" that could eat "$450,000 in six months." The advertisement described the *chivo* growing up, but used the Spanish term *cabrito* to denote this change. A mature *cabrito* becomes a *cabrón*, Tejano slang for a man whose wife is sleeping with another man (*No Se Crean Rumores* and *Se Vende Un Chivo*, in boxes 1977/81-204 and 1977/81-363, respectively; Bentsen to Shivers, July 30, 1954, and Alonso Perales to Elmer Stahl, Sept. 2, 1954, box 1977/81-3631.

40. Yarborough press release, May 31, 1954, and L. D. Ranson notes on Yarborough Corsicana appearance, July 28, 1954, box 1977/81-6; and H. H. Patteson to Carlyle Marney, Aug. 14, 1954, and Marney to Patteson, n.d. (1954), box 1977/81-363, Shivers Papers; Green, *Establishment*, 162.

41. Green, *Establishment*, 156–57; Hagerty diary, entry for July 20, 1954, box 1, James C. Hagerty Papers, DDEL (hereafter Hagerty Papers); Cox, *Ralph Yarborough*, 113.

42. Banks, *Money, Marbles, and Chalk*, 123, 128–29; Cox, *Ralph Yarborough*, 112; Green, *Establishment*, 156, 158–59; Greenhill interview; Ed Syers to Ottis Lock, Aug. 6, 1954, box 1977/81-205; and Weldon Hart to Shivers, Aug. 15, 1954, box 1977/81-373, Shivers Papers.

43. H. E. Chiles Jr. to Shivers, Aug. 13, 1954, box 1977/81-372, Shivers Papers; Osorio interview. Green documents Shivers's campaign finances and finds circumstantial evidence of election law violations (*Establishment*, 162–63). My own review of these confirms this interpretation.

44. Hart to Shivers, Aug. 15, 1954.

45. Bartley, *New South*, 46–47, 59–60, 221, 236–237, 241, 274, 276, 282–86, 301; Frederickson, *Dixiecrat Revolt*, 171–72; Calvert and DeLen, *History of Texas*, 339; Cox, *Ralph Yarborough*, 114–17. For more on anticommunism, see Green, *Establishment*, 121–34; and ibid., 159–60, for the "Port Arthur Story."

46. Cox, *Ralph Yarborough*, 114–17; Green, *Establishment*, 159–60; Schmidt interview; Pickle, interview by author; Kinch and Long, *Allan Shivers*, 158–59. According to Pickle, who disavowed any involvement with the film, Ed Syers handled the Shivers campaign account.

47. *To The Christian People of Texas*, n.d. (1954), and *Ask the People of Port Arthur (Allan Shivers's Home Town) They Know!* n.d. (1954), box 1977/81-204; and "Port Arthur Story Mapped Itinerary," box 1977/81-205, Shivers Papers; Green, *Establishment*, 159–60; Kinch and Long, *Allan Shivers*, 158–59.

48. Syers, Pickle, and Winn, "Duval Story Mapped Itinerary," n.d., box 1977/81-205; "Here's Proof About the Yarborough-Parr Deal," n.d. (1954), box 1977/81-499; Shivers campaign memo, Aug. 26, 1954, box 1977/81-4; and "What Kind of Deal Did He Make With Border Bosses?" n.d. (1954), box 1977/81-204, Shivers Papers; Green, *Establishment*, 162–63; Pickle, interview by author; Voigt interview; Davidson, *Race and Class*, 163.

49. Cox, *Ralph Yarborough*, 119; Bartley and Graham, *Southern Elections*, 245–47, 250–53; Green, *Establishment*, 217–21; Lubbell, *Revolt of the Moderates*, 282.

50. Green, *Establishment*, 163; Pickle, interview by author; Voigt interview; Davidson, *Race and Class*, 163.

Chapter Eight. Scandals and Decline

1. Kinch and Long, *Allan Shivers*, 153; Shivers speech, Austin, Aug. 19, 1954, box 1977/81-4, Shivers Papers.

2. Kinch and Long, *Allan Shivers*, 174, 179; John Osorio to Shivers, June 30, 1954, box 1977/81-334; Dillard to Shivers, memo, Apr. 20, 1955, box 1977/81-372; and Shivers to Fred Nelson, Nov. 23, 1955, box 1977/81-19, Shivers Papers.

3. Ronnie Dugger, "Who Corrupted Texas?" *Harper's*, Mar., 1957, 68; Kinch and Long, *Allan Shivers*, 174; Green, *Establishment*, 168–69.

4. Dugger, "Who Corrupted Texas?" 68; Kinch and Long, *Allan Shivers*, 173, 176–79; Green, *Establishment*, 168–69.

5. Green, *Establishment*, 167.

6. Ibid., 166–67.

7. Ibid., 167–68; Kinch and Long, *Allan Shivers*, 172–73. Acers described a new rule adopted by the board, which prevented "land from being run throughout the Program more than once" (Maurice Acers to Shivers, Mar. 23, 1954, box 1977/81-373, Shivers Papers).

8. Green, *Establishment*, 167–68; John Osorio to Shivers, Feb. 26, 1955; and Acers to Shivers, Apr. 18 and July 8, 1955, box 1977/81-373, Shivers Papers.

9. Green, *Establishment*, 168; Acers to Shivers, Apr. 18, 1955.

10. Acers to Shivers, Apr. 18, 1955.

11. Green, *Establishment*, 167–68. For the close contact between the governor's office and the investigating committee, see Acers to Shivers, Apr. 18, 1955; John Osorio to author, Feb. 8, 1999; *Texas (Austin) Observer*, Feb. 21, 1955.

12. *Texas (Austin) Observer*, Feb. 7 and 21, 1955. Acers and Shivers had known each other since law school. Acers sometimes conducted Shivers's private business while on the public payroll, including attending to business concerns in the Valley and Woodville (Acers to Shivers, memos, Oct. 15 and Dec. 12, 1951, box 1977/81-372, Shivers Papers). As late as June, 1955, Acers worked on the purchase of agricultural equipment for Shivers while a state employee (Acers to Shivers, memo, June 22, 1955, box 1977/81-373, Shivers Papers).

13. Green, *Establishment*, 168; Kinch and Long, *Allan Shivers*, 172; Schmidt interview.

14. Weldon Hart to Shivers, Mar. 4, 1953, box 1977/81-372, Shivers Papers.

15. Green, *Establishment*, 137; Osorio to author, Feb. 8, 1999; Osorio interview.

16. Green, *Establishment*, 163. Letters from Bentsen and Gregory to Shivers indicate a fairly consistent pattern of delaying payment until the exasperated creditor suggested a deal. Gregory forgave $1,000 of a $3,000 tab after waiting fifteen months (Lloyd Bentsen Sr. to Shivers, July 30, 1954, box 1977/81-363; and Lloyd Gregory to Shivers, Sept. 22, 1955, box 1977/81-334, Shivers Papers).

17. Kinch and Long, *Allan Shivers*, 153; *New York Times*, Sept. 19, 1954; Osorio to author, Nov. 12, 1999.

18. *New York Times*, Oct. 21, 1955.

19. "USC Speech Remarks, 1955" folder, box 1977/81-75; and "Resolution of the Student Senate of the University of Southern California, May 25 and 26, 1955," box 1977/81-10, Shivers Papers.

20. "USC Speech Remarks, 1955"; Patterson to Shivers, June 17, 1955, box 1977/81-75, Shivers Papers.

21. "Remarks About New York Speech" folder; and William Peterson to Shivers, July 1, 1955, box 1977/81-75, Shivers Papers.

22. Sherman Adams to Shivers, May 8, 1954, box 1, Administration Series, Papers as President of the United States, 1953–1961 (Ann Whitman file), DDEL (hereafter Whitman file); Kinch and Long, *Allan Shivers*, 199–200; Jonathan Aitkin, *Nixon: A Life*, 230.

23. Aitkin, *Nixon*, 238–42; H. Jack Porter to Eisenhower, May 1, 1956, box 696, Official File, Central Files, Eisenhower Papers; *Houston Press*, Apr. 25, 1956.

24. Green, *Establishment*, 165; Davidson, *Race and Class*, 207; Charles F. Willis to Sherman Adams, Apr. 20, 1954, and Charles M. Dickson to Eisenhower, Oct. 5, 1954, box 530, General File, Central File, Eisenhower Papers. On Porter's plans for a two-party Texas, see Porter to Eisenhower, Jan. 17, 1955, box 696, Official File, Central Files, Eisenhower Papers.

25. Porter to Eisenhower, Jan. 17, 1955, and May 1, 1956; *Dallas Morning News*, Nov. 24, 1954; *Houston Chronicle*, Nov. 24, 1954.

26. Kinch and Long, *Allan Shivers*, 168–69; Coffer to Mitchell, May 31, 1955, and Ralph Yarborough to Stephen Mitchell, Oct. 27, 1955, box 40, Mitchell Papers.

27. Maury Maverick to Mitchell, Oct. 20 and Nov. 18, 1955, and George Nokes to Mitchell, Nov. 21, 1955, box 40, Mitchell Papers.

28. Kinch and Long, *Allan Shivers*, 164; "Memo of Conversation between Governor Allan Shivers and Senator Lyndon Johnson, Boca Raton, Florida," Nov. 15, 1954, box 8, LBJA Famous Names Files, LBJL.

29. Kinch and Long, *Allan Shivers*, 164; Byron Skelton to Stephen Mitchell, Oct. 19 and Nov. 17, 1954, box 35; and Mitchell to Stevenson, Oct. 24 and 28, 1955, box 38, Mitchell Papers; Dalleck, *Lone Star Rising*, 483, 489; Hardeman and Bacon, *Rayburn*, 396.

30. Kinch and Long, *Allan Shivers*, 166, 168–69; *Texas House Journal*, 54th. Leg., reg. sess. (1955), 892; Maverick interview; Green, *Establishment*, 168; Curtis Douglass to Arch Rowan, July 26, 1955, box 1977/81-69, Shivers Papers; Osorio to author, Feb. 8, 1999; Osorio interview; Skelton to Stephen Mitchell, Aug. 12, 1955, box 40, Mitchell Papers.

31. *Brown v. Board of Education* (*Brown II*), 349 U.S. 294 (1955).

32. Calvert and DeLen, *History of Texas*, 344–47; Barkley, *Massive Resistance*, 97–98, 137.

33. Bartley, *Massive Resistance*, 98, 121.

34. Green, *Establishment*, 137; Nan Procter to Shivers, June 25, 1955; Maury Pollard to Shivers, June 29, 1955; Texas Advisory Committee on Segregation in the Public Schools, appointee list, July 27, 1955; and Alonso Jamison to Shivers, Aug. 3, 1955, all in box 1977/81-116, Shivers Papers.

35. Millard Cope to C. R. Granberry, Sept. 27, 1955, and Granberry to Cope, Oct. 6, 1955, box 1977/81-285, Shivers Papers. Curry, who had already noted the sham of black representation on the TACS, wrote committee chair Will Crews Morris to protest the composition of the lily-white subcommittee (Morris to Curry, Aug. 19, 1955, box 1977/81-116, Shivers Papers).

36. Bartley, *Massive Resistance*, 126–28.

37. Ibid., 132. The Tenth Amendment is rarely litigated because of its vagueness. Context and evidence indicates that the framers of the Thirteenth, Fourteenth, and Fifteenth Amendments intended them to alter the relationship between the states and federal government, particularly in the area of individual privileges, immunities, and rights with respect to race. See Henry J. Abraham, *Freedom and the Court: Civil Rights and Civil Liberties in the United States*.

38. *McKinney v. Blankenship*, 282 S.W. 2d 691 (1955), *Race Relations Law Reporter* 1 (1956): 77–85; Wilson interview; Shivers press memo, Oct. 12, 1955, box 1977/81-116; and Stuart Long, *Austin Report*, Oct. 16, 1955, box 1977/81-86, Shivers Papers.

39. Bartley, *New South*, 163–66, 213–22, 191–94; Green, *Establishment*, 187–89.

40. Hart to Shivers, Sept. 20, 1955, box 1977/81-373; and Wallace Savage to Shivers, Oct. 21, 1955, box 1977/81-76, Shivers Papers; Green, *Establishment*, 168.

41. Maverick Jr. to Mitchell, Nov. 18, 1955.

42. "Way to Heart Attack," n.d. (1955), box 1977/81-19, Shivers Papers; Dalleck, *Lone Star Rising*, 483–89.

Chapter Nine. Last Fights and Departure

1. Hart to Shivers, memo, Feb. 18, 1956, box 1977/81-372, Shivers Papers.

2. *Dallas Morning News,* Feb. 22, 1956. Letters pro and con on a fourth term include W. W. Cothran to Shivers and Peter Cheswick to Shivers, Feb. 22, 1956; and Orville Bullington to Shivers, Robert Bluntzer to Shivers, and Swain Burkett to Shivers, Feb. 23, 1956, all in box 1977/81-319, Shivers Papers.

3. *Dallas Morning News,* Mar. 1 and 2, 1956.

4. Hardeman and Bacon, *Rayburn,* 396–97; Dalleck, *Lone Star Rising,* 500; Stuart Long, *Austin Report,* Oct. 30, Nov. 27, and Dec. 4, 1955, box 1977/81-86, Shivers Papers; transcript of NBC's *Meet the Press,* Mar. 25, 1956, box 40, Mitchell Papers; Texas Democratic Advisory Committee, *How to Win Your Precinct Convention in 1956,* box 1977/81-84, Shivers Papers.

5. Hardeman and Bacon, *Rayburn,* 396–97; Dalleck, *Lone Star Rising,* 500; Hart to Shivers, Apr. n.d., 1956, box 1977/81-373, Shivers Papers; *Meet the Press* transcript.

6. Green, *Establishment,* 172; D. B. Hardeman to Mitchell, Apr. 4, 1956, box 40, Mitchell Papers.

7. Shivers, AC74-42, OHC; and Shivers to Johnson, July 31, 1951, box 8, LBJA Files, LBJL.

8. Shivers, AC74-42; Reedy, AC84-40; and Lloyd M. Bentsen Jr., oral history interview by Michael Gillette, June 18, 1975, AC76-11, OHC, LBJL; Pickle, interview by author.

9. Hardeman and Bacon, *Rayburn,* 396–97; Dalleck, *Lone Star Rising,* 165–66; Voigt interview.

10. Hart to Shivers, memo, Apr. 5, 1956, box 1977/81-373, Shivers Papers; Green, *Establishment,* 172; Voigt interview; Maverick interview; Fath interview.

11. Hart to Shivers, memo, Apr. 5, 1956; Dalleck, *Lone Star Rising,* 500.

12. Hardeman and Bacon, *Rayburn,* 399; Dalleck, *Lone Star Rising,* 500; Hart to Shivers, Apr. n.d., 1956.

13. Hardeman, "Shivers of Texas," 55; Gibb Gilchrist to Shivers, Mar. 23, 1956; and G. T. McLaughlin to George Sandlin, Apr. 30, 1956, box 1977/81-84, Shivers Papers; Green, *Establishment,* 172–73, 187; J. A. Hendrix, "The Shivercrat Rebellion: A Case Study in Campaign Speaking Strategies," *Southern Speech Journal* 33, no. 4 (summer, 1968): 289–95.

14. Green, *Establishment,* 174, 187; Cox, *Ralph Yarborough,* 128.

15. Green, *Establishment,* 174–75; Cox, *Ralph Yarborough,* 128–30; Bartley and Graham, *Southern Elections,* 256.

16. Cox, *Ralph Yarborough,* 132–35; Green, *Establishment,* 175–76.

17. Bartley and Graham, *Southern Elections,* 262; Green, *Establishment,* 175–76, 177–78. Daniel's final margin was 3,547 votes (Cox, *Ralph Yarborough,* 135).

18. Hart to Shivers, Aug. 27, 1956, box 1977/81-373, Shivers Papers; Green, *Establishment,* 187, 189.

19. "Report of the Legal and Legislative Subcommittee of the Texas Advisory Committee on Segregation in the Public Schools," in *Race Relations Law Reporter* 1 (Dec., 1956): 1086–91.

20. Robyn Duff Ladino, *Desegregating Texas Schools: Eisenhower, Shivers and the Crisis at Mansfield High*, 6–7, 71–74; John Howard Griffin and Theodore Friedman, *Mansfield, Texas: A Report of the Crisis Situation Resulting from Efforts to Desegregate the School System*, 4–5.

21. Ladino, *Desegregating Texas Schools*, 73–74, 77–80, 82–86; "*Jackson v. Rawdon*, 135 F. Supp. 936 (1955)," in *Race Relations Law Reporter* 1 (1956): 75–77.

22. "*Jackson v. Rawdon*, 5th Circuit Court of Appeals (1956)," in *Race Relations Law Reporter* 1 (1956): 656–57; "*Jackson v. Rawdon*, U.S. DCNDTx (1956)," in ibid., 884–85; Ladino, *Desegregating Texas Schools*, 88–89, 89–91; Griffin and Friedman, *Mansfield, Texas*, 5–7; Green, *Establishment*, 187, 189.

23. "*Jackson v. Rawdon*, 5th Circuit Court of Appeals (1956)," 656–57; Ladino, *Desegregating Texas Schools*, 88–89, 89–91; Griffin and Friedman, *Mansfield, Texas*, 5–7; Green, *Establishment*, 189.

24. *Dallas Morning News*, Aug. 31, Sept. 1, and Sept. 2, 1956. Griffin and Friedman, *Mansfield, Texas*, 6–7; Green, *Establishment*, 189.

25. Shivers statement, Aug. 31, 1956, in *Race Relations Law Reporter* 1 (1956): 885; Green, *Establishment*, 189; Hardeman, "Shivers of Texas," 51; F. Pilot to Shivers, Sept. 17, 1956, box 1977/81-87, Shivers Papers. Concerning the failed integration of the University of Alabama, see E. Culpepper Clark, *The Schoolhouse Door: Segregation's Last Stand at the University of Alabama*.

26. Herbert Brownell, *Advising Ike: The Memoirs of Herbert Brownell*, 194–95, 198, 202, 204–205; Stephen E. Ambrose, *Eisenhower: The President*, 336–38.

27. Ambrose, *Eisenhower*, 336–38; "Press Conference Notes," Sept. 5, 1956, box 61, Hagerty Papers; "President Eisenhower's Radio and Press Conference #94," Sept. 5, 1956, box 5, Press Conference Series, Whitman file.

28. Green, *Establishment*, 189; "Press Conference Notes," Sept. 11, 1956, box 62, Hagerty Papers; "President Eisenhower's Press and Radio Conference #95," Sept. 11, 1956, box 5, Press Conference Series, Whitman file.

29. Hagerty, OH-91; E. Frederic Morrow, interviews by Ed Edwin, Jan. 31, 1968, OH-92, and Thomas Soapes, Feb. 23, 1977, OH-376, DDEL; E. Frederic Morrow, *Black Man in the White House*, 91–93.

30. Sidney McMath, interview by John Luter, Dec. 30, 1970, OH-202; William J. Smith, interview by John Luter, Aug. 20, 1971, OH-240; Orval Faubus, interview by John Luter, Aug. 18, 1971, OH-181; and Amis Guthridge, interview by John Luter, Aug. 19, 1971, OH-186, DDEL.

31. Shivers, OH-238, DDEL; Hart to Shivers, Oct. 16, 1956, box 1977/81-372; and Hubert K. Reese to Shivers, Oct. 18, 1956; Frank Clement to Shivers, Oct. 15, 1956; and Shivers to Clement, Oct. 22, 1956, all in box 1977/81-281, Shivers Papers.

32. Shivers address, Nashville, Oct. 24, 1956, box 1977/81-281, Shivers Papers.

33. Kevin P. Phillips, *The Emerging Republican Majority*, 248–49, 270–79. Green offers evidence of urban labor and African-American voters' preference for Stevenson, but it is perhaps significant to note that Eisenhower did better among labor voters than he did

among blacks (*Establishment*, 220). For Yarborough voting patterns, see Cox, *Ralph Yarborough*, 113–14, 119, 132, 134–35.

34. "Interview With Governor of Texas Allan Shivers, 'The Growth of Texas is Unlimited,'" *U.S. News and World Report*, Nov. 23, 1956, 88–91.

35. Banks, *Money, Marbles, and Chalk*, 151; Calvert and DeLeón, *History of Texas*, 377.

36. Banks, *Money, Marbles, and Chalk*, 150–51; Kinch and Long, *Allan Shivers*, 189–90.

37. Green, *Establishment*, 173; Dalleck, *Lone Star Rising*, 510; Banks, *Money, Marbles, and Chalk*, 151; Kinch and Long, *Allan Shivers*, 190; Calvert and DeLeón, *History of Texas*, 377; Cox, *Ralph Yarborough*, 141.

38. Green, *Establishment*, 181; Cox, *Ralph Yarborough*, 141.

39. Cox, *Ralph Yarborough*, 141; Green, *Establishment*, 181; Kinch and Long, *Allan Shivers*, 189–91, 215.

40. Kinch and Long, *Allan Shivers*, 191.

41. Ibid., 217; Billy Brammer to Nadine Brammer, Feb. 3, 1958, copy courtesy of Nadine Brammer Eckhardt; Nadine Eckhardt to author, Sept. 8, 1997; Billy Brammer's recollections in Lawrence Wright, "The Tide Turns," *Texas Monthly*, Jan., 1986, 330–32; Allan Shivers Scrapbooks, CAH.

42. Wright, "Tide Turns," 330–32. Brammer's recollections to Wright mirror almost exactly his own written record of the dinner (Billy Brammer to Nadine Brammer, Feb. 3, 1958).

Epilogue

1. Cox, *Ralph Yarborough*, 152–54, 203, 206, 268, 270; Banks, *Money, Marbles, and Chalk*, 128–29; Green, *Establishment*, 202–203; Lyndon Johnson and Frank Erwin, telephone conversation, Feb. 1, 1964, Tape WH6402.01, Recordings of Conversations and Meetings, Recordings of Telephone Conversations, White House Series, LBJL.

2. Kinch and Long, *Allan Shivers*, 213, 219–21; *Houston Post*, July 26, 1984.

3. Kinch and Long, *Allan Shivers*, 222–23, 231–36; *Houston Post*, Jan. 9, May 8, and June 26, 1976; and Feb. 12, 1977.

4. Molly Ivins quoted in *Texas (Austin) Observer*, Jan. 17, 1997. Ivins has also lovingly described Texas as a "laboratory for bad government."

SELECTED BIBLIOGRAPHY

Archival Sources

I. Center for American History, University of Texas, Austin.
- Maverick, Maury, Sr. Papers.
- Shivers, Allan. Scrapbooks.

II. Dwight D. Eisenhower Library, Abilene, Kans.

A. Oral Histories
- Anderson, Dillon. OH-165.
- Benedicts, Stephen. OH-210.
- Brownell, Herbert. OH-362.
- Dicker, Edward. OH-178.
- Faubus, Orval. OH-181.
- Guthridge, Amis. OH-186.
- Hagerty, James C. OH-91.
- Hardeman, D. B. OH-213.
- Ingraham, Joe, and H. Jack Porter. OH-349.
- Lane, Alvin. OH-217.
- McMath, Sidney. OH-202.
- Morrow, E. Frederic. OH-96 and OH-376.
- Porter, H. Jack. OH-228.
- Sheldon, Joe S. OH-329.
- Shivers, Allan. OH-238.
- Smith, William J. OH-240.

B. Personal Collections
- Adams, Sherman. Papers
- Brownell, Herbert. Papers

Eisenhower, Dwight D. Papers
Hagerty, James C. Papers

III. Federal Bureau of Investigation, Department of Justice, Washington, D.C.
Shivers, Robert Allan. File 94-42122.

IV. Harry S. Truman Library, Independence, Mo.
A. Oral Histories
Clark, Tom C.
Clifford, Clark.
B. Personal Collections
Clark, Tom C. Papers.
Clifford, Clark. Papers.
Mitchell, Stephen. Papers.
Springarn, Stephen. Papers.
Truman, Harry S. Papers.

V. Lyndon B. Johnson Library, Austin.
A. Oral History Collection
Bentsen, Lloyd, Jr. AC76-11.
Daniel, Price. AC78-40.
Hardeman, D. B. AC89-5.
Pickle, J. J. "Jake." AC81-76.
Reedy, George. AC84-40.
Shivers, Allan. AC74-42.
Skelton, Byron. AC74-252.
B. Personal Collections
Johnson, Lyndon B. Papers.
Pearson, Drew. Papers.
Skelton, Byron. Papers.

VI. Sam Houston Regional Library and Research Center, Liberty, Tex.
Roark, Alf. Papers.

VII. Special Collections Department, University of Houston, Houston.
Allred, James V. Papers.

VIII. Tarlton Law Library, University of Texas School of Law, Austin.
Pope, Jack R. Oral history interview by Bill Brands. February 13, 1986.

IX. Texas Collection, Baylor University, Waco, Tex.
Neff, Pat. Papers.

X. Texas State Archives, Texas State Library, Austin.
Confederate Pension Records.
Good Neighbor Commission Papers.
Jester, Beauford H. Papers.
O'Daniel, W. Lee. Papers.
Secretary of State Records. Elections Division.
Shivers, Allan. Papers.
Stevenson, Coke R. Papers.

XI. U.S. Bureau of the Census, Washington, D.C.

Population Schedule of the Ninth Census of the United States: 1870. Manuscript Returns.

Population Schedule of the Tenth Census of the United States: 1880. Manuscript Returns.

Population Schedule of the Twelfth Census of the United States: 1900. Manuscript Returns.

Population Schedule of the Thirteenth Census of the United States: 1910. Manuscript Returns.

Population Schedule of the Fourteenth Census of the United States: 1920. Manuscript Returns.

Interviews by Author

Berlin, Edgar L. Oct. 17, 1995, Austin.
Carleton, Dr. Don. Sept. 5, 1995, Austin.
Christian, George. July 27, 1997, Austin.
Eckhardt, Robert. July 10, 1997, Austin.
Fath, Creekmore. Feb. 20, 1996, Austin.
Greenhill, Joe, Sr. Jan. 10, 2000, Austin.
Maverick, Maury, Jr. Nov. 28, 1995, San Antonio.
Osorio, John. Dec. 29, 1997, Dallas.
Pickle, J. J. "Jake." Feb. 6, 1996, Austin.
Sanders, Barefoot. Dec. 29, 1995, Dallas.
Schmidt, Fred. Oct. 10, 1995, Fredericksburg, Tex.
Shelton, Emmett. July 10, 1997, Austin.
Voigt, Kathleen. Nov. 28, 1995, San Antonio.
Wilson, Will. Sept. 12, 1995, Austin.

Books, Articles, Theses, and Dissertations

Abraham, Henry J. *Freedom and the Court: Civil Rights and Civil Liberties in the United States.* 4th ed. New York: Oxford University Press, 1982.

Aitkin, Jonathan. *Nixon: A Life.* New York: Regnery, 1993.

Ambrose, Stephen E. *Eisenhower: The President.* New York: Simon and Schuster, 1984.

Atkinson, William Eugene. "James V. Allred: A Political Biography, 1899–1935." Ph.D. diss., Texas Christian University, 1978.

Banks, Jimmy. *Money, Marbles, and Chalk: The Wondrous World of Texas Politics.* Austin: Texas, 1971.

Bartley, Numan V. *The Rise of Massive Resistance.* Baton Rouge: Louisiana State University Press, 1970.

———. *The New South, 1945–1980: The Story of the South's Modernization.* Baton Rouge: Louisiana State University Press, 1995.

——, and Hugh Graham. *Southern Elections: County and Precinct Data, 1950–1972.* Baton Rouge: Louisiana State University Press, 1978.

Barton, David Marsh. "The Governor As Party Leader: Allan Shivers in 1952." (Honors thesis, Austin College, 1968).

Baum, Dale, and James L. Haley. "Lyndon Johnson's Victory in the 1948 Texas Senate Race: A Reappraisal." *Political Science Quarterly* 109, no. 4 (fall, 1994): 595–602.

Berry, Margaret. *UT Austin: Traditions and Nostalgia.* Austin: Shoal Creek, 1975.

Brownell, Herbert. *Advising Ike: The Memoirs of Herbert Brownell.* Lawrence: University Press of Kansas, 1993.

Bryant, Keith L. "Arthur Stillwell and the Founding of Port Arthur: A Case of Entrepreneurial Error." *Southwestern Historical Quarterly* 75, no. 2 (Oct., 1971): 19–40.

Buenger, Walter. *The Path to a Modern South: Northeast Texas between Reconstruction and the Great Depression.* Austin: University of Texas Press, 2001.

——. "Texas and the South." *Southwestern Historical Quarterly* 103 (January, 2000): 309–24.

Bureau of the Census. *Thirteenth Census of the United States: 1910.* Vol. 3, *Population.* Washington, D.C.: GPO, 1913.

——. *Thirteenth Census of the United States: 1910.* Vol. 7, *Agriculture.* Washington, D.C.: GPO, 1913.

——. *Fifteenth Census of the United States: 1930.* Vol. 1, *Unemployment.* Washington, D.C.: GPO, 1931.

——. *Fifteenth Census of the United States.* Vol. 3, *Agriculture.* Pt. 2, *The Southern States: 1930.* Washington, D.C.: GPO, 1931.

——. *Fifteenth Census of the United States: 1930.* Vol. 4, *Occupations by States.* Washington, D.C.: GPO, 1931.

——. *Sixteenth Census of the United States: 1940.* Pt. 6, *Pennsylvania–Texas.* Washington, D.C.: GPO, 1941.

——. *Sixteenth Census of the United States: 1940.* Vol. 1, *Agriculture.* Pt. 5, *West South Central.* Washington, D.C.: GPO, 1941.

——. *1950 Census of Population.* Vol. 2, *Characteristics of Population.* Pt. 43, *Texas.* Washington, D.C.: GPO, 1952.

Calvert, Robert A., and Arnoldo DeLen. *The History of Texas.* Arlington Heights, N.J.: Harlan-Davidson, 1990.

Campbell, Randolph B. *An Empire for Slavery: The Peculiar Institution in Texas, 1821–1865.* Baton Rouge: Louisiana State University Press, 1989.

——. *Gone to Texas: A History of the Lone Star State.* New York: Oxford University Press, 2003.

Carleton, Don. *The Red Scare: Right Wing Hysteria, Fifties Fanaticism, and Their Legacies in Texas.* Austin: Texas Monthly Press, 1985.

Chrisman, David. "The Public Life of Caso March: Anti-Establishment Campaigns in the Democratic Party, 1946–1950." M.A. thesis, Baylor University, 1990.

Clark, E. Culpepper. *The Schoolhouse Door: Segregation's Last Stand at the University of Alabama.* New York: Oxford University Press, 1995.

Cox, Patrick. *Ralph Yarborough: The People's Senator.* Austin: University of Texas Press, 2001.

Dalleck, Robert. *Lone Star Rising: Lyndon Johnson and His Times, 1908–1960.* New York: Oxford University Press, 1991.

Davidson, Chandler. *Race and Class in Texas Politics.* Princeton, N.J.: Princeton University Press, 1990.

DeLeón, Arnoldo. *They Called Them Greasers: Anglo Attitudes Toward Mexicans in Texas, 1821–1900.* Austin: University of Texas Press, 1983.

———. "Our Gringo Amigos: Anglo Americans and the Tejano Experience." *East Texas Historical Journal* 32 (1993): 72–79.

Dugger, Ronnie. "What Corrupted Texas?" *Harper's*, March, 1957, 68–74.

Frederickson, Kari. *The Dixiecrat Revolt and the End of the Solid South, 1932–1968.* Chapel Hill: University of North Carolina Press, 2001.

Genovese, Eugene D. *Roll, Jordan, Roll: The World the Slaves Made.* New York: Vintage, 1976.

Gould, Lewis L. *Progressives and Prohibitionists: Texas Democrats in the Wilson Era.* Austin: University of Texas Press, 1973.

Green, George N. *The Establishment in Texas Politics: The Primitive Years, 1938–1957.* Norman: University of Oklahoma Press, 1984.

Griffin, John Howard, and Theodore Friedman. *Mansfield, Texas: A Report of the Crisis Situation Resulting from Efforts to Desegregate the School System.* New York: Anti-Defamation League of B'nai B'rith, 1957.

Hardeman, D. B., and Donald C. Bacon. *Rayburn: A Biography.* New York: Madison Books, 1987.

Hardeman, D. B. "Shivers of Texas: A Tragedy in Three Acts." *Harper's*, November, 1956, 50–56.

Henderson, Richard. *Maury Maverick: A Political Biography.* Austin: University of Texas Press, 1970.

Hendrix, J. A. "The Shivercrat Rebellion: A Case Study in Campaign Speaking Strategies." *Southern Speech Journal* 33 (1968): 289–95.

"Interview With Governor of Texas Allan Shivers, 'The Growth of Texas is Unlimited.'" *U.S. News and World Report*, Nov. 23, 1956, 88–91.

Jackson v. Rawdon. 135 F. Supp. 936 (1955). In *Race Relations Law Reporter* 1 (1956): 75–77.

———. 5th Circuit Court of Appeals (1956). In *Race Relations Law Reporter* 1 (1956): 656–57.

———. U.S. DCNDTx (1956). In *Race Relations Law Reporter* 1 (1956): 884–85.

Jones, Eugene, Joe Ericson, Lyle Brown, and Robert Trotter Jr. *Practicing Texas Politics.* 7th ed. Boston: Houghton-Mifflin, 1989.

Kennedy, David M. *Freedom from Fear: The American People in Depression and War, 1929–1945.* New York: Oxford University Press, 1999.

Key, V. O., Jr. *Southern Politics in State and Nation.* New York: Alfred Knopf, 1949.
Kibbe, Pauline. *Latin Americans in Texas.* Albuquerque: University of New Mexico Press, 1946.
Kinch, Sam, and Stuart Long. *Allan Shivers: The Pied Piper of Texas Politics.* Austin: Shoal Creek Press, 1973.
Kousser, J. Morgan. *The Shaping of Southern Politics: Suffrage Restriction and the Establishment of the One Party South, 1880–1910.* New Haven, Conn.: Yale University Press, 1974.
Ladino, Robin Duff. *Desegregating Texas Schools: Eisenhower, Shivers, and the Crisis at Mansfield High.* Austin: University of Texas Press, 1996.
Limerick, Patricia. *The Legacy of Conquest.* New York: Norton, 1988.
Lubbell, Samuel. *Revolt of the Moderates.* New York: Harper, 1956.
McCullough, David. *Truman.* New York: Touchstone, 1992.
McKay, Seth. *Texas and the Fair Deal.* San Antonio: Naylor Press, 1954.
McKinney v. Blankenship, 282 S.W.2d 691 (1955). In *Race Relations Law Reporter* 1 (1956): 77–85.
Maxwell, Robert S. "One Man's Legacy: W. Goodrich Jones and Texas Conservation." *Southwestern Historical Quarterly* 77, no. 3 (Jan., 1974): 355–80.
Moak, Lennox Lee. "Manager Government in Port Arthur, Texas." M.A. thesis, University of Texas, 1937.
Montejano, David. *Anglos and Mexicans in the Making of Texas, 1836–1986.* Austin: University of Texas Press, 1987.
Morgan, George T. "The Gospel of Wealth Goes South: John H. Kirby and Labor's Struggle for Self-Determination, 1901–1916." *Southwestern Historical Quarterly* 75, no. 2 (Oct., 1971): 186–97.
Morrow, E. Frederic. *Black Man in the White House.* New York: Coward, McCann, 1963.
Morehead, Richard. *Fifty Years in Texas Politics.* Burnet, Tex.: Eakin Press, 1982.
Moseley, Lou Ella. *Pioneer Days of Tyler County.* Fort Worth: Miran Press, 1975.
Owsley, Frank Lawrence. *Plain Folk of the Old South.* Baton Rouge: Louisiana State University Press, 1949.
Pack, Lindsy. "The Political Aspects of the Texas Tidelands Controversy." Ph.D. diss., Texas A&M University, 1979.
Parmet, Herbert S. *Eisenhower and the American Crusades.* New York: Macmillan, 1972.
Perman, Michael. *The Struggle for Mastery: Disfranchisement in the South, 1888–1908.* Chapel Hill: University of North Carolina Press, 2001.
Phillips, Kevin P. *The Emerging Republican Majority.* New Rochelle, N.Y.: Arlington House, 1969.
Preddy, Jane A. "Port Arthur in 1923." *East Texas Historical Journal* 24, no. 1 (1986): 39–51.
"Report of the Legal and Legislative Subcommittee of the Texas Advisory Committee on Segregation in the Public Schools." In *Race Relations Law Reporter* 1 (1956): 1086–91.
Scott, Allan. "Twenty-five Years of Opinion on Integration in Texas." *Southwestern Social Sciences Quarterly* 48 (September, 1967): 155–63.

Sitkoff, Harvard. "Harry Truman and the Election of 1948: The Coming of Age of Civil Rights in American Politics." *Journal of Southern History* 37, no. 4 (November, 1971): 597–616.

Stewart, William Ford. *Collision of Giants: The Port Arthur Story.* San Antonio: Naylor, 1966.

Texas Almanac: 1947–1948. Dallas: A. H. Belo, 1948.

——: 1954–1955. Dallas: A. H. Belo, 1955.

Wilhoit, Francis. *The Politics of Massive Resistance.* New York: Braziller, 1973.

Williamson, Joe. *The Crucible of Race: Black-White Relations in the American South Since Emancipation.* New York: Oxford University Press, 1984.

Wright, Lawrence. "The Tide Turns." *Texas Monthly,* January, 1986, 330–32.

INDEX

Page numbers in *italic* type refer to illustrations

ISBN 1-58544-407-3

90000

9 781585 444076